THE EXTRAORDINARY
IN THE MUNDANE

THE EXTRAORDINARY IN THE MUNDANE

FAMILY AND FORMS OF COMMUNITY IN CHINA

Edited by

BECKY YANG HSU

Columbia University Press   *New York*

Columbia University Press
Publishers Since 1893
New York   Chichester, West Sussex

Library of Congress Cataloging-in-Publication Data
Names: Hsu, Becky Yang, 1975– editor
Title: The extraordinary in the mundane : family and forms of
community in China / edited by Becky Yang Hsu.
Description: New York : Columbia University Press, [2025] |
Includes bibliographical references and index. Identifiers: LCCN
2024023155 | ISBN 9780231217903 hardback | ISBN 9780231217910
trade paperback | ISBN 9780231561969 ebook
Subjects: LCSH: Communities—China | China—
Social conditions—2000– | Community development—China
Classification: LCC HN740.Z9 C61938 2025 |
DDC 307.720951—dc23/eng

Cover design: Elliott S. Cairns
Cover image: iStock.com/baona

CONTENTS

THE EXTRAORDINARY
IN THE MUNDANE

INTRODUCTION

The Extraordinary in the Mundane

BECKY YANG HSU

O rganized gatherings are subject to strict government control in China, and the chapters in this book outline the varieties of engagement and self-organizing that individuals do to improve their lives. In China there is a long-standing idea that establishing good family relationships is itself a contribution to the greater good. This idea differs from ideas about civic action that envisage civic action in light of a public/private dichotomy, where individuals give up their private time for the greater good, often by opposing the authority of government or big business. (In this dichotomy, the private sphere of the individual, family, and personal life is understood as separate from efforts in the public sphere, which encompasses the collective, citizenry, and the general populace.) That dichotomy doesn't resonate with many individuals in China.

Individuals in China see themselves as influencing a web of social relations that extends outward from themselves and their families to encompass the larger community and the rest of the world. Building up one's family can advance the good of society. This book describes how individuals take part in communities motivated by their experiences, and animated by concepts of family that fall within China's long history of associational life focused on kinship and locality. These forms of community vary in nature and range from short-lived to enduring, project-specific to network-specific, and are sometimes ad hoc.

The authors of the chapters in this collection are witnesses to individuals meeting challenges that are commonly experienced not only in China but also in the United States and in other countries, and the fieldwork reveals specific patterns of interaction rooted in familial relationships. This observation propels the arguments laid out in the chapters. A woman who has an autistic child creates an organization to advocate for more inclusion of autistic children in public schools. A boy is taken by his father to an internet addiction treatment camp—a professional and lay community—in which family interactions are rejiggered to treat the disorder. A pregnant woman who envisages pre- and postpartum care as undertakings led by her mother-in-law is content to have a small circle of individuals make decisions about her medical care: her mother-in-law, her mother-in-law's mother, herself, and her doctor. The compelling details in these studies raise the question, when do various modes of association enhance and hinder the common good?

FROM COMMUNITIES TO ACTS OF ASSOCIATION

Communities are commonly defined as a group of individuals who share characteristics, work toward common objectives, and engage with each other in a manner fostering solidarity or togetherness. However, conceptualizing a community solely as a group or a collection of individuals limits the accuracy of analysis. Individuals are bundles of contradiction and often belong to multiple groups that pursue conflicting goals. Individuals are also in-process and continually changing. Finally, individuals may be harmed by being labeled as belonging to a particular group.

For these reasons, it makes sense to study how individuals associate with one another by examining diverse *acts* of association and the kinds of social relationships they occur in. Each act of community is part of a larger pattern, "a mode of associated living, of conjoint communicated experience."[1] John Dewey's language captures the human experience of associating because it conveys a way of living together. A mode is a way of doing things. More recently, Paul Lichterman and Nina Eliasoph have argued that, while researchers have looked for civic life in a distinct sector, it may be more fruitful to reconceptualize "the civic" as "civic action," where "participants are coordinating action to improve some aspect of common life in society, as they imagine society."[2] The imagination of society—the basis of civic action—is something individuals actively do, with cultural elements. Bin Xu identifies four types of culture that play a role in how individuals create various forms of community: the symbols, meanings, and principles that exist prior to individuals (structure); the agency of individuals in selecting different elements to address specific situations (action); the norms of interaction and communication (interaction); and the embodiment of meaning in tangible objects shaped by social processes (object).[3]

In Chinese contexts, individuals often perceive themselves as influential actors within their network of social ties that progressively extend from their immediate families to encompass larger communities and, ultimately, the world. Fei Xiaotong's theory of the differential mode of association articulates this notion of the self, which has some qualities in common with long-standing philosophical notions.[4] Similar to ripples radiating outward from a stone cast into a pond, individuals occupy the center of their network, starting with close family and friends and extending out to acquaintances and to the rest of the world. In this way, individuals engage in associative acts, constructing their social identity as they intersect with various social networks. Some aspects of Fei's theory have faced critique, but the basic description of individuals in expanding circles of social relationships is an accurate description of how people view themselves in relation to society in China. This perspective, which emphasizes a spectrum of interconnectedness within the societal network, underscores the central roles of the individual and the family in the relationship between the state and society. For many Chinese individuals who do not see things in terms of a strict public/private sphere dichotomy, the choice has not been conceptualized as being between self-interest and the greater good. Rather, the task is to associate skillfully and suitably to simultaneously benefit oneself and contribute to the greater good.[5]

PREEXISTING SYMBOLS OF ASSOCIATION

How individuals associate with one another depends on how they imagine self, society, and the place of family, and they draw on symbols, meanings, and principles that existed prior to them while assessing available options. Civil society in China was formed around family, kin, and localities under dynastic rule, and was constituted by various units such as calligraphy societies, alumni associations, and temple associations.[6] *Jihui* (a gathering) refers to a one-time coming together to celebrate some occasion, whereas *jieshe* (forming an association) has a permanent nature and describes getting things accomplished or discussing issues.[7]

In the late nineteenth century, social life revolved around festivals held at certain times during the year, when the large, influential, and well-to-do families—whose heads included

scholars, bureaucrats, merchants, and military leaders—
organized many of the charities and events in the annual calendar, sponsoring community activities where people would
gather for music and drama, temple-based activities, and competitions, such as races for the Dragon Boat festival. These
large families organized among themselves, watching over a
diverse set of issues. "District orders did not come to the various households but to the local self-governing unit (called, in
Yunnan, the 'public family,' or *kung-chia*). I speak of this type of
organization as a 'self-governing unit' because it was organized
by local people to look out for the public affairs of the community," writes Fei Xiaotong, describing how the large families
organized things like irrigation, self-defense, mediation in personal disputes, recreation, and religious activities.[8] Whereas the
phrase "public family" would be a contradiction in the English
language, it made sense in this context. Trade guilds, benevolent halls, and native-place associations were self-organized
and based on kinship and locality; they were historically aligned
with the imperial state, and their activities did not establish independent political institutions. "In China such things are local
community affairs, and, according to the tradition still preserved,
they are not an affair of the government but are managed by
the local community under the leadership of the better-educated
and wealthier family heads." In the late imperial period, there
was flexibility in relating to the state, though oppressive rigidi-
ties based on gender inequality and clan identities existed.

The twentieth century saw many political shifts. After the
Qing dynasty was overthrown in 1911, the newly established
Republic of China that ended the imperial system saw these
kinds of civic activities as unmodern, and, as Mayfair Yang
writes, "chose to work entirely outside this cultural nexus," opting to work with a new system of political brokers.[9] With the

establishment of Maoist China in 1949, individuals were required to take part in creating a society characterized by a Soviet-type social structure in which all domains of life and property belonged to a single state body. The local modes of association were depleted. "Thus, a potent anticolonial Chinese nationalism and the modern expansionary state together decimated older graduated identities and loyalties woven around three key vectors of traditional China: kinship, religious worship, and locality," writes Yang.[10] In less than three decades, however, the social landscape was dramatically altered again with market reforms and privatization in 1979.

The degree of control has fluctuated, but the government has allowed organized activities deemed nonthreatening to continue. Instead of challenging the state, individuals have consistently built associational life by extending kinship structures, which historically enjoyed a degree of autonomy from government control, and creating networks for accomplishing specific goals. Today, all organizations fall under the Chinese Communist Party's authority, and there is no distinct civic sphere opposing the government.[11] However, social space for individuals to convene within informal groups is allowed, and individuals display certain habits of association.[12] Unregistered organizations are illegal in China, but activities in line with charity are allowed in temples and kinship networks, which thrive in contrast to the nonprofit organizations that face stricter government regulation and control.[13] As Wang Qinsheng, a clan lineage leader, explained, "We help the government to take care of our people and to solve social problems."[14]

The government now embraces family values that align with post-Communist state objectives, shifting away from Maoist antifamily sentiments. Despite the state's emphasis on citizens' adherence to political regulations, it permits activities with these values and employs family imagery itself. Xi Jinping has recently adopted a stern and imposing image as a guardian figure; earlier in his leadership he was referred to as "Uncle Xi" (Xi Dada). Previous leaders, too, drew on family metaphors, including Wen Jiabao, who referred to himself as "Grandpa Wen" to convey his concern after the 2008 Sichuan earthquake.[15] The use of family imagery has limitations, and politically sensitive issues are tightly controlled. In the aftermath of the earthquake, accusations and demands for government accountability regarding substandard construction leading to school collapses were suppressed.[16]

The state grants a degree of legitimacy to family-related topics, and this may have mixed consequences. Instead of restoring local autonomy, it emphasizes an ethical regime rooted in filial respect that in some cases parallels political submission, signaling the reestablishment of top-down authority. In the twenty-first century, "filial piety is undergoing a state-sponsored revival," Yue Du writes, "as the current Chinese government is turning away from Maoist anti-family iconoclasm in favor of traditional values reformulated in service of the postcommunist state."[17] The emphasis on the family at times aligns with, and at other times comes up against, the interests of the state.

CHANGING FAMILIES AND ASSOCIATING ACTS

The system of work units under collectivization after 1949, which took apart the extended family and reduced its size and economic power, was historically unusual. In Chinese society, family has acted as the primary social unit—sustaining social, cultural, economic, and personal well-being. But the family as a symbolic system and a way of ordering reality has changed in response to post-Mao reforms.[18] Chinese individuals have been "demanding the rights of self-development, happiness and security against the backdrop of age-old moral teachings of collective well being," writes Yunxiang Yan.[19]

In the past three decades, kinship networks have again become integral as economic entities. Although individuals no longer live "under the ancestors' shadow," living independently of the family unit is uncommon due to limited alternatives.[20] Norms of interaction and communication reflect this. When the work unit was abandoned and individuals were untied from the state, individuals once again began relying on personal networks composed of family and friends for survival. Aspects of the 1990s and 2000s featured so much negotiation and contestation between holders of capital and political power that it led to the polarization of society and the decline of disadvantaged groups. Demoralization occurred alongside the growing importance of private space in urban life and an emphasis on individual identity, which revolves around living standards and social status.[21] The one-child policy, the need to rely on personal networks, and an emphasis on an individual's internal life all affect how people connect to one another.

Descending Familism

A new hub of family life has emerged in China. Those who live in today's society organize their lives around the youngest members of the family, but the elders are still present. "The grandfather is turned into the grandson," a man in his seventies said, referring to the loss of parental authority and the power and rise of youth autonomy, to Yunxiang Yan who writes of "a national trend of family change wherein the generational and gender axes of patriarchy have been transformed and in many cases even inverted."

To describe this, Yan uses the term "descending familism." Instead of the older, obey-your-elders family style, "the ad hoc and flexible multigenerational household has become the most popular form of family configuration," Yan writes, "and intergenerational dependence, especially downward intergenerational transfer and grandparenting, emerged as a key strategy of family life by the early 21st century."[22]

Family-related emotions pulse under the surface of materialism and ambition, and young adults told me that they can't truly be happy if their parents aren't happy with them. Adult children often seek emotional support and intimacy from their parents. Among the reasons are the implementation of the one-child policy from 1980 to 2016, which gave rise to the "4-2-1 structure" in which one child receives abundant attention from four grandparents and two parents.[23] Although grandparents remain involved, they are not the priority because the overarching goal is the success of the grandchildren. For decades after the policy was implemented, urbanites invested their energy and emotion into raising "one perfect child."[24] In an uncertain job market, growing social inequality, and diminishing social welfare and safety nets, mutual dependence bonds young adults to their parents in new ways. Working adults require assistance with childcare. As the parents age, they need personal care and practical support.

In response to various challenges, some individuals have formed small communities to assist their children, and others have created communities to cope with unfulfilled family aspirations. Sara Friedman's research on communities in Dali, Yunnan, for instance, illustrates the emergence of new community types driven by family concerns as parents seek alternative educational options for their children, such as homeschool communities and Waldorf schools.[25] Although this reaction is considered extreme and very few choose it, it is driven by a commonly felt disillusionment with mainstream education and the intense competitiveness that characterizes it.

In this context, patriarchy no longer defines Chinese families, and expectations no longer revolve around absolute obedience.[26] However, parents still hold significant influence on their adult children's decisions, particularly regarding marriage choices, wedding ceremonies, and divorces.[27] Young adults experience anxiety when their career aspirations clash with their parents' desires.[28] Individuals engage in life-cycle rituals related to family-based ethical obligations as a way to construct identity in the moral universe of the family.[29]

Reliance on Personal Networks

Another development is the increased emphasis on personal networks. The removal of social safety nets when reforms began has made it necessary to rely heavily on personal networks for survival. Despite the vast array of new choices and limitations, "unofficial China" came to be very significant.[30] Chinese society took its present shape in the economic transformations, rapid globalization, a perceived moral void, and the gradual relaxation of restrictions on freedom of speech in the early 1980s and 1990s.

China's wealth inequality has risen dramatically over the past two decades, casting gloom over real material gains. Many Chinese perceive inequality as an unavoidable, albeit undesirable, consequence of economic development. In 1995, the richest 1 percent of adults owned about 40 percent of the assets, and in 2015, the top 1 percent owned about 70 percent of the wealth. China's inequality levels used to be close to those of Nordic countries, but they are now approaching U.S. levels.[31] Various factors have created and maintain this inequality, including geographic income disparity, the household registration (*hukou*) system, the former work units, and social networks.[32] In Chinese political ideology, inequality is accepted, and leaders are rewarded for providing public goods. In the mid-2010s, China entered a new phase of economic development resulting in wage polarization. Professionals in formal skill-intensive industries experienced rising wages, and workers in the informal labor-intensive service sector faced declining wages.[33] This shift was driven by globalization and automation, which have led to a labor migration from manufacturing and construction to the service sector in the informal economy, causing a decrease in wage growth rate in that sector.

Emphasis on Internal Life

Many factors shaped the underside of the Chinese economic juggernaut in the early 2000s.[34] When Chinese individuals experienced a sense of shared restlessness, they noted anger over inequality, injustice, and moral decline. But materialism and mass migration also seemed to lead to a divided sense of self and a feeling of emptiness at the core.[35] After these changes, families in China shifted toward placing greater emphasis on the individual's internal life, with the family serving as an emotional center for well-being. There are many reflections of this, including the experience of family, where raising children is constrained by relatively rigid standards defining success.

Teresa Kuan talked to parents about the experience of raising children, which has been marked by a pervasive sense of anxiety. Parents invest everything they have in securing their children's success, while constantly feeling overshadowed by others who appear to be ahead of them. "The competition will be so fierce later, if you don't have a specialty, you won't be able to adapt to society," one mother said about her daughter's extracurriculars, expressing a common point of view.[36] Nevertheless, there is widespread concern with the psychological well-being of children in Chinese society. As Kuan writes, "the common and pervasive desire for educational achievement is simultaneously accompanied by the specter of psychological unhealthiness."[37]

The nature of these anxieties, and the feelings of moral decline and divided selves in the aftermath of vast social changes, created a growing interest in mental health for both children and adults. Li Zhang writes about the middle class and its pursuit of therapeutic solutions and self-help techniques. The phenomenon known as "psy fever" is a new approach to older problems. Individuals previously sought relief from pain and suffering through Chinese medicine, qigong practices, or solace from family and close friends.[38] Informal conversations served as a form of lay therapy among family members, close friends, and colleagues. Construing problems as mental health issues has increased since the 1980s. Because the Chinese government began officially recognizing "World Mental Health Day" (October 10) in 2000, signaling its acknowledgment of the importance of mental health in the country. In 2004, the Health Ministry issued guidelines to strengthen mental health work, prompting local government health agencies to focus on identifying and treating mental distress and promoting mental health care. These government policies have created an environment in which professional care and forming communities are considered legitimate ways for people to come together to discuss problems. The government has even encouraged the unemployed to use happiness studies and psychological perspectives in a type of "therapeutic governance."[39]

PREVIEW

The chapters in this book offer compelling ethnographic evidence of diverse modes of association, including those that are short-lived, project-specific, or ad hoc in nature. Each chapter provides a detailed case study of a particular way in which family has given shape to certain kinds of associative acts. Individuals navigate their social landscape and confront new problems for families as well as age-old challenges by coordinating and self-organizing to improve their lives according to various imagined communities that they act as members of. Individuals gather in mental health support groups and on social media, for instance, constructing distinct modes of association that positively and negative impact the greater good.

The chapters are organized from macro-level (associational life that intersects with broader Chinese society) to micro-level activities (involving tightly knit circles of individuals) to show the diversity of associating at multiple levels. All the associational lives examined here are highly personal. Three key social domains in China where forms of community exist in relation to family are highlighted: the formal domain (political and economic), health care (including mental health), and personal networks. Collectively, the chapter authors provide a broader range of study than any single ethnography could cover.

The first two chapters examine the family imagination and its effect on policies and economy, respectively. In chapter 1, Yunxiang Yan examines three groups of parents in China who advocate for the social inclusion of their children who have been marginalized on the basis of cognitive difference, sexual preference, and untimely death. These activist parents fight against the notion that adult children who cannot complete their life tasks—which includes continuing the family line—are therefore not "complete persons." They began forming grassroots organizations in the 1990s, and they now engage in advocacy work, taking issue with problematic social stigmas and, in the case of *shidu* parents, with the consequences of the government's one-child policy when parents lose their only child. Motivated by kinship with their children, these parents reach out to strangers—other parents in similar situations and activists in global networks—with support and also work to educate the public. These parent-led groups have managed to avoid triggering the strict control the Chinese government exerts on most other formally-organized civic groups, even allowing them to establish nationwide organizations. This might be, in part, because they have not abandoned the discourse of familism, which the government cannot contradict for fear of undermining its own use of family-values discourse as an instrument of governance.

Richard Madsen's argument in chapter 2 demonstrates how individuals in China perceive themselves as connected to others through a complex system of kinship networks intertwined with the economy. This familial metaphor is not positive; it reflects a grim reality of rising inequality and unequal distribution of power and resources. In China, people view the economy as a network of powerful individuals rather than as an impersonal market, assuming that the country's leaders have close relationships. Creating connections with powerful individuals is necessary for economic advancement. The religious imagination in China echoes the unequal power structure, with powerful legendary figures worshipped in small temples and shrines as part of a hierarchical system all the way up to the Jade Emperor. This hierarchy mirrors the earthly hierarchy of state functionaries, adding a sacred inevitability to the imagined power structure of the Chinese state. Madsen describes a mode of association, a way of relating to one another in the context of the economy, that arises from a specific conceptualization of family, which has major consequences for social and economic relationships in China.

The next two chapters examine the coordinated action in semi-professional spheres within the temporary communities that form in health care and self-care in response to relational problems, highlighting the agency of individuals in selecting modalities to handle difficulties. In chapter 3, Teresa Kuan examines how psy-training courses generate mutual support among women training to be counselors, creating small circles of "we-ness" in which participants share their troubles and potentially counteract alienation. The inflexibility of family norms in China shapes the experience of marital trauma among middle-aged women in distinctive ways. However, in the "safe space" of a psy-training course, strangers can transform their gendered suffering and sense of isolation into solidarity and alignment, a unique mode of association that is not based on kinship or political belonging.

In chapter 4, Yichen Rao explores a unique type of short-term mode of associating that has emerged in response to concerns about adolescent internet addiction in China. These activities are driven by Chinese innovations and offers treatment through a combination of health care, psychological therapy, and a philosophical perspective that views internet addiction as a problem of the whole family. The camp motivated families to change by inviting "rebooted" ones to come back to the camp to tell their own journeys of change, and by hosting presentation sessions every night (usually led by psychologists) to enable group discussions among parents and children. Coordinated action intersecting with professional providers occur between psychologists, parents, and children, as well as between families, as they entrust their family lives to this larger network and solve problems related to how they imagine their children ought to function in the larger society.

The final three chapters of this volume show how individuals confront problems using associative acts, to various degrees of success. Among young adults, a part of life that has now become indispensable is the use of social media platforms, which individuals actively participate in during their leisure time. In chapter 5, Lynn Lin Sun highlights the problem of social demands for perfection as defined by marriage and childbearing experienced by young, middle-class, urban women in Shanghai. Despite aspiring to the ideal of marital happiness, they often find it unattainable. In response, they turn to digital communities in social media. Social media platforms facilitate interactions in a way that presses them to present an idealized image of themselves, seeking temporary relief from the pressure. However, this exacerbates the tension they feel and ultimately deepens their unhappiness as they experience the dissonance between their projected image and their actual reality.

The case examined by Gonçalo Santos in chapter 6 examines the medical decision of whether to get a cesarean section. In China, medical decisions are conceptualized as decisions to be made by a small community rather than an individual. Close study of a particular case shows how and why a small circle of individuals—her mother-in-law, her mother-in-law's mother, herself, and her doctor—interact and coordinate to make decisions about a pregnant woman's medical care. For pregnant women, making decisions in a vulnerable situation on their own without the support of their network would be isolating rather than empowering, and it would be viewed as neglectful rather than as a recognition of her individual rights. The requirement for family consent in major medical decisions, such as childbirth, is not only a bureaucratic and legal matter but also reflects a cultural model of what is considered good and appropriate care.

The act of association rooted in the imagination of the family that is examined in chapter 7 is the preparation of burial clothing for those still in good health in small towns and mid-sized cities across China. The burial clothing is a set of tangible objects that facilitates coordination among those who are aging as they imagine themselves as part of a larger community that includes both the living and the departed. A woman in her seventies showed me the burial clothes she has prepared for herself while a group of friends admired them merrily. Preparing burial clothing is "a happy thing," someone told me. Our little ad hoc gathering echoed the coffin and burial clothing viewing parties people still sometimes hold. A lineage, conceived as a stable social structure, interweaves life (new births and living members) alongside the names of the deceased on a lineage chart. In preparing burial clothing, individuals anticipate remaining in circles of family and friends living in the past, present, and future, though taking on a different status as an ancestor.

Ethnographic detail is offered on multiple domains of Chinese society, covering various perspectives in the rural/urban divide and including the LGBTQIA+ community, but perspectives from non-Han ethnic groups are missing with the exception of one case in chapter 7 involving an individual of the Dai minority ethnicity. The non-Han minority experience is necessary in any comprehensive assessment of China as a country, and I regret being unable to include a chapter on Uyghurs in Xinjiang.

CULTURE AND THE COMMON GOOD

Within the chapters in this book, the remarkable impact of seemingly ordinary social interactions is unveiled. Through fieldwork, the authors explore diverse modes of self-organizing, both temporary and enduring, that are inseparable from symbols and meanings, individual actions utilizing them, and interactional norms. The impact on individual well-being and how these modes contribute to a greater good are explored. With a critical lens, the authors examine the influence of family imaginary on various forms of community, uncovering both positive and negative consequences. By carefully evaluating how culture shapes the act of associating, light can be shed on the underlying factors that drive the formation and dissolution of communities. In authoritarian settings with restricted formal avenues, the significance of these acts becomes more pronounced. Understanding these cultural mechanisms becomes vital in the pursuit of the common good.

NOTES

1. John Dewey, *The Middle Works of John Dewey, 1899–1924*, vol. 9, *1916, Democracy and Education*, ed. Jo Ann Boydston (Carbondale: Southern Illinois University Press, 2008), 93.
2. Paul Lichterman and Nina Eliasoph, "Civic Action," *American Journal of Sociology* 120, no. 3 (2014), 809.
3. Bin Xu, *Culture of Democracy* (Cambridge: Polity, 2022), 179–80.
4. Fei Xiaotong, *From the Soil: The Foundations of Chinese Society*, trans. Gary G. Hamilton and Wang Zheng (1947; repr. Berkeley: University of California Press, 1992). See also Philip J. Ivanhoe, *Oneness: East Asian Conceptions of Virtue, Happiness, and How We Are All Connected* (Oxford: Oxford University Press, 2017).
5. The idea that being good in family relationships has good consequences for the public is very old: individuals who develop good character in fulfilling their duties to family also becomes good citizens. For example, *Xiao Jing*, in the Classic of Filial Piety (from around 500 BCE), states: "He who loves his parents does not dare to do evil unto others; he who respects his parents does not dare to be arrogant to others. Love and respect are exerted to the utmost in serving the parents, and this virtue

and teaching is extended to the people; the example is shown to the whole world beyond China." Xiao Jing, "The Classic of Xiao," trans. Xin-ming Feng, chap. 2, page 5, accessed January 12, 2024, http://tsoidug .org/Xiao/Xiao_Jing_Comment.pdf.

6. Mayfair Yang, *Re-enchanting Modernity: Ritual Economy and Society in Wenzhou, China* (Durham, NC: Duke University Press, 2020).

7. Yang, *Re-enchanting Modernity*, 257. A gathering is a temporary alliance, and an association has a more lasting nature. "Association" and "gathering" are brought together to make the phrase "associational gathering" (*shehui*, modern term for "society").

8. Fei Xiaotong, *China's Gentry: Essays in Rural-Urban Relations*, trans. and ed. Margaret Park Redfield (University of Chicago Press, 1953), 81.

9. Yang, Reenchanting Modernity, 260.

10. Yang, *Re-enchanting Modernity*, 260–61.

11. Although there is no civic sphere opposing the government, there are activists who challenge the government. See Chih-Jou Jay Chen, "Deriving Happiness from Making Society Better: Chinese Activists as Warring Gods," in *The Chinese Pursuit of Happiness: Anxieties, Hopes, and Moral Tensions in Everyday Life*, ed. Becky Yang Hsu and Richard Madsen (Berkeley: University of California Press, 2019), 131–54.

12. Environmental issues are also somewhat tolerated by the state for organizing, in contrast to issues related to human rights and religion. See Jean Lin, *A Spark in the Smokestacks* (New York: Columbia University Press, 2023).

13. Anthony Spires, "Regulation as Political Control: China's First Charity Law and Its Implications for Civil Society," *Nonprofit and Voluntary Sector Quarterly* 49, no. 3 (2020): 571–88. Strict government control and monitoring over organizing activities is likely to further intensify with the passage of a nationwide Charity Law in 2016.

14. Yang, *Re-enchanting Modernity*, 264.

15. Bin Xu, "Grandpa Wen: Scene and Political Performance," *Sociological Theory* 30, no. 2 (2012): 114–29.

16. Bin Xu, *The Politics of Compassion: The Sichuan Earthquake and Civic Engagement in China* (Stanford, CA: Stanford University Press, 2017).

17. Yue Du, *State and Family in China: Filial Piety and Its Modern Reform* (Cambridge: Cambridge University Press, 2021), 19.

18. William R. Jankowiak and Robert L. Moore, *Family Life in China* (Cambridge: Polity, 2017).

19. Yunxiang Yan, "Introduction: The Rise of the Chinese Individual," in *The Individualization of Chinese Society*, ed. Yunxiang Yan (New York: Berg, 2009), xvii–xviii.

20. Francis L. K. Hsu, *Under the Ancestors' Shadow: Kinship, Personality, and Social Mobility in Village China* (1948; repr. New York: Doubleday, 1967).

21. Yan, "Introduction: The Rise of the Chinese Individual," xv–xl.

22. Yunxiang Yan, "Introduction: The Inverted Family, Post-Patriarchal Inter-generationality and Neo-Familism," in *Chinese Families Upside Down: Intergenerational Dynamics and Neo-Familism in the Early 21st Century*, ed. Yunxiang Yan (Leiden: Brill, 2021), 3.

23. Teresa Kuan, *Love's Uncertainty: The Politics and Ethics of Child Rearing in Contemporary China* (Berkeley: University of California Press, 2015).

24. Thomas Gold, "After Comradeship: Personal Relations in China Since the Cultural Revolution," *China Quarterly* 104 (1985): 671.

25. Sara Friedman, "Opting Out of the City: Lifestyle Migrations, Alternative Education, and the Pursuit of Happiness Among Chinese Middle-Class Families," *Journal of the Royal Anthropological Institute* 29, no. 2 (2023): 383–401.

26. Stevan Harrell and Goncalo Santos, eds., introduction to *Transforming Patriarchy: Chinese Families in the Twenty-first Century* (Seattle: University of Washington Press, 2016), 1–36.

27. Deborah Davis, "Performing Happiness for Self and Others," in *The Chinese Pursuit of Happiness: Anxieties, Hopes, and Moral Tensions in Everyday Life*, ed. Becky Yang Hsu and Richard Madsen (Berkeley: University of California Press, 2019), 66–83.

28. Becky Yang Hsu, "Having It All: Filial Piety, Moral Weighting, and Anxiety Among Young Adults," in *The Chinese Pursuit of Happiness: Anxieties, Hopes, and Moral Tensions in Everyday Life*, ed. Becky Yang Hsu and Richard Madsen (Berkeley: University of California Press, 2019), 42–65.

29. Ellen Oxfeld, "Life-Cycle Rituals in Rural and Urban China: Birth, Marriage and Death," in *Handbook on Religion in China*, ed. Stephan Feuchtwang (Cheltenham, UK: Edward Elgar, 2020), 110–31.

30. Perry Link, Richard Madsen, and Paul Pickowicz, introduction to *Unofficial China: Popular Culture and Thought in the People's Republic* (Boulder, CO: Westview, 1990).

31. Thomas Piketty, Li Yang, and Gabriel Zucman, "Capital Accumulation, Private Property, and Rising Inequality in China, 1978–2015," *American Economic Review* 109, no. 7 (2019): 2469–96.

32. Yu Xie, "Understanding Inequality in China," *Chinese Journal of Sociology* 2, no. 3 (2016): 327–47.

33. Scott Rozelle, Yiran Xia, Dimitris Friesen, Bronson Vanderjack, and Nourya Cohen, "Moving Beyond Lewis: Employment and Wage Trends in China's High- and Low-Skilled Industries and the Emergence of an Era of Polarization," *Comparative Economic Studies* 62 (2020): 555–89.

34. Perry Link, Richard Madsen, and Paul Pickowicz, "Restless China: An Introduction," in *Restless China* (Washington: Rowman & Littlefield, 2013), 1–9.

35. Arthur Kleinman, Yunxiang Yan, Jing Jun, Sing Lee, Everett Zhang, Pan Tianshu, Wu Fei, and Guo Jinhua, eds., "Introduction: Remaking the Moral Person in a New China," in *Deep China: The Moral Life of the Person* (Berkeley: University of California Press, 2011), 1–35; and Li Zhang, *Anxious China: Inner Revolution and Politics of Psychotherapy* (Berkeley: University of California Press, 2020).

36. Kuan, *Love's Uncertainty*, 4; also see Vanessa Fong, *Only Hope: Coming of Age Under China's One-Child Policy* (Stanford, CA: Stanford University Press, 2004).

37. Kuan, *Love's Uncertainty*, 5.

38. Zhang, *Anxious China*.

39. Jie Yang, *Unknotting the Heart: Unemployment and Therapeutic Governance in China* (Ithaca, NY: Cornell University Press, 2015).

1

LOVE FOR A CHILD

Parental Advocacy for Social Inclusion

YUNXIANG YAN

In this chapter I explore how the advocacy actions of three groups of urban Chinese parents intersect with the values of Chinese neo-familism—especially intergenerational solidarity and identity integration. The first group consists of straight parents who support their LGBTQIA+ adult children and fight for the rights of sexual minorities in public life; they are referred to as rainbow parents (彩虹父母) in the Chinese media, a label these parents accept as their new social identity. The majority of the second group are parents of children with autism (or other intellectual disabilities) who advocate for their children's rights to education and social inclusion. The third group are *shidu* parents (失独父母), those past their fertility years whose only child has died.[1] They advocate not only for themselves but also on behalf of their deceased children. Among all three groups of parents, the primary drive behind their engagement in social advocacy (and, less commonly, in activism) is the increasingly strong intergenerational dependence and solidarity valued by Chinese neo-familism.[2]

An overwhelmingly downward flow of care and support from the senior to the junior generations is common practice in the private sphere of life in China.[3] Parent-child bonds have become so powerful that, by the early twenty-first century, parents were tending to perceive their own personhood and that of their children as one integrated relational entity, commonly known in Chinese discourse as *qinzi yiti* (亲子一体), which can be translated as the "integrated wholeness of parents and children."[4] Consequently, when children face disrespect or discrimination, their parents perceive themselves to be similarly victimized and feel compelled to fight back.[5] When parents publicly advocate through civic engagement for the social rights of their children, their family-oriented actions contribute to the common goods of diversity and social inclusion. This observation leads to the necessity of reconsidering the interactive relationship between the family and civil society.

Until recently the family institution and civil society were intellectually conceived of and theoretically treated as separate fields, with the former belonging to the private sphere and the latter constituting the core of the public sphere.[6] Social activism for the common good can be interpreted as alternative to, and often in opposition to, family activities characterized by self-interest and nepotism.[7] Edward Banfield famously observed that an ethos of amoral familism in a southern Italian village led to the villagers' inability to act on behalf of their common good because they only cared about the immediate, material interests of their families.[8] In other words, their private virtue of family solidarity resulted in a public vice of social and political apathy. Banfield's critique of amoral familism has been quite influential in the social sciences. It fits well with Western liberal thinking, which accentuates the centrality of the autonomous and self-choosing individual within all aspects of the modernization process, including in the formation of civil society. Consequently, the family and other primary groups in modern societies have been widely regarded as obstacles to civic engagement and political mobilization.[9] Similarly, reform-minded Chinese intellectuals and political elites at the turn of the twentieth century treated familism as an obstacle to China's pursuit of modernity;[10] later in the century, the same was said of the state-sponsored Mao-era campaigns of family reform.[11] In current Chinese scholarship, the idea that public life and civic engagement are separate from and in opposition to familism remains the dominant view.[12]

This narrow and rigid perspective has begun to change, however, among scholars who study civil society. The 2013 volume *The Golden Chain: Family, Civil Society and the State*, edited by Jurgen Nautz, Paul Ginsborg, and Ton Nijhuis, represents perhaps the first systematic attempt to examine the multifaceted links among individuals, families, civil society, and a democratic state.[13] It is not uncommon for activists, especially women and parents, to strategically contravene or bridge the private/public divide in their advocacy work by, for example, focusing their activism on goals that would benefit both their own families and society or by taking collective action alongside family members.[14] Equally important, within the Catholic understanding of the common good, family and kinship are not viewed as liabilities in public life. The common good is primarily defined as relational and is derived from the close ties among individuals; there is no irreconcilable conflict with private virtues.[15] Now is the time, therefore, to reassess the same set of issues from the perspective of family studies.

The central question I ask is this: Under what conditions, by what mechanism, and to what extent might the private virtues of familism contribute to the common good in the public sphere? This question is particularly important in China, where family values, albeit in the form of neo-familism, still play a key role in guiding individual behavior. I first present a brief introduction to three types of urban parent advocates as well as the four developmental stages of their advocacy careers. I then take a close look at the role of certain values in familism, with a particular focus on intergenerational solidarity and the integrated personhood between parent and child. Although traditional familism has been chiefly responsible for the stigmatization and marginalization of these parents, the values of neo-familism enable them to search for alternative ways to protect their children and to engage in social advocacy for diversity and inclusion. I conclude by discussing some implications of the link between the family and civil society in China.

I draw on data from a variety of sources. The analysis of rainbow parents is primarily based on ethnographic data from my fieldwork in 2019, supplemented by documentary research. I conducted in-depth interviews with more than twenty rainbow parents in July and December 2019, and I participated in a number of events organized by the PFLAG (Parents and Friends of Lesbians and Gays) branch in Shanghai, China. My discussion about the other two groups of parents draws on data primarily from the scholarly literature and media reports. In addition, during my fieldwork in Beijing and Shanghai over the past two decades, I have met with and interviewed several *shidu* parents and parents of children with intellectual disabilities; these experiences provided me with limited concrete information to complement the documentary research.

CHARTING PARENT ADVOCACY FOR SOCIAL INCLUSION

Parent advocacy emerged in urban China in the early 1990s, and it has grown gradually in the public sphere during the past few decades. Few of the parents had prior experience with any sort of civic engagement. Because of the absence of institutional support, most of them were forced to seek alternative ways to help themselves and their children combat social stigmas, discrimination, and exclusion. They were subsequently transformed by their own work into proud parent advocates who proactively embrace their advocacy work in the public sphere—their "activities for the public interest" (公益活动).

These activities consist of three major categories: self-advocacy against stigmas at the individual level, organized parental advocacy for inclusion and diversity on behalf of vulnerable children at the group level, and social advocacy for normative and policy changes at the societal level. Whereas self-advocacy is the starting point for all parent advocates, the other two types of advocacy are not necessarily carried out by all. In addition, the shift from advocacy to activism is ad hoc rather than planned, a result of the unique position of any one group at a given time. For example, the advocacy work of *shidu* parents developed into activism for a short period, with a well-defined policy change goal; however, they were ultimately forced to retreat by the authoritarian state. Therefore, it is far too early to identify a developmental trajectory with clearly visible stages and dimensions.

Self-Advocacy Against Dual Stigmas

All three groups of parents began their advocacy journeys as a result of adversity. My interviews with rainbow parents typically began with their recollections of the initial shock after learning of their children's nonnormative sexual orientation and continued with their painful experiences of being stigmatized and marginalized. The parents blamed themselves for being incompetent and failing to raise their children properly, and they deeply feared any critical public opinion or unfavorable moral judgments from their immediate social circles. What they reported is the rather common social phenomenon of a courtesy stigma; that is, those who are closely associated with stigmatized individuals and groups are also stigmatized, albeit with diminishing intensity.[16] For example, parents of autistic children in Australia and nonprofit organization (NPO) workers providing services for sex workers in Canada have encountered various types of courtesy stigma.[17]

In China, in addition to courtesy stigma, the three groups of parents are subject to direct stigmatization (and discrimination) for being incomplete and flawed persons. They are typically criticized as individuals who in some ways have failed in their child-rearing responsibilities; thus they face disrespect, ridicule, and harsh judgment within their social circles. They also encounter various forms of discrimination because they are perceived to have preordained bad luck, inauspiciousness, or other contaminating forces. Driven by fear, anxiety, guilt, and grief, these parents often end up cutting off their social ties and enduring a prolonged state of isolation, self-blame, and depression.[18] Their self-protective behavior is commonly perceived as evidence of guilt or an antisocial nature, which exacerbates their isolation and further reduces them to a kind of nonperson in the eyes of others.[19]

Such dual stigmas (associated and direct) may render the daily lives of these parents intolerable. For example, to escape from the festive New Year's celebratory atmosphere that would only highlight their personal grief and misery, one group of *shidu* parents arranged to spend New Year's Eve together in a hotel restaurant—only to be informed at the time of their arrival that their reservation had been canceled. The manager had found out who they were and did not want to host a group of unfortunate

people on the holiday for fear it might adversely affect his business in the new year.[20] Next I analyze the cultural premises of
such dual stigmas; suffice it to note here that it was against such
a prejudicial social environment that these determined parents
decided to fight back, an unusual and uneasy beginning on their
journeys of parent advocacy.

In 1993, Tian Huiping, the mother of a four-year-old autistic
boy, quit her job to establish the first self-help organization in
China for the parents of children with autism because she had
not found any support from the public sector or from state agencies. Thus began her twenty-five-year-long crusade to promote
autism understanding. Facing similar frustration, other parents
(mostly mothers) have embarked on the same path. The Xinxin
Center for Children in Special Education was established in 1998
in the city of Xi'an by Zhang Xiaoqiang, a mother with an autistic
son. Her original idea was simply to create a space where mothers
and their autistic children could meet and support one another.
But by the early 2010s hundreds of similar parent organizations
had mushroomed in cities all over the country, and in 2014 a
national consortium was established.[21]

One of the earliest nongovernmental organizations (NGOs)
for *shidu* parents began at a dinner party in July 2003, with parents from ten families. Some of them were already connected
through an online forum run by a major funeral and cemetery
service company in Shanghai. Ms. Wang, a veteran social worker,
had initiated the gathering with no specific purpose other
than to meet other bereaved parents, but the guests received
so much moral and emotional support from one another that
they decided to organize a group of their own. To highlight their
belief that their deceased children had become like stars in the
sky, they named their organization *Xingxing Gang* (Harbor of
Stars). The group itself was the harbor, indicating the parents'

continuing protection of and caring for their children. In the city of Wuhan, Li Minglan, a female entrepreneur who had lost her twenty-year-old daughter to a rare disease, established the Heart-Connecting Home organization in 2007 to help other bereaved parents and as a way to overcome her own grief and personal sense of loss. These organizations of *shidu* parents tend to be small in scale and localized, but they share a uniting, politicized claim for government compensation. In 2010, *shidu* parent representatives from all over the country resorted to collective action—a sit-in in Beijing—thereby amplifying their social advocacy into social activism, with unexpected repercussions (more on this to come).

Unlike the other two groups, rainbow parents began their journey of social advocacy by partnering *with* their adult children who had announced their nonnormative sexuality. Wu You-jian, a retired magazine editor and mother who had immediately accepted her gay son with open arms, was invited to appear on a live television program in November 2005. Risking social ostracism, she courageously endorsed her son and the entire *tongzhi* community.[22] Her story and opinions were subsequently covered by mainstream media outlets. She also took full advantage of the new internet culture to start blogs and establish a hotline to help parents who had been morally and socially crushed by the coming out of their LGBTQIA+ children. On June 28, 2008, Wu and Ah Qiang (Hu Zhijun), a gay man who once ran the popular online blog "Husband-Husband Life," established PFLAG China in Guangzhou.

During the subsequent decade, PFLAG grew into a de facto national organization with thirteen full-time employees, seventy-seven local groups spanning the country, more than seven thousand registered volunteers, and tens of thousands of members. By the end of 2019, more than one thousand of those volunteers were rainbow parents, among whom ninety-one had received intensive leadership training at PFLAG headquarters or at partner organizations in the United States and had become leaders of local chapters.

As many parent-activists recall, their first and most important victory during this initial stage of self-advocacy was to rediscover the sense of dignity and self-confidence necessary to contend with the injustice of their situation: stigmas, bigotry, and open discrimination from the outside world, as well as their own personal sense of guilt, grief, and inferiority. Gathering with other parents facing similar challenges—and reclaiming a social life with this new group—provided vital help, enabling them to establish their own new moral community. *Shidu* parents refer to one another as "people with the same fate" (同命人); the term emphasizes both their shared hardships and their group solidarity. Living with their prolonged grief and sense of guilt after losing their singleton child, *shidu* parents have shared psychological problems because they do not allow themselves to have any moments of joy in their everyday lives. But in groups such as Harbor of Stars and Heart-Connecting Home, leisure activities are carefully choreographed to reintroduce hope for happiness. The bereaved parents learn how to replace their previous perceptions of not deserving a good life after the loss of their son or daughter with a new perception that they ought to live their lives *well* on behalf of the child.[23]

Rainbow parents and parents of children with intellectual disabilities regard fellow members of their respective organizations as people from the same family (一家人), with whom they can freely share various forms of pain, anger, joy, and mutual aid. Rainbow parents I studied in Shanghai invested heavily in self-advocacy work to help fellow parents struggling to accept their children's nonnormative sexual orientation and to cultivate their sense of pride and confidence. They shared information and opinions in their own WeChat groups, established telephone hotlines to help others in need, and organized groups to build positive community experiences through speeches and art performances. In the events I attended, veteran rainbow parents had a well-planned division of labor among themselves: some were busy organizing and participating in group activities, and several others engaged in one-on-one soul-searching conversations with new participants. Organized activities of singing, dancing, dining out, and sightseeing trips—or simply getting together to chat—were common among all three groups of parents because these activities have been shown to help stigmatized individuals restore their self-esteem and confidence. Parents of children with intellectual disabilities found that sharing their hands-on experiences of providing special education for their children was an important way to boost their self-respect and self-assurance.

Parents' Advocacy on Behalf of Their Children

Rainbow parents stand out as the most vocal and active advocates for their adult children with nonnormative sexuality. Working within the *tongzhi* communities, they provide moral and emotional support to LGBTQIA+ individuals who suffer hostility, meddling, and oppression from their own parents. In parent-to-parent conversations, they find ways to share their personal experiences of moral transformation with these uninformed (and thus judgmental) parents. Rainbow parents also carry out their work through the PFLAG China telephone hotline and their WeChat groups.[24] Such communication encounters are particularly useful for answering questions and providing advice on parent-child relations amid coming-out issues within the family. Three of the fifteen rainbow parents I interviewed in Shanghai had worked or were still working with the hotline service. They recalled many cases when phone calls had led to in-person encounters and various kinds of practical assistance as fellow rainbow parents voluntarily provided additional support.

Rainbow parents also proactively engage the general public to promote better understanding of nonnormative sexual orientation and to support equal rights for their LGBTQIA+ children.[25] A number of rainbow parents have been featured in documentary films, TV programs, and news media reports, which helps to bolster their advocacy work.[26] Their position as straight persons is an advantage on this front because they are advocating for diversity and inclusion from the perspective of the sexual majority. They speak the language that all parents share—the unbreakable and irreplaceable parent-child bonds, the importance of helping their children to be happy, and the central value of intergenerational solidarity—which allows their version of *tongzhi* activism to be heard by an empathic public. When a rainbow mother heard two women making offensive comments about a feminine-like man passing by in a park, she told me that she criticized the two women and defended homosexuality as a natural phenomenon. Their quarrel soon attracted a crowd of onlookers, some of whom joined the two women to lash out at my informant for being a shameless lesbian. Once they learned that my informant was actually a straight mother of a lesbian daughter, however, the attitude of the originally hostile crowd changed; as parents themselves, they became more willing to listen to my informant's pro-diversity perspective.

Parents of children with intellectual disabilities have the challenge of providing (or procuring) special education for their children. This undertaking, requiring devotion, time, knowledge, and material resources, has created practitioners out of these parent advocates. As part of their routine advocacy work, they must train themselves in special education and learn how to secure funding from private donations, deal with various government regulations, and build alliances with professionals in mental health, social work, and special education.

Because autism was not recognized by the Chinese medical profession until 1982, many parents have little knowledge about it. Hence, they often delay pursuing a diagnosis and obtaining treatment. The Chinese Law on Protection of Persons with Disabilities and related policies guarantee, on paper, the right to an education for children with intellectual disabilities. In reality, however, they are regularly turned away from public schools. This leaves the parents of autistic children as the sole providers of an education for their children. By 2019, there were 1,345 NGOs and service facilities for autistic children registered with the China Disabled Persons Federation, and nearly half of these organizations were created by parents.[27] Researchers surveyed sixty-nine NGOs devoted to autism in 2017 and found that only one predated 2000, and thirty-six had been established by the parents themselves.[28] Although their original goal was simply to help their own children thrive, these parents have helped raise public awareness about the special needs of more than ten million people in China with intellectual disabilities.

Unlike parents in the other two groups, *shidu* parents no longer have an opportunity to advocate for their child's needs. Yet they have found a unique way to deepen parent-child bonds through their devotion to proactively fulfilling their child's last wishes or personal goals. This can take the form of volunteer work, monetary donations, or social action. In so doing, their activities shift from advocacy for their own status to a type of nonconfrontational activism in the name of their children. The best-known example in this connection is Yi Jiefang, a Chinese national living in Japan. After her son died in an automobile accident, Yi and her husband sold their clinic in Japan and returned to China to complete two wishes of their late son: to promote educational exchanges between Japan and China, and to help contain sandstorms by planting trees in Inner Mongolia. They completed the first of their son's wishes in 2003 by donating funds to a primary school. They then set up a foundation for the tree-planting project. For the next fifteen years, Yi spent most of her time in the desert areas of Inner Mongolia, and her commendable work attracted thousands of volunteers to the project—many of whom were also *shidu* parents. By 2018, they had together successfully planted nearly five million trees.[29] As Yi reflected, "Had it not been for my son, I probably would never have thought of planting trees for the public, or anything like that."[30] Similarly, Mao Aizhen, who lost her son to suicide in 2011, established a private foundation to help other *shidu* parents as well as people suffering from bipolar disorder, which had gone undiagnosed in her son. One *shidu* father began studying a foreign language: "My son was not able to fulfill his dream. So, I am doing this for him, and this makes me feel as if he is still alive."[31] A couple in Guangzhou city donated 300,000 yuan to help a primary school in central Jiangxi province in the name of their deceased daughter, an active volunteer who had desired to help rural schools. This monetary sacrifice showed their parental devotion, and they felt like their daughter was still alive and working together with them.

Such intergenerational solidarity seems to breach the veil between life and death and, at the same time, between the private and public sectors. As noted previously, the key turning point in self-advocacy among *shidu* parents occurs with the shift from survivor's guilt to a sense of living for two. Many parents speak about having the eyes of their child when they take sightseeing trips; in this way, their child accompanies them, and they experience new things together.[32]

Personal Growth and Advocacy Expansion

Many parents experienced personal growth along with the development of their advocacy work. They reported that their empathy toward others, concerns about social issues, and social activities outside their immediate circle of family and close friends all increased significantly. Consequently, they began to engage in activities focusing on society as a whole, effectively moving parental advocacy on behalf of their children into social advocacy for social inclusion, diversity, and justice. For example, all the rainbow parents I interviewed reported that engaging in advocacy work for the sake of their children had brought new meaning to their lives. They appreciated the opportunities for both becoming better parents and contributing to the common good of society. Mom Xiaoyang, who volunteers answering the rainbow hotline of PFLAG China, recounted her journey of personal growth in detail. With visible pride she expressed gratitude that her son had opened the door for her to participate in social activism: "I just found the true self inside me; so now I am doing this [i.e., engaging in activism], both for myself as well as for others." A rainbow father told me, "We call ourselves 'meikui mom and meikui dad,' because the word meikui means 'without a closet.' . . . Our family is a family without a closet [wugui jiating]. We also hope that one day there will be no more closets in society." Personal growth alongside others progressing in the same way can contribute to durable relational bonds, and rainbow parents often enjoy a strong sense of belonging within their moral community. In a rather dramatic case, the rainbow mother of a bisexual daughter felt a second loss after her daughter announced her decision to marry a straight man. The mother reached out to the leader of the local rainbow parent group: "What am I going to do now? May I still be a rainbow parent and continue to participate in our group activities?!"[33]

According to Director Hu, PFLAG China regularly offers training programs for parent leaders and activists. In this way, they acquire new ideas about justice, diversity, and inclusion at the societal level, gain awareness that a more progressive society is the best protection for their children, and receive training to carry out advocacy work outside their own social circles. Rainbow parents have also expanded their advocacy to universities, public parks, and private and state-owned enterprises in the form of public lectures, sharing of stories, roundtable discussions, and artistic performances for fund-raising campaigns.

In one of the more dramatic efforts, a group of eleven rainbow mothers from various cities marched to the famous matchmaking corner of People's Park in downtown Shanghai in May 2017. Unlike other parents gathered there to negotiate potential spouses for their straight sons and daughters, these mothers were raising awareness about the dating and marital challenges faced by their adult children in a society intolerant of their lifestyle.[34] The group leader explained that her son was already married to a man and was living with him in the United States, but the cause was still important to her: "I am not here to do any matchmaking for my son. I just want to make my voice heard and to let the entire society know that our children are by no means pathetic or just being faddish."[35]

These highly devoted and publicly self-identifying rainbow parents have also developed their own networks with fellow parents who have joined their advocacy work but do not wish to go completely public with their new identities. These parents are known as shadow rainbow parents. In 2019, PFLAG China organized more than one thousand events and activities in public spaces, attracting 78,000 people, although estimates show that their advocacy work reached more than ten million in some way. Working together, rainbow parents and other volunteers have helped more than 400,000 families accept members of sexual minority groups into family life.[36] Not all of the parents are comfortable, however, with this degree of exposure; by 2019, tens of thousands of shadow rainbow parents had joined the advocatory work more discreetly through networks initiated by more self-identifying rainbow parents.

Members of all three groups appear to follow a similar path of personal development, accompanied by an expansion of their advocacy focus from a more intuitive, single-focus concern to a more intentional interest in the common good of wider society. One parent of a child with autism told researchers, "At first, I did this for my own child, but then later, I felt I could help other children too. Now I feel I am promoting fairness in society. If our children do not have social fairness, they won't have high-quality lives."[37] Note the shift from "my own child" to "our children," demonstrating how this parent had begun to embrace a broader vision of societal change.

Several years after its establishment in 1998, the above-mentioned Xinxin Center for Children in Special Education in Xi'an city expanded its mission from providing a basic special education to autistic children to "realizing the rights of disabled children and calling for more care and inclusion from the whole society."[38] In pursuit of this higher goal, Inclusion China was founded in 2014 as a national consortium of parent organizations for children with intellectual disabilities. In light of the core principles of the UN Convention on the Rights of Persons with Disabilities (CRPD), Inclusion China advocated respect for dignity and difference, accessibility and equality of opportunity, and nondiscrimination and full inclusion in society; it has also brought the previously scattered parent organizations together and helped many parent advocates complete the shift from self-help and parent advocacy to a more inclusive social advocacy. By 2020, in partnership with other volunteer organizations, it had developed a national network in more than eighty cities with 242 parent organizations that covered about 100,000 families of children with intellectual disabilities.[39]

From Advocacy to Activism—and Back

Social advocacy among *shidu* parents takes two major forms, one of which has developed into activism. In the first form, many of these parents have realized that they can add value to their own lives by helping others in need. As Li Minglan, the founder of Heart-Connecting Home in Wuhan, put it, "Although my child is gone, there are many other children in the society who need our love." Li regularly organized members of her organization to visit local institutions for orphans and disabled children, spending time playing with these children as well as donating toward their welfare. After the devastating 2008 earthquake in Sichuan left many children orphaned and many parents childless, Harbor of Stars, the Shanghai-based NGO, sent three teams of volunteers to the quake area to offer person-to-person care of both children and parents.[40]

The second form of social advocacy among *shidu* parents is the pursuit of fairness and justice by way of demanding compensation from the Chinese government. They argue that when they answered the government's call to have a single child in the 1980s and 1990s, and thus help the country reduce its population, they were told that the government would take care of them in their old age. Sweeping reforms have altered eldercare policy, however, and aging parents are once again relying heavily on adult children to provide for them. *Shidu* parents feel abandoned by the government through what they see as piddling compensation: a small sum allocated to the category of "families with special difficulties due to the birth-planning policy."[41]

These parents demanded to be treated by the government as exemplary citizens and to be compensated properly for their sacrifice.[42] As one protestor shared with researchers, "When our country needed to control population growth, we shared the state's concerns and burdens. . . . Now at this time, we very much need our country to bear witness to our suffering, to give us its care!"[43] Their claims were supported by a number of scholars who noted that the government had used its administrative power to limit the rights of an individual to bear children, and as a consequence they had had only a single child, so the government should take responsibility and compensate them.[44]

After sharing their grief, distress, and disappointment with government policies through social media and online chat groups for years, *shidu* parents launched their first offline collective action in May 2010. A delegation of twenty-four parents from different cities staged a sit-in in front of the National Health and Family Planning Commission (NHFPC) in Beijing to deliver their demands for official recognition of their contribution and associated compensation. The following year, eighty elected representatives of *shidu* parents from all over the country staged a second protest. They presented an open statement, "About the Demands and Application for Compensation from Parents Who Have Lost Their Only Child," which had been signed by 2,341 parents. Disappointed with passive responses from the NHFPC, these parents continued to stage sit-ins, take part in marches, and issue appeals to the government through open statements or petitions. In 2013, there were three protests in Beijing alone, each involving hundreds of parent-activists. Other grieving parents in provincial cities in Jiangsu, Hubei, Liaoning, Shanxi, and Shandong led protest demonstrations in front of their local NHFPC offices.[45]

In April 2014, a group of 240 parent-activists not only returned to Beijing to protest but also *sued* the NHFPC for violations of the administrative procedure law. Within several months, their lawsuit was rejected as inadmissible, first by the Beijing Intermediate Court and then by the Higher Court. Because the Chinese state regards the social activism of *shidu* parents as potentially harmful to political and social stability, it immediately pushed back. Policy-oriented research singled out several organizations of *shidu* parents and their leaders from elite social backgrounds as serious risk factors.[46] Organizations of *shidu* parents were either shut down or were forced to redirect their activities to areas that were approved by the local governments. Media coverage of *shidu* parents was dramatically reduced as well. For example, Harbor of Stars, one of the earliest *shidu* parent organizations (and arguably the best known after it sent volunteer teams to help earthquake victims in 2008), was ordered to close in 2014. After restructuring and reorienting its work agenda, the organization was allowed to reopen—but under the watchful eyes of the state. Some local governments internally classified *shidu* parents as dangerous individuals in the local community who required close monitoring during the 2019 "strike hard" campaign against organized crime.[47] By early 2020, I could find little information about members of Harbor of Stars conducting volunteer work, and their previously rich online presence was now nonexistent.

The Chinese state could not tolerate, much less legitimate, the claim by *shidu* parents that they were owed compensation because according to official ideology individuals and groups must surrender their personal interests to the supremacy of the interests of the state. Compliance with the one-child policy had been a universal duty, and thus *shidu* parents' assertion of their sacrifice as particularly heroic was judged groundless. In addition, a challenge to state ideology was considered a challenge to state authority, which could not possibly be conceded.

THE JANUS-FACED FAMILY AND THE CATALYST OF NEO-FAMILISM

As indicated at the beginning of this chapter, the family (as an institution) has long been viewed in social theory as incompatible with, or even in opposition to, civil society. Familism is considered especially so. As civic society theories rightly blame, emphasizing an individual's loyalty to family over allegiance to any outside social organization leads to political apathy and individual selfishness in the public arena. This is not to suggest, however, that familism is individualistic. Familism in traditional societies (especially peasant societies) places family interests over those of any individual member, including the family head. It is ethically constructed through a discourse on obligations and self-sacrifice rather than personal rights and self-realization.[48] In familism, the individual is a means to a higher end: the continuation and prospering of the family group. Thus it is antithetical to individualism.

In social practice, familism is manifested as a cooperative organization dedicated to the survival and flourishing of the family, which plays crucial economic, sociocultural, and political functions. For both ideological and practical reasons, familism relies on a hierarchical arrangement of gender and generational relations, and so it exists in opposition to equality and relational intimacy among family members.

It should also be noted that traditional familism does not value the interests of the individual. The family is a Janus-faced institution and, if necessary, it could turn a hostile face toward those individuals who are deemed unfit to follow the family script and punish them through stigmatism, discrimination, and oppression.

The Hostile Face of the Family and Familism

Traditional China is widely referenced as a classic example of peasant society based on the principles of familism; it was the primary principle of association in public life as well as the foundational ideology of the imperial state.[49] As an all-encompassing value system, it dictated an individual's life course. Moral obligations both inside and outside the family were fulfilled by way of a well-elaborated and fixed family script. In Chinese, this process is known as *zuoren*, which means literally "making oneself a human being." According to this script, no one is born as a socially accepted person; everyone must earn the right to be a person by constantly fulfilling one's obligations toward other people, including parents, children, other family members, other relatives, neighbors, friends, and other related persons in public life—which can be reckoned to include the emperor and the imperial state. In actual practice among ordinary people, *zuoren* involves, first and foremost, the completion of one's life tasks as a child and a parent: obedience to parents; growing up to work for one's parents; getting married in order to become a parent; taking care of aged parents; and receiving, in old age, the joy of being taken care of by children and grandchildren. This well-defined series of actions should be carried out in strict accordance with the family script, with the right timing and in the proper manner. In rural north China, a grandparent who has many children and grandchildren is referred to as *quanke ren*, a complete person. With the title comes the right to sit in the honorary seat during community events. Conversely, an individual who has failed to complete these obligatory tasks has not earned the right to be treated as a complete person, and the more unfulfilled one's obligations, the more is the personhood of the individual incomplete.[50]

One cannot succeed in *zuoren* by merely accomplishing one's own individual goals in family life. Instead, people must control their desires and self-interests, place a priority on the interests of the family, and then proactively enable other members of the family to fulfill their obligations as proper persons also. Each major family obligation (like those mentioned previously) is considered an enabling act to benefit others. Part of becoming a complete person is making sure close relatives and friends also become complete persons.[51]

Their perceived failure to act out the family script is the main reason parents of children with intellectual disabilities, rainbow parents, and *shidu* parents face the dual stigmas and various forms of bigotry and discrimination discussed earlier. Children with intellectual disabilities are typically viewed as inferior, abnormal, and hopeless because they cannot and will not fulfill their moral obligations to make themselves into proper persons. Adults with nonnormative sexuality are regarded as abnormal not only because of their sexual orientation but also because of the unlikelihood that they will become parents, which then leads to their failure to fulfill that set of important family obligations.

Because of their association with their "incomplete" adult children, rainbow parents are marginalized by a courtesy stigma.

This is a rather common social phenomenon.[52] But in the Chinese case, parents also suffer the *direct* stigma of failing to act out the family script because their adult children are failing to do so. These parents are thus regarded as incomplete persons in their own right. Such dual stigmas strike the *shidu* parents most acutely because they have completely lost their only hope for achieving complete personhood. In addition, folk beliefs associate the unexpected loss of adult children with the parents' own moral deficiency in a previous life. The possibility that their bad fate might be contagious adds yet another layer to the stigma.

In other words, the dual stigmas against these three groups of parents are rooted in the conservative values of traditional familism that hold the parents responsible not only for their own failures to fulfill their moral obligations in the prescribed way but also for the failures of their children. This is why many of these parents choose to cut off their social ties and reduce their interactions with family members. They may even move away to avoid encountering anyone who knows of their "flaws," "failures," or "inauspicious fates."

It is equally important to note, however, that the Chinese family institution and the values of familism are by no means static or unchangeable; both have undergone radical changes over the last several decades in response to the social transformations taking place at the macro level.[53] Chief among these changes is the transformation of the family into a haven of private life by the early 1990s and the rise of neo-familism with the centrality of children by the 2010s.[54] Under neo-familism, the family remains the identity-holder for its members, but the ways of performing a family-based identity have become more flexible and creative, and the previously fixed family script has been subjected to improvisation.[55] With respect to our three groups of parents, in fact, the values of neo-familism—especially those of intergenerational solidarity—have inspired and enabled them to fight back against the dual stigmas and to engage in advocacy for social inclusion. To illustrate the new potential of intergenerational solidarity after the rise of neo-familism, let me revisit a tragic case from 2014 that I have examined elsewhere.

Aunty Liu, who lived in a village close to my field site, was a single mother who was widowed in her early thirties. This hardworking independent woman had raised her son on her own and had supported him so that he could receive the best possible education and eventually land a decent job in Beijing. He was filial and regularly sent money home from the capital. Aunty Liu thus became one of the most respected persons in her village, exemplifying the moral career of both motherhood and *zuoren*. Yet because her son wanted to focus on his career and seemed disinterested in marriage, gossip began to circulate in the community that he was abnormal. Aunty Liu was deeply worried by this, and she felt ashamed for failing in her obligation to help her son progress on the normal track of life. She did not want to force her son to marry, and in front of her friends and relatives she defended his decision to remain single. But she kept her true feelings to herself: she had let her husband down and failed in her duty to *zuoren*. Aunty Liu became severely depressed, and shortly after confiding in her two best friends, she committed suicide.[56]

It would be tempting to attribute Aunty Liu's tragic end to Goffman's social bigotry of courtesy stigma. There is indeed a strong stigma against unmarried adults (men and women alike) in traditional familism. These individuals deviate from the normal track and, more important, their lack of marriage puts an end to the moral growth of their parents, who cannot fulfill their obligations of becoming grandparents by helping their adult children get married. As a result, these adult children are regarded by the community as incomplete persons, and if they die unmarried they will not be allowed to be buried in the family or kinship cemetery.[57]

However, courtesy stigma alone unlikely contributed to Aunty Liu's suicide because public opinion was critical only of her son. It did not affect her reputation as a dutiful single mother. What eventually drove her over the edge, according to her friends, was the entanglement of two strong feelings existing in Aunty Liu's heart and mind. On one hand, she felt shame and guilt for raising a son who did not want to marry like everyone else. On the other, she loved her son so much that she simply could not force him to do anything against his will; instead she would do anything necessary to help him succeed in his life goals. These female villagers added that being a good person also meant being sensitive to others' feelings and helping others achieve what they yearn to have. Aunty Liu was the perfect parent in that respect. "Her son was just too selfish to consider his mother's feelings," concluded one female informant. "He was unable to feel his mother's heart because he is a man. He let his mother down."[58]

Aunty Liu's experience presents the same dual stigmas suffered by the three groups of parent advocates. These stigmas write off and discredit anyone who has failed to act out their social role fully, as prescribed by the fixed family script and the cultural expectations of *zuoren*. Unlike urban parents—who have better access to information and social capital outside their family circles—Aunty Liu lived in a close-knit rural community where traditional values of familism and the social pressures of conformity are substantially stronger. Before community gossip could turn against her, she had already inflicted on herself the stigma of being a failed parent. Her final act was a radical effort to defend her reputation.[59]

Equally noteworthy is the fact that Aunty Liu chose not to force her son to give up his own choices and to marry for the sake of family, which would be proper parental behavior as coded in the traditional family script. Instead, she continued her unconditional support of her son and eventually sacrificed herself for his best interests. Her actions were radical but not entirely inconceivable to her fellow villagers at the time, hence the empathetic comments from other mothers of her generation. As I document elsewhere, by 2010, the foci in family life in rural northeast China had shifted from ancestors to grandchildren.[60] Such an unreserved devotion to the well-being of one's child is indeed a defining feature of neo-familism, which plays a much more important and active role in the case of parent advocacy than in the individual tragedy of Aunty Liu.

Now let us take a closer look at how certain values of neo-familism enable urban parents to stand up for and fight against the social stigma and bigotry that is rooted in traditional familism.

Neo-Familism as the Catalyst of Change

By "neo-familism" I refer to the new discourses and practices of Chinese individuals since the early 2000s that invoke familial values as the primary strategy for pursuing both individual happiness and family prosperity. Like traditional familism, it involves the collective efforts of a multigenerational domestic group. Other similarities include the foundational idea that the interests of the family take precedence over the interests of its individual members. But in neo-familism there is a nuanced difference in balancing family and individual interests across generational lines.

In today's competitive and risky social environment, many people find themselves unable to put their traditional values into practice. Others employ familism but merely as a resource to pursue individual happiness. The rise of neo-familism is also indicative of important social and political developments far beyond the boundaries of the domestic group. The party-state, as a means of governance, has been proactively evoking the political aspects of traditional familism, advocating integration of the family and the state, incorporating familism into patriotism, and drawing on the family.[61]

Elsewhere I have sketched the contours of Chinese neo-familism and offered a detailed ethnographic account of certain practices of neo-familism in the everyday life of ordinary people.[62] As far as urban parental advocacy is concerned, four features of neo-familism are particularly noteworthy. First, the focus of family life has shifted at both the spiritual and the material levels from glorifying ancestors to enabling the youngest family members to succeed. The continuity of the descent line has lost its spiritual significance, and the core value of filial piety no longer demands self-sacrifice by the junior generations. Second, parent-child mutual dependence and intergenerational solidarity have gained a new saliency in both the pragmatic and the emotional aspects of family life—so much so that a new intergenerational identity is in the making that ties together parents and adult children. This identity is known in both family discourse and practice as the "integrated wholeness of parents and children" (亲子一体).[63] Third, an "intimate turn" has occurred in family life that significantly undermines the emphasis on hierarchy and discipline in traditional familism. An increasing number of people across generational and gender lines maintain that familial emotions (亲情) are the most important values referenced in their lives.[64] This in turn reshapes the foundation of parent-child bonding and mutual dependence from the obligation-centered traditional familism to the affection-centered neo-familism. It has effectively reshaped the everyday interactions of family life.[65] Last, the practice of neo-familism relies on and encourages individual improvisation instead of the coded behavior of the conventional family script. Since the early 2000s, Chinese individuals have been utilizing whatever familial resources are available to them to deal with myriad challenges in an increasingly precarious social context; they improvise their family lives creatively, flexibly, and persistently, on an ad hoc basis.[66] This situational improvisation, native to neo-familism, is diametrically opposed to conventional familism, which demands universal conformity to a fixed family script (and vilifies any deviation). Individual agency, emotionality, and personhood gain a new importance with neo-familism, and they awaken and embolden individuals to break through the constraints of the old family script and innovate toward a new kind of normal.

These features of neo-familism naturally serve as catalysts for parental advocacy in urban China. The centrality of the child opens new interpretations and redefinitions of nearly all major social roles. The conventional script of family life and the *zuoren* process were invariably based on the centrality of ancestors and the superiority of senior generations. Parents were responsible for teaching children to glorify their ancestors. But new understandings about parental obligation—to enable children to succeed and be happy—provide today's parent advocates with an ethical foundation as they reject social stigmas and morally justify their unconditional acceptance of their children.

In traditional familism, only "normal" is acceptable. It would be inconceivable for any individual parent to redefine normality with regard to their children. The criteria for normal were established by ancestors and are not subject to personal interpretation. Yet rainbow parents accept their children's sexuality as a different kind of normal, advocating that the sexual orientation of their children is determined by their genes and thus is another normal alongside heterosexuality.[67] In a similar way, parents of children with intellectual disabilities educate the general public that their children were born with special conditions because of their genes, and thus they are different than most but not abnormal.

The new identity of an "integrated wholeness of parents and children"(亲子一体) and the intimate turn in family life provide parent advocates with additional ethical motivation and a strong emotional drive when taking actions on behalf of their children. *Shidu* parents are the most dramatic example of the strength of this motivation when they spend money and time on behalf of their deceased children. They consider their children to be existing still within themselves and so they are their "child's eyes in this world."[68] Parent advocates from the other two groups will often make great sacrifices for the sake of integrated wholeness with their child. Many parents (mostly mothers) of a child with intellectual disabilities give up their own careers to spend more time with their child, doing all that they can to make improvements to the larger social environment so that their child is treated with respect. Parents in this group dread the breaking of this parent-child integration by their death because their child will then be left without their protection and care.[69] During my interviews with rainbow parents, it was common for a parent to use the plural pronouns of "we" and "us" to describe their adult child's individual activities. And they referred to any achievement by their child as "ours." Parents full identification with their child enabled them to overcome social bigotry and stigma. When I asked a father if he worried about losing face (i.e., his reputation and prestige) because he openly supports his gay son, he responded, "How much is my face worth? Compared to my child's health and happiness, my face is worthless." The personal growth of all three groups of parents is closely related to their shared identification with their child, and they are particularly proud to have pursued a moral career of social advocacy alongside their beloved offspring, even if the child is present only spiritually.

The intimate turn in neo-familism also motivates nonheterosexual children to come out to their parents and to form a parent-child alliance in the fight for diversity and inclusion. As one gay college student told me, "I think they [my parents] are always my family. I should and I must tell them something about me." Another young gay man drove home the point: "When my parents did not know, I felt the entire world had abandoned me, and I worried my parents would not want me anymore. After [coming out], even if the whole world indeed were to abandon me, the people about whom I care the most would still want to be with me."[70]

The improvisatory feature of neo-familism helps to reduce social pressures on parent advocates; the moral goal of fighting for the well-being of one's children, considered admirable from all perspectives, preemptively justifies the unconventional means that these parents have adopted. Actions such as openly supporting LGBTQIA+ persons as normal individuals, petitioning for the education and inclusion of persons with intellectual disabilities, and especially breaking away from one's immediate circle to reach out to strangers facing similar challenges might be socially devastating if not for the fact that the people doing these actions are parents who are fulfilling familial values in a neo-familism way.

Improvisation of family-like relationships can also help mitigate social pressures for members of the advocacy groups. As soon as these groups are established at the grassroots level, they tentatively cultivate a family-like atmosphere in their activities and begin to treat their organizations as alternative family forms.

The strong sense of solidarity among members can promote family-like loyalty. One set of bereaved parents, for instance, were concerned about who would honor them as ancestors because their son had died and could not tend to their future graves. At the funeral of their son, they expressed hope that they might count on their relatives to handle those tasks that would normally have been his duty. A relative complained that this would be too much to ask. At that moment, several *shidu* parents told the grieving couple not to worry: "Harbor of Stars is your family, and we will take care of you."[71]

I have described neo-familism as only one catalyst—although a crucially important one—for successful parent advocacy in China. The initial spark that begins the advocacy is older than China itself—the love of a parent for a child. Whether this spark can flame into real change (that is, parents can organize to take social-advocacy action) depends on a number of factors in the larger social setting, including exposure to more liberal ideas through education, travel, and career opportunities. Like many of the urban rainbow parents, for example, Aunty Liu had refused to pressure her son to unwillingly play the role prescribed by the old family script. Unlike the rainbow parents, however, she lived in a close-knit rural community where narrower views (including traditional familism) still prevailed. She was not able to debunk the convention that only married heterosexual adults are normal people because she could not conceive of any alternative reality.

In contrast, the three groups of parents I have described all live in cities where social life is more open and mobile, so they have easy access to alternative ideas. The founders of the major parent organizations all had previous exposure to more liberal ideas from outside their familiar communities. Huiping had studied in Germany before she established the first parent

organization for children with autism in 1998. Wang, who organized the first gathering of *shidu* parents in Shanghai and played
a key role in the Harbor of Stars organization, was a veteran
social worker with rich experience in community building. Minglan was a successful woman entrepreneur who relied on both
her financial resources and her broad social network to lead the
Heart-Connecting Home group in Wuhan city. Youjian, the
cofounder of PFLAG China, was a retired editor and author
who had read the story of Jeanne Manford and her friends in
the United States; this inspired her to establish an NGO for sexual minorities in China. The idea for the nationwide advocacy
group Inclusion China, begun in 2014, came from the overseas
experiences of its two founders.

Although neo-familism has emerged as a leading trend in
family change during the last two decades, it does not automatically protect the parent advocates from scorn. Many individuals
who practice neo-familism still uphold the values of conventional familism, such as the supremacy of the descent continuity,
the patrilineal structure of the household, and the fixed standards
for a "normal" person. For them, nonheterosexual individuals
and those with intellectual disabilities are always abnormal—
as are families with a stunted family tree because of the death
of an only child. This explains why the three groups of parents
encounter stigmas and harsh moral judgments even among their
immediate social circles with similar practices and priorities.

Neo-familism does not automatically result in parent advocacy for social inclusion; it merely serves as a catalyst—an
enabling factor—for those parents with the necessary social
resources to embark on such a moral career. Even among parents in the three groups who uphold values of neo-familism,
only a small minority participate in collective advocacy action,
suggesting some ambivalence about more traditional views of

personhood. Yet as I have shown, the absence or presence of this enabling factor makes a huge difference in the rise of parent advocacy. This alone prompts further reflection on interactions between the family and civil society.

CONCLUDING REMARKS

The three groups of urban parents I have described engage in collective action and social advocacy in the interests of their respective families, first and foremost—especially the interests of their children, who are at the center of family life. Traditional familism, and the fixed family script of making oneself a decent person (*zuoren*), pushes these parents out from under the previously protective yet conservative umbrella of their immediate social circles. Traditional familism discredits and imposes dual stigmas on these parents, whereas neo-familism—especially the centrality of children and the intergenerational integration of personhood between parents and children—provides them with a new ethical foundation on which these parents seek alternative ways to preserve their identities and social standing alongside unrelated individuals who face similar challenges. By creating a new moral community of parent organizations, the members of which are perceived as their new extended family circle, these parents can stand up for themselves as well as for their children and begin their subcultural careers of social advocacy.

These parents retain familism's centrality of the family unit, which is ultimately expressed as the unbreakable parent-child bond, and they equate the work of social advocacy with their moral duties as parents.[72] Yet their familial orientation expands outward. A lack of individual autonomy does not prevent them from moving beyond the initial stages of self-advocacy and parent advocacy to experiencing moral growth in public life. There they begin to embrace and express the values of diversity and social inclusion in society at large.[73] One might speculate, if the political climate permits, that some of these parental advocacy organizations will grow more active politically and move to the arena of social activism, as demonstrated by the short-lived actions of some *shidu* parents from 2012 to 2014. Parent advocacy can begin to bridge the divide between private and public life, between the family and civil society.

In the past decade, the Chinese state has further tightened its control over civil society organizations through new laws and regulations. Organizations working on pragmatic issues such as community building or environmental protection have been co-opted into becoming service providers with government funding, but most rights-advocacy organizations, such as labor NGOs, have suffered from government hostility and oppression.[74] Despite the unfriendly political tide, rainbow parents and parents of children with intellectual disabilities have been able to establish a de facto national network for more coordinated activities among different cities.

As many parent advocates report, the moral authority and cultural capital of parenthood in Chinese culture begets a special strength for their advocacy work. Both parent advocates and the general public recognize that parents are selfless providers and protectors of their children, and even those who object to the specific cause of parent advocacy agree that such advocates have good intentions. These parents express their causes primarily in terms of the values of neo-familism, such as the centrality of children or the parental duty to protect their children, and they have certain advantages vis-à-vis the government authorities because the Chinese state has also been promoting its own version of neo-familism as a new tool for governing.[75] Thus the government authorities are unlikely to reject their advocacy unless it crosses some sort of political red line.

The goals of current-day parent advocacy remain to seek justice and social inclusion primarily for their children and themselves, not to challenge the status quo of government policies or undermining the authority of the state. They do this by appealing for help from the state. Such parent advocacy promotes trust and collaboration among otherwise unrelated people and pursues the common good of various social groups. In some cases, parent advocacy has transformed group-specific issues into broader public issues of social justice and inclusion, creating a new space for public life between the private family and the authoritarian state. More group-based advocatory activities then resulted in more lively civic engagement but not necessarily confrontational politics against state authority. Despite the unfriendly political climate, a modest civil society can grow from advocacy efforts.

It is important to add a family perspective to my analysis of civic engagement and civil society in contemporary China. The first step is to recognize that neither the values of the family nor the values of familism are immutable. The earlier neglect of the interactions between the family and civil society might not have been entirely ungrounded because traditional familism does not tolerate behavioral deviations from the fixed family script (hence the stigma against the three groups of parents described in this chapter). Individuals living in close-knit communities with little mobility are not able to seek support outside their immediate social circles (recall the case of Aunty Liu). But the emergent neo-familism offers a normative alternative, and the more open and mobile urban milieu makes it possible for the parents described in this chapter to establish civic organizations and engage in social advocacy.

In this sense, this study does not necessarily negate early social theories on family behavior.[76] Instead, it calls for more attention to the new reality and the shift to a new perspective that does not arbitrarily exclude the family from civic society. As indicated at the beginning of this chapter, current scholars of civic societies recognize the earlier neglect of the close links between the family, civil society, and the state, thus motivating them to conduct more empirical studies on parental activism.[77] But few efforts have been made from the perspective of family studies, and this scholarly blind spot seems to be particularly salient in the field of China studies.[78] This chapter seeks not only to fill the gap with an empirical study but also to experiment with a new normative approach by examining and highlighting values of neo-familism as catalysts for social advocacy and the common good. Whereas individualism and the discourse on rights serve as the guiding spirit of civic society in modern Western societies, Chinese parents engage in civic activities as representatives of their respective families instead of as autonomous individuals; and in their advocacy work, they primarily rely on the discourse on moral obligations. This may be indicative of a more deeply rooted connection between the family and civil society in the Chinese (versus Western) context, an interesting and broader issue that deserves more scholarly attention.

NOTES

1. In this study, I retain the Chinese term *shidu* because there is no English-language equivalent that adequately captures the unbearable and unmeasurable loss of one's only child in Chinese culture. The parents in the second group are often referred to as "*xingxing fumu*" (星星父母), or parents of children from the stars, because autistic children were called "children from the stars," first in Taiwan and then in mainland

China. I will not, however, adopt this Chinese expression as one may infer the misleading English term of being parents of celebrities.

2. Yunxiang Yan, "Neo-Familism and the State in Contemporary China," *Urban Anthropology and Studies of Cultural Systems and World Economic Development* 47, no. 3–4 (2018): 181–224.

3. Yunxiang Yan, "Intergenerational Intimacy and Descending Familism in Rural North China," *American Anthropologist* 118, no. 2 (2016): 244–57.

4. Wenrong Liu, "转型期的家庭代际情感与团结" (Intergenerational affection and solidarity in families during social transition), 《社会学研究》 (*Sociological Studies*), no. 4 (2016): 145–68; and Yunxiang Yan, "Introduction: The Inverted Family, Post-Patriarchal Intergenerationality and Neo-Familism," *Chinese Families Upside Down: Intergenerational Dynamics and Neo-Familism in the Early 21st Century*, ed. Yunxiang Yan (Amsterdam: Brill, 2021), 1–30.

5. Although they uphold the value of filial piety in social discourse, in general urban adult children tend to receive more support from their parents for financing their marriages or for child-rearing than they can offer in terms of elderly support. In the public sphere, there has been sporadic advocacy work on behalf of an awareness of Alzheimer's disease, such as the TV show *Forget Me Not Café*, but there has been no organized social activism on behalf of the parents by adult children.

6. Paul Ginsborg, "Uncharted Territories: Individuals, Families, Civil Society and the Democratic State," *The Golden Chain: Family, Civil Society, and the State*, ed. Jürgen Nautz, Paul Ginsborg, and Ton Nijhuis (New York: Berghahn, 2013), 17–39; and Karen Hagemann, "Gendered Boundaries: Civil Society, the Public/Private Divide and the Family," *The Golden Chain: Family, Civil Society, and the State*, ed. Jürgen Nautz, Paul Ginsborg, and Ton Nijhuis (New York: Berghahn, 2013), 43–65.

7. Elżbieta Korolczuk, "When Parents Become Activists: Exploring the Intersection of Civil Society and Family," *Civil Society Revisited*, ed. Kerstin Jacobsson and Elżbieta Korolczuk (New York: Berghahn, 2017), 129–52.

8. Edward L Banfield, *The Moral Basis of a Backward Society* (New York: Free Press, 1958).

9. For a brief review, see Martin King Whyte, *Small Groups and Political Rituals in China* (Berkeley: University of California Press, 1974), 6–11.

10. Susan L. Glosser, *Chinese Versions of Family and State, 1915–1953* (Berkeley: University of California Press, 2003).

11. Yunxiang Yan, *Private Life Under Socialism: Love, Intimacy, and Family Change in a Chinese Village, 1949–1999* (Stanford, CA: Stanford University Press, 2003); and Yunxiang Yan, "Three Discourses on Neo-Familism," in *Chinese Families Upside Down: Intergenerational Dynamics and Neo-Familism in the Early 21st Century*, ed. Yunxiang Yan (Amsterdam: Brill, 2021), 253–74.

12. Everett Zhang, "China's Sexual Revolution," in *Deep China: The Moral Life of the Person*, ed. Arthur Kleinman, Yunxiang Yan, Jing Jun, Sing Lee, Everett Zhang, Pan Tianshu, Wu Fei, and Guo Jinhua (Berkeley: University of California Press, 2011), 106–51.

13. Jürgen Nautz, Paul Ginsborg, and Ton Nijhuis, eds., *The Golden Chain: Family, Civil Society, and the State* (New York: Berghahn, 2013).

14. Sara O'Shaughnessy and Emily Huddart Kennedy, "Relational Activism: Reimagining Women's Environmental Work as Cultural Change," *Canadian Journal of Sociology* 35, no. 4 (2010): 551–72; and Korolczuk, "When Parents Become Activists."

15. David Hollenbach, "The Glory of God and the Global Common Good: Solidarity in a Turbulent World," *Proceedings of the Catholic Theological Society of America* 72 (2017): 51–60.

16. Erving Goffman, *Stigma: Notes on the Management of Spoiled Identity* (Englewood Cliffs, NJ: Prentice-Hall, 1963).

17. In Australia, see David E. Gray, "Perceptions of Stigma: The Parents of Autistic Children," *Sociology of Health & Illness* 15, no. 1 (1993): 102–20; and in Canada, see Rachel Phillips, Cecilia Benoit, Helga Hallgrimsdottir, and Kate Vallance, "Courtesy Stigma: A Hidden Health Concern Among Front-Line Service Providers to Sex Workers," *Sociology of Health & Illness* 34, no. 5 (2012): 681–96.

18. Ying Chen and Chih-Jou Jay Chen, "The State Owes Us: Social Exclusion and Collective Actions of China's Bereaved Parents," *Modern China* 47, no. 6 (2021): 740–64; Helen McCabe, "Parent Advocacy in the Face of Adversity: Autism and Families in the People's Republic of China," *Focus on Autism and Other Developmental Disabilities* 22, no. 1 (2007): 39–50; Lihong Shi, "Losing an Only Child: Parental Grief Among China's Shidu Parents," in *Chinese Families Upside Down: Intergenerational Dynamics and Neo-Familism in the Early 21st Century*,

ed. Yunxiang Yan (Amsterdam: Brill, 2021), 176–93; and Wei Wei and Yunxiang Yan, "Rainbow Parents and the Familial Model of Tongzhi (LGBT) Activism in Contemporary China," *Chinese Sociological Review* 54, no. 5 (2021): 451–72.

19. Jinhua Guo and Arthur Kleinman, "Stigma: HIV/AIDS, Mental Illness, and China's Nonperson," in *Deep China: The Moral Life of the Person, What Anthropology and Psychiatry Tell Us About China Today*, ed. Arthur Kleinman, Yunxiang Yan, Jing Jun, Sing Lee, Everett Zhang, Pan Tianshu, Wu Fei, and Guo Jinhua (Berkeley: University of California Press, 2011), 237–62.

20. Chen and Chen, "The State Owes Us," 11.

21. Inclusion China "家长组织联盟 2017 年年报" (2017 Annual Report of the National Consortium of Parent Organizations for Children with Intellectual Disabilities), accessed March 2, 2021, http://www.inclusion-china.org/informationdisclosure/annals/; and Yuntian Yi, "国内100个人中就有1个自闭症患者？背后真正的原因你知道多少？" (One of a hundred people suffers from autism; how much do you know about the deep causes?), 2020, accessed March 2, 2021, https://zhuanlan.zhihu.com/p/114837498.

22. LGBTQIA+ people in Greater China are commonly referred to as *tongzhi* (meaning comrade or comradeship in English). In a way, this is similar to the appropriation of the word "queer" in Western LGBTQIA+ communities, but it is derived from the respected revolutionary usage in the International Communist Movement rather than from any derogatory term. See Wah-Shan Chou, "Homosexuality and the Cultural Politics of *Tongzhi* in Chinese Societies," *Journal of Homosexuality* 40, no. 3–4 (2001): 27–46.

23. Shi, "Losing an Only Child."

24. Fangjing Tu, "WeChat and Civil Society in China," *Communication and the Public* 1, no. 3 (2016): 343–50.

25. Wei and Yan, "Rainbow Parents and the Familial Model of Tongzhi (LGBT) Activism in Contemporary China."

26. Elisabeth Lund Engebretsen, "'As Long as My Daughter Is Happy': 'Familial Happiness' and Parental Support-Narratives for LGBTQ Children," in *Chinese Discourses on Happiness*, ed. Gerda Wielander and Derek Hird (Hong Kong: Hong Kong University Press, 2019), 86–106.

27. Yi Yuntian, "国内100个人中就有1个自闭症患者？背后真正的原因你知道多少？" (1 percent of the Chinese suffers from autisms; how much do you know the causes of this phenomenon?), accessed March 2, 2021, https://zhuanlan.zhihu.com/p/114837498.

28. Helen McCabe and Guosheng Deng, "'So They'll Have Somewhere to Go': Establishing Non-Governmental Organizations (NGOs) for Children with Autism in the People's Republic of China," *Voluntas* 29, no. 5 (2018): 1019–32.

29. Mingyue Ma and Hong Zeng, "'大地妈妈' 易解放的十五年生死承诺" (Mother Earth's life-devotion commitment during the past 15 years), March 8, 2018, 凤凰网公益 (*Phoenix Net for public interest*), accessed February 20, 2021, https://gongyi.ifeng.com/a/20180308/44899816_0.shtml.

30. Shangjun Li, "'大地妈妈'易解放和她的五百万棵 '绿色生命树'" (Mother Earth and her five-million trees of green life), December 1, 2017, 中国青年网 (*China Youth Net*), accessed February 20, 2021, http://qclz.youth.cn/znl/201712/t20171201_11091092.htm.

31. Shi, "Losing an Only Child," 187.

32. Shi, "Losing an Only Child," 187–89.

33. All quotes are from my fieldwork notes in 2019. Also see Danxu Yang, "失独家庭被'黑恶化', 舆论忧成打压民众工具" (Shidu families demonized; Public opinion at risk of becoming an oppressive tool), 《联合早报》 (*Lianhe zaobao [Singapore]*), April 1, 2019, accessed April 16, 2019, https://www.zaobao.com.sg/znews/greater-china/story20190401-944756.

34. LRela, "同志家长为孩子相亲被驱逐后，大家在讨论什么？" (After the tongzhi parents engaging in matchmaking for their gay children were dispersed, what have people said about it?), May 22, 2017, accessed November 10, 2019, http://www.sohu.com/a/142660741_660608; and Vista K, "'出柜'的父母：我要告诉全世界，我的孩子不是妖怪" (The coming-out parent: I want to tell the whole world that my child is not a freak), 每日头条 (*Everyday Headline News*), July 7, 2017, accessed November 6, 2019, https://kknews.cc/zh-my/baby/ogyq5e5.html.

35. Tianyi Wen, "同性恋家长为子征婚" (Parents of homosexuals matchmaking for their adult children), 《中国新闻周刊》 (*China News Weekly*), June 21, 2017, accessed October 2, 2019, http://www.chinanews.com/sh/2017/06-21/8256976.shtml.

36. PFLAG China, "同性恋亲友会2019年报" (The 2019 annual report of PFLAG China), accessed March 26, 2020, http://www.pflag.org.cn/h-nd -2166.html#_np=148_469.

37. McCabe and Deng, "'So They'll Have Somewhere to Go,'" 1026.

38. Huiru Li, "张晓强和她的孩子们" (Zhang Xiaoqiang and her children), Shaanxi Net, January 16, 2020, accessed January 3, 2021, http://m .cnwest.com/xian/a/2020/01/16/18382339.html.

39. Cishanjia Zhongguo, "疫情中，心智障碍者的集体自救" (Collective self-rescue of parents of children with intellectual disabilities during the COVID-19 pandemic), 新浪网 (*Sino.com*), March 6, 2020, accessed January 26, 2021, https://k.sina.com.cn/article_2015391145_78206da900100u2m7 .html.

40. Xiaoxing Huang, "'星星港'抚平丧子之痛" (Appeasing the pain of losing one's child at "Harbor of Stars"), 《都市快报》 (*City Post*), October 23, 2011, accessed November 16, 2020, https://hzdaily.hangzhou.com.cn /dskb/html/2011-10/23/content_1155989.htm.

41. Xiangli Kong, "风险社会视角下失独家庭的政策支持机制" (The policy-support mechanism for *shidu* families from the perspective of a risk society), 《北京行政学院学报》 (*Journal of Beijing Administration Institute*), no. 5 (2018): 101–9.

42. Rui Ba, "部分失独者申请国家补偿" (Some *Shidu* parents demanding state compensation), 法制晚报 (*Evening News of Rule of Law*), April 25, 2014, accessed March 13, 2021, http://news.sina.com.cn/c/2014-04 -25/141530011113.shtml; and Kong, "风险社会视角下失独家庭的政策 支持机制."

43. Chen and Chen, "The State Owes Us," 15.

44. Guangzong Mu, "失独父母的自我拯救和社会拯救" (Self-help and social rescue of *shidu* parents), 《中国农业大学学报社会科学版》 (*China Agricultural University Journal: Social Science Edition*) 32, no. 3 (2015): 117–21.

45. Ba, "部分失独者申请国家补偿"; and Chen and Chen, "The State Owes Us."

46. For example, see Bichun Zhang and Baojun Xu, "失独父母的非制度 化政治参与及其分类治理" (The noninstitutional political participation of *shidu* parents and the differentiated governance), *Jianghan Forum*, no. 8 (2015): 132–37.

47. "Yang, Danxu. 2019. "失独家庭被'黑恶化', 舆论忧成打压民众工具" (*Shidu* families demonized; Public opinion at risk of becoming an oppressive tool). 《联合早报》 (Lianhe zaobao [Singapore]), April 1. https://www.zaobao.com.sg/znews/greater-china/story20190401-944756 (accessed April 16, 2019)."

48. Adela Garzón, "Cultural Change and Familism," *Psicothema* 12 (suppl.) (2000): 45–54.

49. Xiaotong Fei, *From the Soil: The Foundations of Chinese Society*, trans. Gary Hamilton and Wang Zheng (1948; repr. Berkeley: University of California Press, 1992).

50. Guo and Kleinman, "Stigma: HIV/AIDS, Mental Illness, and China's Nonperson"; Yunxiang Yan, "Doing Personhood in Chinese Culture: The Desiring Individual, Moralist Self, and Relational Person," *Cambridge Anthropology* 35, no. 2 (2017): 1–17; and Heng-hao Chang, "From Housewives to Activists: Lived Experiences of Mothers for Disability Rights in Taiwan," *Asian Journal of Women's Studies* 15, no. 3 (2009): 34–59.

51. For example, in the village where I have been doing field research since the late 1980s, a couple was widely praised as exemplary in making themselves decent human beings (i.e., *zuoren*) because they worked and lived extremely frugally. For decades, they had refused to buy good food or new clothing for themselves. Yet they had built the best homes in the village for their two sons and financed the sons' marriages in style. Another couple was known to be generous on gift-giving occasions, which was especially virtuous because they were childless and thus had many fewer opportunities to host gift-receiving ceremonies themselves.

52. Goffman, *Stigma*.

53. William R. Jankowiak and Robert L. Moore, *Family Life in China* (Cambridge: Polity, 2017); Gonçalo Santos and Stevan Harrell, eds. *Transforming Patriarchy: Chinese Families in the Twenty-First Century* (Seattle: University of Washington Press, 2017); and Martin King Whyte, "Continuity and Change in Urban Chinese Family Life," *China Journal*, no. 53 (2005): 9–33.

54. Yan, *Private Life Under Socialism*; Yan, "Neo-Familism and the State in Contemporary China"; and Yan, "Introduction: The Inverted Family, Post-Patriarchal Intergenerationality and Neo-Familism."

55. Yan, "Neo-Familism and the State in Contemporary China."

56. Yan, "Doing Personhood in Chinese Culture."

57. See Goffman, *Stigma*. In one case I witnessed when I lived in rural northeast China in the 1970s, a deceased unmarried man in his early thirties was not dressed in appropriate funeral clothing and was placed in a thin box instead of a proper coffin; he was then buried in the middle of a field far away from the community cemetery. This was because he was not considered a complete person. It was sad to watch him being treated so heartlessly, yet no one, his parents and siblings included, felt there was anything wrong with such cruelty. The villagers were simply doing exactly what was prescribed for them by traditional familism.

58. Yan, "Doing Personhood in Chinese Culture," 5.

59. Wu Fei, "Suicide, a Modern Problem in China," in *Deep China: The Moral Life of the Person, What Anthropology and Psychiatry Tell Us About China Today*, ed. Arthur Kleinman, Yunxiang Yan, Jing Jun, Sing Lee, Everett Zhang, Pan Tianshu, Wu Fei, and Jinhua Guo (Berkeley: University of California Press, 2011), 213–36.

60. Yan, "Intergenerational Intimacy and Descending Familism in Rural North China."

61. Yan, "Three Discourses on Neo-Familism."

62. Yunxiang Yan, "Parents-Driven Divorce and Individualization Among Urban Chinese Youth," *International Social Science Journal*, nos. 213–214 (2015): 317–30; Yan, "Intergenerational Intimacy and Descending Familism in Rural North China"; and Yan, "Neo-Familism and the State in Contemporary China."

63. Liu, "转型期的家庭代际情感与团结"; and Yan, "Introduction: The Inverted Family, Post-Patriarchal Intergenerationality and Neo-Familism."

64. Becky Yang Hsu, "Having It All: Filial Piety, Moral Weighting, and Anxiety Among Young Adults," in *The Chinese Pursuit of Happiness: Anxieties, Hopes, and Moral Tensions in Everyday Life*, ed. Becky Yang Hsu and Richard Madsen (Berkeley: University of California Press, 2019), 42–65.

65. Harriet Evans, "The Intimate Individual: Perspectives from the Mother-Daughter Relationship in Urban China," in *Chinese Modernity and the Individual Psyche*, ed. Andrew Kipnis (New York: Palgrave, 2012), 119–47; Yan, "Intergenerational Intimacy and Descending Familism in Rural North China"; and Jinghui Zhu and Zhu Qiaoyan, "温和的理性：当代浙江农村家庭代际关系研究" (Mild rationality: A study of

intergenerational relationships among rural families in Zhejiang province), 《浙江社会科学》 (*Zhejiang Social Sciences*), no. 10 (2013): 99–105, 129, 158.

66. Yan, "Neo-Familism and the State in Contemporary China," 211–15.

67. Wei and Yan, "Rainbow Parents and the Familial Model of Tongzhi (LGBT) Activism in Contemporary China."

68. Shi, "Losing an Only Child."

69. Leilei Dai, "遗嘱，透露出'星星父母'们的悠悠家愁" (Anxiety in the will of parents of children with intellectual disabilities), 《法治周末报》 (*Weekend Post of Rule of Law*), July 10, 2019, accessed January 28, 2021, https://www.sohu.com/a/325865012_99923264.

70. Jiudao, Hailun, and Chenxing. "中国父母：当我得知孩子是同性恋后" (Chinese Parents: After learning my child is a gay), Voice of America, July 23, 2016. https://www.voachinese.com/a/chinese-lgbts-parents-opens-up-20160722/3431124.html.

71. Huang, "'星星港'抚平丧子之痛."

72. See Kim McBrayer, "Plotting Confucian and Disability Rights Paradigms on the Advocacy-Activism Continuum: Experiences of Chinese Parents of Children with Dyslexia in Hong Kong," *Cambridge Journal of Education* 44, no. 1 (2014): 93–111.

73. Wei and Yan, "Rainbow Parents and the Familial Model of Tongzhi (LGBT) Activism in Contemporary China."

74. Ivan Franceschini and Elisa Nesossi, "State Repression of Chinese Labor NGOs: A Chilling Effect?," *The China Journal*, no. 80 (2018): 111–29; and Anthony J. Spires, "Regulation as Political Control: China's First Charity Law and Its Implications for Civil Society," *Nonprofit and Volunteer Sector Quarterly* 49, no. 3 (2020): 571–88.

75. Yan, "Three Discourses on Neo-Familism."

76. See Banfield, *The Moral Basis of a Backward Society*.

77. See Nautz, Ginsborg, and Nijhuis, eds., *The Golden Chain*; and for a brief review see Korolczuk, "When Parents Become Activists."

78. See Ginsborg, "Uncharted Territories."

2

FAMILY METAPHORS

Inequality, Culture War, and Imperiled Common
Good in China and the United States

I n the past forty years, with the collapse of the Communist bloc, a globalized market economy has pervaded all
parts of the world. Its net result has been a decrease in economic inequality among nations. Thus the gap between the
American and Chinese economies has greatly decreased; the
Chinese economy has grown spectacularly because of its market reforms and its participation in global trade. The Chinese
GDP is second only to the United States and by some defini-
tions of purchasing power parity may even now exceed that of
the United States.[1] At the same time, globalization has led to
much greater inequality *within* nations. In the United States,
the rate of inequality has constantly accelerated since 1979, and
now the top 400 billionaire families own more wealth than the
entire bottom 60 percent of the population. In China, the level
of inequality has also been rising dramatically. The initial effect
of Deng Xiaoping's movement to reform the socialist economy
beginning in 1979 was actually to narrow the gap between rural
and urban China, with result that "around 1983–1984, China was
probably more equal than it has ever been, even more equal than
under socialism." In Mao's China, the measure of inequality, the

"Gini coefficient," was one of the lowest in the world. But after the mid-1980s, the rate of inequality in China soared. According to Barry Naughton, the "size and speed of China's increase in inequality are unprecedented. . . .[T]here may be no other case where a society's income distribution has deteriorated so much so fast."[2] Now, the Gini coefficient is almost as high and perhaps even higher in China than in the United States.[3] Although the overall per capita income is much lower, by some measures there are more billionaires in China than in the United States.[4]

In both societies the inequality generates the potential—and currently in the United States the actuality—of considerable social unrest. Marx would have predicted that the rising levels of inequality would lead to class conflict. But here I argue that in everyday life in both the United States and China the inequality is not *experienced* as class conflict.

In the United States, about 60 percent say that inequality is a serious problem—a view emphasized by political leaders such as Bernie Sanders—but only about 40 percent say that addressing inequality is a top political priority. There is not strong support for addressing inequality by redistributing wealth from the top of the income distribution to the bottom. Preferred policies are those that would allow those in the lower half of the income distribution to better themselves by access to better paying jobs through education and training and by being secure against personal disaster by having affordable health care. These attitudes are perhaps connected to a particularly American optimism about prospects for upward mobility—although such prospects have actually diminished relative to many European countries and Canada. Another factor is widespread distrust (although more concentrated among Republicans than Democrats) of the federal government's ability to fairly and justly redistribute wealth.[5]

Thus, in the United States concern about inequality seems rather abstract, removed from the concerns of daily life. What ignites more intense passions are "culture wars": struggles over moral visions stereotypically attributed to "liberal elites" and "populists," battles over science and education, religion and secularism, gender and sexuality, racial inclusion and exclusion.

In China, too, surveys done by Martin Whyte and colleagues show a relative lack of concern about inequality, even among people at the lower end of the income spectrum.[6] However, although public conflicts—or at least the news about them—are suppressed, there is evidence of animus over "corruption"—perceived personal decadence coming together with an immoral use of personal guanxi—and within various sectors, against gender discrimination, religion, the civic inclusion of migrant laborers, and freedom of intellectual and emotional expression. So despite rising inequality, daily life is afflicted more by culture conflicts than by class struggle.

I argue here, however, that in both societies these cultural conflicts are connected with rising inequality, and indeed in their current intensity are a manifestation of it. A simple Marxist explanation for this would be that ruling elites foment conflicts over culture to distract the masses from becoming mobilized against the rich. I don't doubt that this is some part of the story, but I argue that there is another important part: the social foundation for elite manipulation. Rather than drawing on Marx, I invoke Max Weber's account of the cultural conflicts of modernity.

Max Weber described the modern moral condition as beset by irreconcilable tensions between competing values. Perhaps ever since human societies achieved a level of complexity beyond small hunter-gatherer groups, people have been faced with some form of this existential pluralism: some of the various goods to which we have been taught to aspire are incompatible. But in the modern world, according to Weber, the major value spheres have become increasingly differentiated. The spheres of religion, kinship, economics, politics, art, sex, and science have become increasingly rationalized, and the values governing these spheres are increasingly at cross purposes. Our world, Weber said, is fundamentally polytheistic—a world of "warring gods."[7]

Without necessarily agreeing with Weber's theoretical explanation of the tensions, I do hold that his description of modern tensions—between work and family, politics and the economy, religion and science—is accurate, and I argue here that the effect of rising inequality generated by the globalized market economy is to increase the conflict among these warring gods, leading to social discontents that in the United States and Europe are manifesting themselves in angry populist movements. Such forces are being held in check for now in China by the "stability maintenance" mechanisms of an authoritarian state. As long as levels of domestic inequality not only persist but keep rising, however, I believe that neither the United States nor the Chinese system—and indeed the world system—will be able to maintain stability. I conclude by linking this predicament to the challenges of seeking a global common good.

But if rising inequality is an important factor for the discontents, why does it often manifest itself not in clear class consciousness but in value conflicts—"culture wars"? Let us first build a theoretical framework that we can then use to compare tensions endemic to the United States and China.

COMPARATIVE FRAMEWORK

In Max Weber's classic presentation, the conflicts presented to modern people are among abstract "values" that become logically

differentiated from one another by becoming more systematically articulated through a process of "rationalization." Individuals are then faced with existential dilemmas in trying to choose
among competing values.[8] But here I present these value spheres
in less abstract terms, seeing them embedded in distinct kinds
of communities, both communities of everyday life and "imagined communities" extending, with the aid of modern media, the
experiences of daily life into a "social imaginary" of encompass-
ing communities embodying different facets of ordinary life.[9]
The "existential dilemmas" people face are the result of being
pulled by competing social pressures from these communities.

By "communities of everyday life," I mean first of all the network of personal relationships. These networks generate common experiences, articulated through common moral languages
that can be expanded into imagined communities through
modern social media. We can know ourselves as a national community of family communities, a part of a universal religious
community, a business community, a political community, a scientific community, and so forth. The common narratives of such
imagined communities capture us to the extent that they resonate with our experience within our interpersonal networks.

We can make a distinction between communities of everyday life that are relatively closed (most of my associates are
also associates of each other) and those relatively open (most
of my associates have their own networks not associated with
me). The anthropologist Mary Douglas observed that people
within densely intertwined closed networks would understand
their social relations though a "condensed" moral language. Such
a form of speech uses multilayered, metaphorical symbols that
condense many meanings gained through the common experience of relatively closed groups. Some of these condensed symbols are felt to be so intrinsically powerful that in the very act of

being expressed they bring about what they signify. Such forms of speech are the basis for sacramental religions.[10]

According to Douglas, people in relatively open networks use an "elaborated" moral language. These are, first, based on symbols with clearly defined meanings, which individuals can use to communicate their unique interests and feelings with the hope of reaching agreement with someone with complementary interests and feelings. It also leads to a religion of inner experience rather than an external form and to a critical consciousness that frees individuals from habitual following authority, even as it allows them to calculate ahead in a complexly organized world.[11]

In Chinese societies, the language of kinship found in local agrarian communities organized through familial lineages would be an example of a condensed moral language. In America one would especially find such language in localized rural communities and long-standing urban neighborhoods whose members share common bonds of ethnicity, religion, and occupation. A difference between the American and Chinese style of condensed languages is that the American sort is more inflected with individualism. It is less oriented toward the common obligations of kinship and more on flattering and derogatory terms for individual character—ways of articulating who in your circle of acquaintances is loyal and disloyal, who can be counted on, who will have your back in the rough and tumble of daily life.

The elaborated moral language is more universal and found wherever in the world there is a complicated division of labor coordinated by large bureaucracies. In the United States, it is the language of "bureaucratic individualism," of individuals trying to advance themselves through the maze of degrees and certifications and standards and regulations that define corporate and political hierarchies.[12]

Of course no modern society is composed solely of closed or open communities. None use a purely condensed or elaborated moral language to understand social relations. We need a mix to live a satisfactory life. But I suggest that rising inequality tends to pull such a mix apart, leading to a polarization between parts of the society that use more condensed or elaborated moral languages.

In the framework presented here, the different spheres of family, economy, politics, religion, and science are each expressed through a kind of imagined community; but they are imagined differently when proceeding from a relatively closed community with a condensed moral language or an open community with an elaborated language. I first illustrate how this might work in the United States before proceeding to a comparison with China.

UNITED STATES

Open and Closed Communities

In the United States—at least those parts invested in its hegemonic white European cultural traditions—many people see themselves as part of a national community of family communities, a business community, a political community, a universal religious community, and perhaps a scientific community. The common narratives and rituals of these communities capture us to the extent that they resonate with our experience within our interpersonal networks. When narratives and rituals are understood in terms of dense moral language, one may get a different interpretation than if they are understood in terms of an elaborated language. For example, for Christians using a dense emotionally resonant, multilayered language, the stories of the Bible might be interpreted in a literal way, and rituals like the

Eucharist might be seen as containing the Real Presence rather being just symbolic. Those using the elaborated language may make distinctions between factual history and poetic myths, symbol and substance, and see moral rules less as sacred external constraints and more as guidelines to shape the promptings of one's heart. This can lead to different ways of imagining one's religious community, which sets the stage for struggles over those imaginations. All imagined communities, not just religious ones, get split by such battles.

Different imagined communities represent different life directions, different sets of hopes and fears, different imagined goals for one's energy and ambition. To some degree, perhaps everyone feels the tension imposed by these different life directions. But the tensions may be experienced differently by people at different levels of an economically unequal society. The tightly intertwined local networks, with their condensed speech codes, are more common toward the bottom. Those near the top tend to live within relatively open, branching networks with elaborated speech codes learned especially through higher education.

In the more tightly intertwined local networks with their condensed speech codes, the boundaries between different spheres of life may be blurred. People may have jobs in large corporations but don't harbor realistic ambitions of moving up the organizational hierarchy and away from their community. Work is a job to get enough income to raise one's family and maintain a decent level of consumption within the local community. Within the community some are more affluent than others, particularly local business owners, but they (like Howard Newton, the owner of a car dealership portrayed in *Habits of the Heart*[13]) are tied to poorer members by bonds of familiarity and friendship, and they gain pride not simply by being economically successful relative to the nation's population as a whole but relative to their local community. Local churches are focal places for meeting community acquaintances and celebrating the rhythms of life together even if, like most of one's friends, one may not actually be able to adhere to one's religion's moral ideals. Politics is local, and the leaders are people most community members would know, with virtues and foibles that most share, tasked with delivering some benefits from a distant impersonal government bureaucracy while shielding the community from outside restrictions. Science is a world for people able to master a lot of fancy jargon and stands apart from community common sense although it can generate some useful technology. There are certainly tensions between these different parts of community life, but they are held in check by the interlocking affiliations of community members. A side effect is suspicion and hostility toward outsiders—especially those of a different race or lifestyle. Slogans about "building walls" may be a resonant metaphor for the need for exclusion.

For people within more open, branching networks with their elaborated speech codes (consistent with the languages of utilitarian and expressive individualism), the tensions between the demands of different imagined communities are more sharply defined. The family is tied together by bonds of mutual affection and interest rather than obligations of kinship and is unsupported by a stable network of long-time acquaintances. Work becomes a career whose demands can contradict maintaining the bonds of affection needed to keep the family together. The requirements for economic advancement may contradict the call to love thy neighbor given by one's church. The imperatives of politics may interfere with the need for economic advancement and may also run contrary to the standards of one's church. Science may bring knowledge necessary to power the economy and heal the family and manage the government and even the church, but it can also impose inconvenient demands. Those living in more open networks, which tend to be found toward the upper ends of the income distribution, may have different relationships from those in more closed networks to the imagined communities that define our modern lives.

In the United States, those in relatively closed networks certainly feel the pressure of a massive, globalized corporate capitalist economy. Jobs arise and disappear because of the unfathomable interplay of global financial transactions. Government bureaucrats mandate rules and regulations—for instance about mining coal—that may disrupt whole communities for the sake of some difficult to imagine common good. Economic pressures cause collapses in nuclear families beset with epidemics of drug abuse and domestic violence, and heavy-handed welfare bureaucracies can afflict victims with distress and pain.

But in an interlocking network understood by its members in terms of a condensed language, "family values" remain strong, with family being imagined not so much in terms of companionate marriage as kinship—blood kinship and fictive kinship— with its particular bonds of loyalty. Even if most of one's relatives or neighbors may be feckless, there is more chance that someone from within that network will stand by you than anyone on the outside. In *Hillbilly Elegy*, J. D. Vance describes his Appalachian family as incredibly dysfunctional, beset with domestic violence, adultery, and substance abuse, but at the same time as an intensely loyal web of kin—grandparents and uncles and aunts, each deeply flawed, but some willing in their own way to help a vulnerable young man when one or another part of his immediate family fell apart. In this context, problems are created and solved—if they are solved at all—through personal connections to kin, or to neighbors acting as quasi kin. It is through such connections that one gets a job—if any are available—at the local factory or gets a favor from the local government or a reprieve after a brush with the law as embodied in one's local sheriff.[14]

All of the imagined communities that pull at one tend to be imagined in terms of networks of strong personal connections, loyal and disloyal people. Such is the American political community. Donald Trump's words and deeds have resonated strongly with this imaginary. He has told his followers that their problems are due to dishonest, disloyal people taking cover behind the formal rules of a "deep state." The country's problems will be solved if a leader with a big personality like Trump cuts through the wall of rules and gets rid of these disloyal people. That's how your badass uncle would do it to defend your family's honor from some arrogant bureaucrat. There is not a clear-cut boundary between public and private life. Relationships with work or government are governed by the same kinds of personal loyalties and feuds that govern one's family and local community.

This way of thinking can apply to one's imagined religious community. In the Catholic Church, for example, there are now websites criticizing the authority of the Catholic Bishops' Conference (with its own quasi-bureaucratic policy proposals based on consensus documents) and promoting allegiance to strong, outspoken bishops appointed by the more conservative popes, John-Paul II and Benedict XVI, against bishops appointed by the more liberal Pope Francis. At issue is less the fine points of doctrine than a perceived willingness on the part of the conservatives to defend Catholics from "liberals" who challenge the Church on the role of women, dialogue with other religions, and support for the rights of non-Christian migrants.[15]

In contrast are people whose social connections are comprised of more open networks, typically the new middle classes who have gained their status through mastering technical skills through higher education and whose ways of talking were reflected in the *Habits of the Heart* portraits of American individualism.[16] They certainly feel stress from competing demands of work, politics, religion, and family life. In their world, understood through an elaborated code of abstract categories negotiated through the logic of cost-benefit analysis or expressive affinity, individuals take responsibility for themselves by leaving home, choosing intimate partners and congenial friends who best fit the inclinations of their personality, negotiate trade-offs between career and family—sometimes favoring one or the other—participate in politics according to the same cost-benefit logic, and find in religion and other leisure activities a voluntarily chosen community life that resonates with their inner feelings. The felt tensions in this world are due more to "structural" issues than to interpersonal benevolence or malevolence, and one's personal success in life involves balancing the requirements of these structures and maybe sometimes changing them. This way of living brings one into contact with people who have a wide variety of personal beliefs and lifestyles—although they will mostly share similar levels of education and income—and the emphasis is on tolerating this diversity and even learning from it as long as it doesn't impede the smooth functioning of one's workplace or the sanctuary of one's private life.

Political tensions in the United States arise at least in part because of the differences between these two kinds of community, of imagining the social world, and of confronting the tensions between the larger imagined communities that shape modern life. The different kinds of community are connected with different levels of income and education. As income inequality increases, the different kinds of community are pulled further apart and the tensions between them are exacerbated. The different sides end up speaking in different languages about the social world.

Modern media brings them into contact with each other but magnifies the difference. Social media, especially, expands interpersonal networks but also encourages a condensed moral language. Much of the communication on the internet is not rationally articulated argument but emotionally charged memes that serve as markers for particular prejudiced identities. This helps foster the imagination of extended closed communities.

The net result is various forms of culture war rather than class struggle, although it is indeed intimately tied to social class.

Rising Inequality and Cultural Polarization

How has the rise of economic inequality since the late 1970s affected this? It first of all destabilized the arrangements that people had made to reconcile the competing demands of communities to which they are attached. In the United States, for example, from the end of World War II to the late 1970s, many working-class people (at least the white working class) could see a relatively high degree of harmony between the aspirations of their families, the mission of their churches, and the economic striving of the corporations that employed them. The corporation provided enough pay to sustain a middle-class lifestyle, as well as a stable job structure through which one could progress from apprentice to journeyman toward a retirement funded by a decent pension, to enjoy one's children and grandchildren, most of whom could find work locally, sometimes in the same corporation. The local churches could provide a sense of partially closed but mutually supportive community that might sustain one's family in times of difficulty—as the local Catholic parish did by providing food and fellowship and moral support for my working-class family when my father was laid off during periodic recessions. There was thus an overlap between the narratives that gave meaning to family, religion, and economic livelihood. Within a working-class milieu there may have been a sense that more open communities, such as found in university towns, represented a different way of life. "Don't go to Berkeley," my father used to tell me in the 1950s, "there are a bunch of Commies there"; but they seemed far away and for many effectively walled off by the social pressures of one's intertwined local community. But their research was leading to technologies that could benefit ordinary people. The same was true of the bohemian artists who were isolated a safe distance away in San Francisco.

But with rising inequality, that overlap began to pull apart. In the early 1980s a cause and consequence of rising inequality was a transformation in economic life. The steel foundry in Oakland where my father had worked until retirement was shut down, its products now made in Korea. Some in the younger generation (like myself) got enough higher education to achieve well-paying knowledge-based jobs, but in so doing we had to move far away from home. Those from working-class families who didn't do well in school have struggled with unstable jobs in service industries. The local parish was now mostly attended by immigrants from the Philippines who came to the neighborhood because housing was relatively cheap. But with gentrification the local demographics are changing again. The social life that once complemented the sacred liturgy of the church—its weekly bingo games, dances, charity fiestas—is no longer there. A shortage of priests left the parish thinly staffed, and one pastor had to leave suddenly when he was accused of sexual misconduct. Meanwhile those of us who have moved away have to negotiate new ways to reconcile work in demanding jobs with fragile family life and religious narratives that don't fit with the stories told in the scientific and artistic communities to which we belong.

The economic transformations left people at all social levels unsettled, but new gaps arose in the means by which people in different social strata handled the unsettledness. People with a relatively high level of education are now familiar to a higher degree than ever before with the various narratives that constitute the imagined communities of business, politics, religion, and science. They take part in institutions animated by these different narratives and associated rituals: the business corporation, the political campaign, the university research lab, the religious polity. If they don't participate in the formation of some of the narratives and rituals, they have friends and associates who do. So their imagination becomes filled with a potentially exciting array of possibilities but also a confusing cacophony of stories, instantiated in rituals, that pull one's identity in different directions.

With the help of the social capital that comes from diverse social networks and the cultural capital that comes from higher learning, relatively privileged people can follow various strategies to handle the tensions between these imagined communities. They can personally compartmentalize—for example, acting like a cutthroat competitor during the workweek and a benevolent churchgoer on Sunday, or a sober scientist in the lab and an uninhibited reveler at the rock concert. They can develop an attitude of tolerance toward acquaintances committed to particular different narratives while reserving close friendships for those invested in similar narratives. They can take pride in a cynical relativism, or they can earnestly try to reconcile different community attachments by searching intellectually and emotionally for higher principles.

For people in lower social strata—and even for those with a fairly high income based on work that required little education— it may be more difficult to reconcile the various narratives that modernity presents. They may not be familiar with the narratives or know them only as vague abstractions. They may find the vaguely understood pluralism more frightening than stimulating. They may try to block off discordant voices by limiting their associations to people perceived to be very similar to themselves. They may develop insular narratives that depict them and their friends as part of beleaguered imagined communities set in opposition to elites whose immorality is manifested in relativism, cynicism, and decadence. Resentment filled divisions grow, based not on differences in wealth but on perceived differences in moral integrity. This, of course, feeds into racism, sexism, homophobia and a host of other social phobias, all leading to angry pushback and recrimination—and all material for manipulation by aspiring politicians.

The different narratives are increasingly carried along by the imagined communities' own media. But there are also media that have historically tried to find a reconciling platform for diverse narratives. In the United States at the national level this is done by "mainstream media" such as the *New York Times*, *Washington Post*, and *Wall Street Journal*. However, in their news pages, if not in editorial pages, they tend to present many opposing viewpoints in a form of detached objectivity, an elaborated moral language mostly drained of emotional resonance and reconciled under a rubric of rationalized tolerance for ambiguity. It is just this style of reconciliation that will be offensive to people with limited resources to cope with many competing narratives. Newer forms of media, especially available through the internet, are readily adapted to a robust condensed language loaded with emotionally powerful memes that dispense with such plurality and reject ambiguity and stir the hearts of those disgusted with the imagined relativistic immorality of cosmopolitan elites.

The economic pressures in the United States have intensified since the turn of the century. Advances in technology have enabled corporations to replace many of their workers with robots and to outsource the rest of their blue collar jobs to countries with lower wages, particularly China. This hollowing out of manufacturing industries has left whole communities devastated, especially in the upper Midwest. These working-class communities were precisely those interlocking networks of relatives, friends, and neighbors, often working in the same factories, that provided mutual support, a sense of personal dignity, and a meaningful common life. Classical economic theory would assume that once the old industries declined workers could migrate to jobs in new industries, based on new technology. But this would have required workers to move around freely, and it was precisely the densely interlocking nature of mutually supportive networks that made it difficult for unemployed workers to migrate in search of new jobs. Economists were slow to recognize this. It means one thing for an economics professor with national and international networks of fellow professionals to move from, say, the University of Michigan to the University of California, and another for an automobile worker from Detroit with a long-standing, supportive local network to move to California where the person has no acquaintances. Afflicted with concentrated unemployment, such closed communities became prone to "deaths of despair" from suicides and opium addiction.[17] Meanwhile Wall Street financiers prospered as never before in what superficially looked like a healthy growing economy—until the financial crash of 2008, and then the COVID crisis of 2020. But as the economy recovered from the crisis of 2008, the owners of finance capital regained their wealth while all too many displaced workers stayed behind.[18] Given the current class and race-based disparities in infections and deaths from COVID, it is all too probable that we may see a similar pattern in the economic recovery.

Under such circumstances, the tensions between family, economy, politics, and science became stronger and sharper. But they were experienced in different ways by different kinds of communities located toward different ends of the economic spectrum. People in closed, interdependent networks may have different ways of imagining the national community, the business community, the political community, the religious community, and the scientific community than those in open networks.

Workers in such communities, now devastated by unemployment and underemployment, may have once imagined the business community as a benevolent force, led by tough minded, if stingy, owners who nonetheless managed to create world dominating companies that provided good jobs with decent pay even though it had to be squeezed out of them by strong unions. But now they may come to imagine the business community as a predatory force led by greedy owners working in collusion with foreign powers like China to make money while sacrificing the workers whose toil had made them rich. A vivid story with personalized villains.

Within this framework there may indeed be strong disagreements. Exactly who are the villains? Business owners or "expert" bureaucrats from the deep state who have enabled the nefarious activity?

There is the same kind of framework for imagining and criticizing the political community. The political community may have once been seen as a powerful protective force with tough leaders—some tougher than others—who protected the blessed American way of life against foreign Communists and jihadists, managed immigration, especially from the global south, kept domestic unrest low or at least confined to inner cities, and provided a decent social safety net to those who deserved it and through no fault of their own needed it. But now the community may be dominated by selfish leaders with cozy relations to top business elites and foreign enemies like China to enrich themselves at the expense of ordinary hard working people. But who exactly are the selfish leaders? Some say Donald Trump is a selfish leader. Is he or is he not? There may be strong debates about this, but they hinge not so much on whether he respected institutional rules, or even the Constitution, but on whether he "gets things done" with sufficient toughness for the benefit of "people like me."

In the same vein, the religious community may have been imagined as a set of mutually tolerant Protestant, Catholic, and Jewish denominations, all led by competent leaders affirming central values of the American Way. But now it is divided between robust preachers against confusing forces of moral relativism and intellectual skepticism. For Catholics, for instance, who are the true shepherds: the uncompromisingly orthodox Pope Benedict or the sentimentally pragmatic Pope Francis?

Finally, those within this way of imagining may have once seen the scientific community as a collection of somewhat eccentric individuals, unlike themselves, who could invent powerful weapons and household products that would keep America great. But they may now see them as an assemblage of mostly foreigners, especially Asians, who are producing technologies that put ordinary workers out of work and are arrogantly propagating talk about global warming—and with the COVID-19 pandemic, the need for social distancing—that would lead to a decline in the American standard of living.

On the other hand, those in more open networks—usually beneficiaries of higher education and in occupations with more income and prestige than manufacturing jobs—may certainly feel the pressures of balancing family, work, politics, religion, and science in their ordinary lives. But having networks of contacts that cut across business, government, religion, and science, they might imagine these communities as systems of roles individuals occupy for parts of their lives while striving for balance with other parts. In each imagined community, the roles are structured by common rules: in the family, for example, by rules for effective communication and negotiation; in the business community by rules for maximizing efficiency and profit; in the political community by rules for maintaining power in an effective but legitimate way; in the religious community rules for being an active congregant; and in the scientific community, rules for discovery, verification, and publication.

Problems with these communities are less the problem of identifiable malevolent actors than of the rules, that is, the "structure." In times of economic stress, the problem is not greedy business owners—the "system" forces everyone to compete to achieve efficiency and profit—but the rules governing the system, which may be improved by better regulations, better insurance for the downside, and better protocols for communication and coordination. For politics, better channels of communication, better polling and advertising, better methods for managing consent, and more effective bureaucracies. For religion, better training for ministry, better supervision, better transparency of decision-making, and fuller congregational engagement. For science, clearer standards for peer review, stricter rules to prevent fraud, and better practices for communicating findings to the public.

This is not to say that there is simple consensus about these issues. Indeed there are often strong controversies. Should there be more or less regulation of businesses? Should government bureaucracies be beefed up or slimmed down? Taxes decreased or increased? Religious ministry based on better theology or warmer pastoral care? Science focused more on theoretical questions or applied technologies? But even when they are heated, the debates take place within a common framework and with a common style of discourse.

Whatever resolutions might be achieved to the tensions between family, economy, politics, religion, and science by either those embedded in closed or open networks, they are in the end unsatisfying. To borrow a phrase from Clifford Geertz, people are trapped in webs of significance that they themselves have spun, but none of these are strong enough to withstand the tensions placed upon them. This leads to more intense spinning of one's own webs and more intense hostility toward the different webs of others.

These different ways of imagining the "warring gods" and coping with conflict among them lead to increasing conflict between parts of the society embedded in closed solidary networks with condensed speech codes, on one hand, and those in open ended networks with elaborated codes on the other.[19] They tell the story of their lives and their struggles differently, and they have different imaginations of the larger communities that constitute the national society. This then leads to the "culture wars" between "liberals" and "populists" that currently afflict American society. The society is not divided by contending interests within a common understanding of what those interests are and a common moral vocabulary for arguing about a just resolution of contending interests. It is rent by different ways of imagining the nature of interests and arguing about the requirements of justice.

Although connected to different forms of community life, different opportunities for social mobility, and different levels of education, in the United States the different forms of social imagination are both influenced by a particularly strong tradition of individualism. It is a vision that sees society as a collection of independent individuals, each responsible for their success or failure. The two visions have different understandings of the proper forms of responsibility. One vision holds that individuals need to be tough and bold in standing up for relatives and friends. The other holds that they have to be competent in following the rules of large corporate organizations and fair in applying the rules. It is the difference between familial individualism and bureaucratic individualism. But the emphasis on the individual fosters a lot of self-righteousness. This intensifies the battles of a culture war.

Rising inequality also intensifies the battles. Pressure at the top forces the people there to work harder to reach and stay on top. A culture of individualism encourages the idea that success is the result of superior talent and hard work, which in turns engenders arrogant and condescending attitudes toward those whom they perceive as "losers." Meanwhile, those mobile individuals with wide networks who succeed in the increasingly unequal economy draw further away from the relatively closed communities of those below. Upward mobility declines. The two visions inhabit social worlds that do not touch. An effective public dialogue about the common good becomes increasingly difficult.

I lay out this rough framework for research on the United States to form a heuristic basis for comparison with China. Are there similar tensions between the life spheres in China, and have they been affected by a rapid rise in inequality? And how might this affect relations between the United States and China, and more broadly, the quest for a global common good?

CHINA

Closed and Open Communities

To a large extent, China before 1980 was a society of relatively closed networks in which family, economy, politics, religion, and science were fused together in an undifferentiated whole.

Premodern Chinese society was dominated by the inter-twined kinship networks of corporate lineages based in agrarian villages. The moral language used to understand these relation-ships was indeed a condensed one, full of categories about dif-ferent degrees of kinship and about the virtue that should be exercised to maintain harmony among all of these relationships. To be sure, Chinese village communities were never completely closed. They depended on trading and temple worship networks, mostly centered on local market towns, and also on an educa-tion system that for a few offered a path to recruitment into the imperial civil service. These were further opened by the collapse of the imperial regime, the advent of industrial modernity, and the displacements of war and revolution in the first half of the twentieth century.

After being disrupted in a turbulent early twentieth century, these forms of community and their associated moral languages were transformed by the Maoist regime. One change was that relatively closed corporate communities were made even more closed. Under the residency policies of the Maoist state, it became virtually impossible for villagers to move. In the cities, life was lived in "work units" that provided not only employment but most social welfare services, and from which, for most peo-ple, there was no exit, unless one joined the army or was sent to a prison camp for a political mistake. Primary and eventually even secondary education became universally available, but there was only a minuscule chance of expanding one's horizons through higher education.

Under party propaganda, the moral languages used to under-stand these densely intertwined closed relationships changed. Older languages about filial piety and harmony were suppressed and replaced by new languages about revolutionary spirit, prog-ress, and class struggle. But the new moral languages remained very dense, not so much a matter of careful Marxist analytic distinctions but of deeply layered, emotion laden calls to annihilate enemies and achieve unending progress through struggle. Even though the Marxist vision was supposed to be "scientific" and analytic and to describe universal laws of history, in the hands of the Maoist propagandists it was interpreted through an experience of deeply personal struggle against morally good and evil members of tightly intertwined communities in a kind of condensed speech code. One element the Maoists added to this was the notion of struggle. When you substitute harmony for struggle within a closed community, the struggle has to take on life and death dimensions. You cannot afford to let your foe survive to fight another day.

Nonetheless, under the surface of the propaganda, older moral languages continued to be used. The language of class struggle could be used by one part of a kinship network to attack another, or by variously defined insiders to scapegoat outsiders.

The party-state consisted of hierarchical layers, each layer a fairly closed community of comrades. At the top it was something like the aristocracy at an imperial court. Top officials went to the same schools, lived in proximity, attended the same leisure events, and arranged marriages between each other's children. Even as they split into factions they talked of their social relations in languages of loyalty and deference under the guise of Marxist rhetoric.

The Cultural Revolution temporarily opened closed communities; Red Guards roamed the country denouncing family ties, even with their parents, and attacking people deemed to have special privileges, all in a hypermoralized, quasi-Marxist language. But its end result was a further closure of the society. As far as possible, local communities hunkered down. Red Guard factions pitted those accused of having privileged

family connections against those who felt relatively less privileged. After the chaos was over, the old closed circles of loyalty
and deference returned.

The Reform Era: Rising Inequality in a
Globalized Economy

An opening of both community relations and moral language
began to occur with Deng Xiaoping's reforms after 1979. Movement restrictions were loosened, educational opportunities were
expanded together with a new emphasis on expertise, constraints
on media communication were relaxed, and students and scholars were sent to study abroad to increase the exchange of ideas
with foreign cultures.

This led to a rapid differentiation between family, economy,
politics, religion, and science. The rapid pace of this differentiation ("compressed modernity") was extremely unsettling.
The spheres were not as separate as in the United States, and
the peculiar mixture of separation and fusion led to mixtures
of experiential freedom and despair. There are multiple ways
to imagine these experiences. In the ferment leading up to the
June 4, 1989, movement, Li Shengzhi, a leading intellectual, told
me that "our problem is not that we don't have ideas—we have
plenty of ideas. The problem is that no one has the same ideas."
This problem persists in China, even as the mix of ideas changes.
In the United States rising inequality has been leading to polarization into two main forms of discourse, whereas in China it
has created more fragmentation. Culture conflict in China has
become more like a persistent guerilla insurgency, a scattering
of skirmishes in the interior of a society held together by the
integument of a powerful state.

As in the United States, people imagine the separate spheres as extended communities that mirror their experience in their primary communities. These communities are constituted by relatively closed networks, imagined through a familistic language of hierarchical responsibilities and obligations. Not only in premodern China but in the present, the dominant metaphor has been that of the family. But the concept, and indeed felt reality of the Chinese family, is not the same as the dominant modern Western idea. Chinese social scientists still acknowledge the relevance of the great anthropologist Fei Xiaotong's account. As he observed, if a friend in England or America wrote a letter saying that he was going to "bring his family" to visit, the recipient knows very well who will be coming with him. But "in China, although we frequently see the phrase 'Your entire family is invited,' very few people could say exactly which persons should be included under 'family.'" A wealthy, powerful person may include in his family anyone who is related in any way. But with a reversal of fortune, one's family could shrink to a very small group. The configuration of Chinese society is "like the rings of successive ripples that are propelled outward on the surface when you throw a stone into water. Each individual is the center of the rings emanating from his social influence. Whenever the ripples reach, affiliations occur. The rings used by each person at any given time or place are not necessarily the same."[20]

This way of understanding one's social relations as open-ended relationships imagined in terms of an infinitely expandable family has been practically constricted by the political economy that came into being under the Communist regime. Because of the household registration laws enacted in the late 1950s, farmers could not leave their local communities and urban workers could not leave their work units. In the countryside, this led to tightly bounded relations, with clear distinctions between in-groups and out-groups, most imagined in terms of familistic ties. It is a kind of thinking that has always led to building walls around villages, around urban residential compounds, around universities, and around all sorts of government buildings. The size of the wall is a symbol of the importance of those within it.[21]

It is a mentality that could lead to extreme brutality toward those who did not belong, illustrated most grotesquely at the intimate level in the story by Liao Yiwu about the village that burned a woman to death who contracted leprosy and was suspected of harboring an evil spirit.[22] But on the national level it can also foster grotesque brutality toward non-Han ethnic minorities, especially the 1.5 million Uyghurs in concentration camps and the Tibetans being subjected to repression.[23]

Although villages in the post-Mao era have been opened up, indeed in many places hollowed out as residents migrate to the cities for work, the migrants often have little inclination or cause to trust those who employ them. The owners of factories who employ these workers have a great incentive to cultivate thick personal relationships (*guanxi*), which often are articulated in quasi-familistic terms, with networks of party officials linked all the way to the top to Big Daddy Xi Jinping, but they have little incentive to treat their workers as anything other than cogs in a machine. The Dongguan factory girls portrayed in Leslie Chang's book *Factory Girls* constantly lie to their employers, producing all sorts of phony credentials, and their employers constantly lie to them, making empty promises about pay raises and job security.[24] Everyone uses everyone else, each gaining some money while often losing basic human dignity. As a poem by the migrant worker Xie Xiangnan expresses it: "My finest five years went into the input feeder of a machine, I watched those five youthful years come out of the machine's asshole—each formed into an elliptical plastic toy."[25]

Because of the way the household system (*hukou*) works, most migrant workers can never completely sever their ties with their families and natal communities. They can never be full urban citizens, with access to urban educational and social welfare services. Thus they continue to remit some of their earnings to their parents and grandparents, who in turn are often the primary caregivers of their children, but their daily lives are lived apart from those families, at the mercy of employers who use them only as cogs in a profit-making machine. They are faced with the indifference of urban permanent residents who would not want to socialize with them and of urban governments that drive them out of cities to make the cities look beautiful when hosting major international events. As a Tibetan migrant woman in a documentary by Joselyn Ford puts it, "I have nowhere to call home."[26]

The primary experience for people in the upper end of the unequal society is that of a relatively closed community imagined through familistic metaphors. Exposés in the American media (censored in China) have revealed how billions of dollars in wealth have been amassed by the ramifying kinship networks of China's top leaders.[27] Here indeed are the elastic families that Fei Xiaotong theorized. Their wealth comes from the desire of other entrepreneurs to establish guanxi with them, connections based on a particularistic exchange of favors and cemented in elaborate banquets and other rituals. Such relationships are a way to break into relatively closed relationships, but they never allow for complete entry; that is, a strong moral relationship based on the ethics of familial loyalty and responsibility. The exchange of gifts, aka bribes, creates fragile relationships. Both sides often want to stabilize the relationship with receipts and secretly recorded videos that can be used for mutual blackmail.[28]

The reliance on guanxi extends deep into the urban middle classes. Although family networks were disrupted during the

Maoist regime when the closed work units of the state took over the roles families might have provided, these networks have now revived as the state has pulled back from its provision of housing and welfare. People must fall back on the support of parents and grandparents. For many people, getting a good job or getting a license to start a small business or getting access to any kind of scarce resource depends on building good guanxi, either directly or through the extended family of someone from whom one needs a favor.

Fragmented Social Imaginaries

All the while, families, both rural and urban, are faced with competing pressures from the economy, politics, religion, and science. What do these look like in the imagination of people who have historically and culturally been embedded in relatively closed familistic communities?

The economy does not look like an impersonal market guided by an invisible hand but like an intertwined network of people with money and power becoming evermore intertwined toward the top and more loosely articulated at the bottom. If you are at the bottom, coming from the countryside with no resources other than your labor power, you can scramble to get paying jobs in factories and shops whose profits go to the better connected middle and upper classes. The strong do what they will, and the weak suffer what they must.

But there is perhaps more commonality of vision up and down the economic ladder in China than in the United States. At all levels people use a condensed language of moral responsibility toward extended families and people treated like family. It is a thicker language of moral interconnection than American individualistic discourse. But it is also a language of particularistic exclusion that justifies predatory behavior by the well connected to those in the exclusion zone and a frantic amoral scramble for resources among the excluded. However, the productivity of the system has brought enough wealth to those near the bottom that they may consider themselves lucky compared to their forebears.

One exception to this picture in China may be the young generation—millennials and younger, especially children of the urban middle classes. According to some social researchers—and maybe exaggerated complaints of parents—many of these children, influenced by consumer culture and spoiled by doting parents under the one-child policy, seem particularly self-centered. Having sacrificed so much for their children, parents complain that the children don't reciprocate with sufficient filial piety. One researcher says "people in this generation have an individualistic and egoistic self."[29] But it may be that people in this generation have an "elastic self" made possible by the ability to enter a wider network of relations through the internet.[30] There seems to be a divide between youth with good family connections and enough cultural capital to get a high level of education and access to stable jobs, on one hand, and "slackers" who have neither and seem especially prone to egoistic and disruptive behavior, on the other. In any case, a generational divide may complicate the cultural fragmentation exacerbated by rising inequality.

There is another important exception to this picture, which is currently a more politically consequential one. Professionals of all kinds—scientists, teachers, doctors, social workers, journalists, lawyers, clergy—are inducted into an ethic of professional autonomy and taught to evaluate themselves by standards integral to the profession attributed to individual achievement, not personal connections. Work in the profession often requires movement far away from parents and relatives and service to clients without prejudice to family background or status. This produces a vision of an economy inhabited ideally by meritocratic individuals acting responsibly according to a universalistic ethic.

Examples would be the social workers I interviewed who tried to proudly follow their motto to "help people help themselves."[31] More heroic examples would be the "rights lawyers" daring to help oppressed clients seek justice, even at the risk of being imprisoned themselves.[32] There are many people like this in China, and because they are the ones most likely to be interlocutors with American scholars, their hopes and aspirations often come to be seen as the wave of the future in China. But this professional imagination of the economy is not hegemonic in China. Professionals themselves complain, most with a sigh, a few with angry determination, that they have to cultivate guanxi with influential business and political leaders to do their work. Without compromising the values of their profession, they are ineffective. Steadfastly refusing to compromise, as some rights lawyers and investigative journalists do, can land one in prison.

The economy, however, wreaks cruel havoc with many families. For those at the bottom, it separates parents from children, and its fluctuations bring instability that makes it difficult to carry out familial responsibilities. For those in the middle classes, it has led to an inflationary explosion of housing prices that make it difficult for parents to provide the money their children need to have a home of their own for a spouse. And the stressfulness of jobs pressures children to neglect responsibilities of caring for parents in old age.[33] The pressures also contribute to a high divorce rate, which is aided by the proclivity of men in the higher reaches of the economy to enjoy themselves by acquiring mistresses.[34]

In China, any imagination of the economy has to overlap with politics. The Communist Party espouses a professional ethic. Membership is supposed to be based on a commitment to developing a socialist society, and party members are supposed to advance themselves through constant study of party documents and rigorous discipline in following the directives of the party center. Thanks to propaganda, almost everyone in China knows the content of these ideals and also knows that the reality is far different. Today, people join the party not mainly to advance socialism but to advance themselves. Students commonly plagiarize their application to join the party, as well as the regular self-reviews to evaluate their party discipline.[35] Advancement within the party depends on favorable reviews from one's superiors, which leads to clientalist relationships. At the highest levels, the party is dominated by scions of interconnected "old revolutionary" families. These arrangements fit the vision imagined by people brought up in closed communities of tightly intertwined networks, and they validate that vision.

When I taught at Fudan, I was surprised that most of the best students didn't want to become entrepreneurs or get jobs in innovative organizations. Instead they wanted to become government bureaucrats (which in most cases would also include being party members) because that offered the most stable income and a regular path to advancement. The bureaucracy's work is often imagined as being paternalistic—the official as *fumuguan*, a parent to the people. This entails "maintaining stability" by providing social services and controlling any disruptive voices or actions, which is now made possible using increasingly sophisticated and intrusive surveillance technologies.

As an imagined community, the paternalistic party-state both supports and comes into tension with the family and economy. The official ideology of the party, now depicted on countless posters throughout the country, celebrates the extended family; typical posters, done in a faux woodblock style, depict children serving parents and the parents serving the grandparents. But the ideology also depicted in ubiquitous posters upholds the ideal of Lei Feng, the mythical soldier who wrote that he just wanted to be a small cog in the great locomotive of the revolution. The needs of this great locomotive to maintain its power can clash with the welfare of families, as it did when covering up the beginnings of the COVID-19 epidemic. The great locomotive also protects certain industries while chocking off innovation. Those tempted to protest such conflicts face the intimidating power of modern surveillance technologies.

In the imagination of those with the perspective of closed kinship dominated communities, making progress in this system depends on one's level in the economic hierarchy. For the well positioned, it will involve creating some good personal relationships with powerful people within the state. For those migrant workers at the bottom who don't have any resources to build such relationships as long as they work in the city, the best approach may be simply to avoid politics altogether. The factory girls in Leslie Chang's book didn't even know the name of the Chinese president. (Workers forced back home during the COVID-19 crisis had to rely on extended family members for support because there was only minimal government social safety net support.[36]) For those a bit higher up, effort may be made to build connections through favors or flattery. Those with more resources to give can be more successful in the favor and flattery game, which leads to criticisms from those lower down about corruption. Thus political conflict gets personalized, but the personalization takes place closer to the middle levels of the party-state; the aura of the personality cult surrounding the top leader makes the state as a whole seem unassailable.

The personality cult, built out of incessant propaganda and solidified through vast state rituals, gives the state a religious aura, which puts it in tension with the many other forms of religion that have flourished in the Reform era.[37] Local deity worship, the form of popular religion that flourishes in the countryside, is in some ways complementary to the state's pretensions. The objects of worship in millions of small temples and shrines around the country are powerful legendary figures—generals, warriors, and scholars, imagined as part of a hierarchy all the way up to the Jade Emperor. In the imagination of tightly intertwined closed familistic communities, this sacred hierarchy reflects the earthly hierarchy of functionaries of the state. The state used to try to eradicate this worship in the name of combating "superstition," but today it increasingly tolerates it in the name of preserving "intangible cultural heritage."[38] It in fact imparts a sacral inevitability to the imagined hierarchy of powerful persons that for people grounded in closed familistic communities constitute the Chinese state.

There are other forms of religion, however, that exist in more complicated patterns of tension with the spheres of family, economy, and state. These include Buddhism, Christianity, and Islam. In each case, they worship a universal deity or savior that links believers into vast imagined communities that transcend earthly family ties. Although membership can be virtually ascribed in some instances—a Huimin is by default a Muslim, a village Catholic inherits the religion of his parents—there is a strong voluntaristic element in all of these religions. Even though many Buddhists, Christians, or Muslims may be passive believers, their faith traditions call them to active participation, which connects them with a broad transcendent community of believers. Such broad imagined communities potentially threaten the state, and they potentially inculcate an ethic of solidarity that is in tension with the modern economy. Thus the state is exerting effort to co-opt and "sinicize" these religions, but each religion has followers who carry out varieties of belief in defiance of the state.[39]

Rising economic inequality increases these tensions. Relatively poor and devout religious believers have some cause to criticize members who are relatively rich and hypocritical, especially when they get some of their position by cooperating with state authorities who want to constrain the religion. The ensuing controversies are not about class directly but about the morality of fellow believers who have made compromises with money and power: class conflict as culture conflict.

Finally, rising inequalities intensify conflicts between science and the other social spheres. In the last thirty years, the Chinese scientific community has flourished, thanks to very generous government funding and to open exchange programs through which many Chinese scientists have received excellent training abroad. Some have stayed to make major contributions to global science, but others have returned to develop science in their motherland. Almost by definition, scientists are part of an open community of colleagues united by common expertise rather than personal kinship. More than most other communities in China, it's scientists who see themselves as part of a global community, with methods of research and standards of excellence that are universal. This is true of social scientists as well as natural scientists. Such universalism is in tension with the state and the economy.

Some parts of the party-state want its scientists to serve national development, if necessary by stealing intellectual property or by hiding their own research from colleagues abroad. Powerful corporate interests do the same. Scientists are faced with the moral dilemmas of being faithful to ethical requirements of their profession and forces of the economy and the state. Some cynically give in to the temptation to serve wealth and power, but many feel genuinely conflicted. The pressures increase as inequality increases. Getting near the top end of the distribution requires compromises with the forces of wealth and power. Meanwhile the power gets personalized; access to research grants and journals is still heavily dependent on subservient relations with senior mentors.

The scientific community in China also comes into tension with many aspects of religion, especially those practices aimed at bringing about healing. Increasing inequality leads to a growing gap between those who have access to advanced scientifically based health care and those who do not. The have-nots may come to trust the personal care of local folk healers and resist the pretensions of aloof scientists, and scientists may return the favor with condescension toward ignorant, superstitious people. There is also tension between the dynamics of family solidarity and impersonal clinical science, as illustrated in chapter 6 in this book on a conflict over giving birth by C-section.

CONCLUSION

Common Challenges Within Different Visions of the Common Good

What might be the consequences of class inequality leading to cultural conflicts for U.S. and Chinese mutual quests for a global common good?

Liberal democracy has, in theory, a way for a society to work toward the common good. The common good is never fully achieved, but a tentative, imperfect version may be gained through rational debate among members of civil society in the public sphere. Civil society is made up of many different kinds of communities with many different conceptions of the good life, so no one conception of the good is possible in such a society. If there is enough overlap among the different groups and a general commitment to mutually intelligible reasoned discourse and effective media to facilitate that discourse, it may be possible to arrive at tentative understandings of goods shared in common—especially support for institutions that can resolve differences through reasonable compromise rather than violence. Individuals will remain pressured by the competing demands of the various communities to which they are connected, but if the pressures are not overly severe, they may accept as a common good the virtue of living with such tensions as a way to enable a general peace and interdependent prosperity. In this vision, the common good arises from the bottom up, from a pluralistic civil society to the institutions of the state. It is not a singular common good, the kind that might be envisioned as proceeding from an almighty God or the kind envisioned by "perfectionist" moral philosophies such as Catholic natural law, and for that matter Confucianism and Islam. It is a "good enough" good coming from flawed human beings.[40]

We have seen that rising inequality in the United States has intensified the tensions between family, economy, politics, religion, and science that are endemic to modern life. At the same time, inequality has led to different ways of understanding and coping with the tensions among forms increasingly separated within an expanding economic spectrum. In *Habits of the Heart*, the authors argued that the liberal vision, in its pure form, would not be sustainable, especially under conditions of extreme inequality, but it had been made viable by the partial diffusion of moral commitments carried by the condensed languages of religion and civic republicanism. But today inequality has engendered a cultural and social polarization that is difficult to be reconciled within democratic institutions, and even a good enough common good is difficult to discern.

According to current Chinese ideology, the Communist party-state is the power responsible for realizing the Chinese common good. Meanwhile, rising economic inequality is helping to exacerbate the modern tensions between family, economy, politics, religion, and science. The legacies of traditional Chinese culture give a different tone to common understandings of the nature of these tensions, but the tensions certainly persist. The absence of an open public sphere makes it difficult for rational discussion about the common good to rise from the bottom up. A powerful intrusive state holds the tensions in place and prevents the kind of polarization that we have in the West. The party-state now clothes itself in a "perfectionist" ideology composed of a mixture of Marxist and Confucian rhetoric, but the rhetoric seems superficial and the Chinese Communist Party seems to have more interest in maintaining power than in promoting a genuine social common good. The party-state maintains control more through overwhelming power than through deeply felt legitimacy. How long can such a state maintain its control? Already, popular anger over the government's response to the coronavirus outbreak—anger that may be more difficult to suppress than the virus itself—is challenging propaganda and control.[41] If the state should crack apart, cultural polarization would probably ensue, making it difficult to imagine achieving a good enough common good through democratization.

But the United States is having its own problems in achieving a democratic resolution of its tensions. The long run solutions for achieving a world safe for democracy would involve transforming global economies to mitigate current extremes of inequality.

What are implications of this for U.S.-China relations? A basis for cross-cultural dialogue is that there are important similarities underlying our differences. Both societies suffer tensions among different value spheres, even though the specific patterns of tensions may differ. In both cases, these tensions have been exacerbated by rising inequality. Although these tensions are leading to visible turmoil in the United States (and in other liberal Western societies), in China they are contained for now, but the containment under authoritarian control will not last forever. Both societies face common problems because of rising inequalities and face challenges in how to create more just societies. One issue is that inequality in both societies is connected to patterns of trade between the societies. It should be in the enlightened self-interest of elites on both sides to adjust trade in ways that lead to more equitable wealth distribution in each society. I don't expect enlightenment to happen soon, but both societies have cultural resources that could counter the tendencies of neo-liberal ideology. This would be another fruitful area for dialogue.

NOTES

1. According to Investopedia, 2020, the U.S. GDP in early 2020 (before the pandemic outbreak) was 21.44 trillion and China's nominal GDP was 14.14 trillion. But in PPP, China's was 27.31 trillion.

2. Barry Naughton, *The Chinese Economy: Adaptation and Growth*, 2nd ed. (Cambridge, MA: MIT Press, 2018), 246–47.

3. In December 2018, the Chinese Gini was .468. (Statistica), but some economists estimate that the true Gini could be significantly higher; at the same time, for the USA, it was .49.

4. According to a 2020 Hunrun Global Rich List report, China now has 799 billionaires vs. 629 in the USA. But Forbes 2020 has different numbers with the USA first and China second.

5. Pew Social Trends, January 2020, https:pewresearchcenter.org/2020/01/09.

6. Martin King Whyte, *Myth of the Social Volcano: Perceptions of Inequality and Social Injustice in Contemporary China* (Stanford, CA: Stanford University Press, 2010).

7. Max Weber, "Science as a Vocation," in *From Max Weber: Essays in Sociology*, ed. and trans. Hans H. Gerth and C. Wright Mills (New York: Oxford University Press, 1949), 129–56, esp.151–55; and Max Weber, "Religious Rejections of the World and Their Directions," in *From Max Weber: Essays in Sociology*, ed. and trans. Hans H. Gerth and C. Wright Mills (New York: Oxford University Press, 1949), 323–59, esp. 327–57.

8. Weber, "Religious Rejections," 327.

9. See Benedict Anderson, *Imagined Communities* (New York: Verso, 1991).

10. Mary Douglas, *Natural Symbols: Explorations in Cosmology* (New York: Vintage, 1973), 19–58.

11. Douglas, *Natural Symbols*, 19.

12. Alasdair MacIntyre, *After Virtue* (South Bend, IN: University of Notre Dame Press, 1984), 22–33.

13. Robert N. Bellah, Richard Madsen, William M. Sullivan, Ann Swidler, and Steven M. Tipton, *Habits of the Heart: Individualism and Commitment in American Life* (Berkeley: University of California Press, 1985), 170–77.

14. J. D. Vance, *Hillbilly Elegy: A Memoir of a Family and Culture in Crisis* (New York: Harper Collins, 2016).

15. Tom Roberts, "The Rise of the Catholic Right," *Sojourners*, March 2019, https://sojo.net/magazine/march-2019/rise-catholic-right.

16. Bellah et al., *Habits of the Heart*.

17. Anne Case and Angus Deaton, *Deaths of Despair and the Future of Capitalism* (Princeton, NJ: Princeton University Press, 2020).

18. David H. Autor, David Dorn, and Gordon H. Hanson, "The China Shock: Learning from Labor-Market Adjustment to Large Changes in Trade," *Annual Review of Economics* 8, no. 1 (October 2016): 205–40.

19. Relatively embedded. Practically no one could survive in a modern industrial society in a completely closed community and make any sense of the modern world through a condensed speech code; nor could anyone survive the social and psychological alienation that would come from completely open networks and a completely elaborated speech code. But important differences arise from the relative balance of the two forms of modern life.

20. Fei Xiaotong, *Xiangtu Zhongguo* (Shanghai, 1948), translation from "Chinese Social Structure and Its Values," in *Changing China: Reading in the History of China from the Opium War to the Present*, ed. J. Mason Gentzler (New York: Praeger, 1977), 211–13.

21. Sun Longji, "The Deep Structure of Chinese Culture," in *Seeds of Fire: Chinese Voices of Conscience*, trans. Geremie Barme and John Minford (New York: Farrar, Straus, and Giroux, 1988), 30–35.

22. Liao Yiwu, "The Leper," in *The Corpse Walker: Real Life Stories, China from the Bottom Up* (New York: Anchor, 2009), 49.

23. Darren Byler, "Spirit Breaking: Uyghur Dispossession, Culture Work, and Terror Capitalism in a Chinese Global City" (PhD diss., University of Washington, 2018).

24. Leslie T. Chang, *Factory Girls: From Village to City in a Changing China* (New York: Spiegel and Grau, 2008).

25. Xie Xiangnan, *Iron Moon: An Anthology of Chinese Worker Poetry*, trans. Eleanor Goodman and ed. Qin Xiaoyu (Buffalo, NY: White Pine Press, 2017). Quoted in Megan Walsh, "The Chinese Factory Workers who Write Poems on their Phones," May 1, 2017, http://lithub.com, 8.

26. Joselyn Ford, dir., *Nowhere to Call Home: A Tibetan in Beijing*, China documentary film, 2014.

27. See David Barboza, "Billions in Hidden Riches for Family of Chinese Leader," *New York Times*, October 25, 2012.

28. X. L. Ding, "'The Only Reliability Is That These Guys Aren't Reliable'": The Business Culture of Red Capitalism," in *Restless China*, ed. Perry Link, Richard Madsen, and Paul Pickowicz (Lanham, MD: Rowman and Littlefield, 2013), 37–57.

29. See Richard Madsen, "Making the People or the Government Happy? Dilemmas of Social Workers in a Morally Pluralistic Society," in *The Chinese Pursuit of Happiness: Anxieties, Hopes, and Moral Tensions in Everyday Life*, ed. Becky Yang Hsu and Richard Madsen (Berkeley: University of California Press, 2019), 110–30.

30. Tricia Wang, *Talking to Strangers: Chinese Youth and Social Media*, Ph.D. Dissertation, University of California, San Diego, 2014

31. Madsen, "Making the People or the Government Happy?," 110.

32. Chih-Jou Jay Chen, "Deriving Happiness from Making Society Better: Chinese Activists as Warring Gods," in *The Chinese Pursuit of*

Happiness: Anxieties, Hopes, and Moral Tensions in Everyday Life, ed. Becky Yang Hsu and Richard Madsen (Berkeley: University of California Press, 2019), 131–54.

33. Madsen, "Making the People or the Government Happy?," 110.

34. Haiyi Monica Liu, *Seeking Western Men: Email-Order Brides under China's Global Rise* (Stanford: Stanford University Press, 2022).

35. Tricia Wang, *Talking to Strangers*.

36. Off the Epi-center: How Rural China is coping with COVID 19. Lecture by Scott Rozelle, UCSD 21st Century China webinar, May 6, 2020, https:china.ucsd.edu.

37. Ian Johnson, *The Souls of China: The Return of Religion After Mao* (New York: Pantheon, 2017).

38. Vincent Goossaert and David A. Palmer, *The Religious Question in Modern China* (Chicago: University of Chicago Press, 2011).

39. Richard Madsen ed., *The Sinicization of Chinese Religions* (Leiden: Brill, 2021).

40. See William A. Galston, "Liberal Egalitarian Attitudes Towards Ethical Pluralism," in *The Many and the One: Religious and Secular Perspectives on Ethical Pluralism in the Modern World*, ed. Richard Madsen and Tracy B. Strong (Princeton, NJ: Princeton University Press, 2003), 25–41; and Chandran Kukathis, "Ethical Pluralism from a Classical Liberal Perspective," in *The Many and the One: Religious and Secular Perspectives on Ethical Pluralism in the Modern World*, ed. Richard Madsen and Tracy B. Strong (Princeton, NJ: Princeton University Press, 2003), 55–77. For perfectionist accounts of the common good, see John H. Haldane, "Natural Law and Ethical Pluralism," in *The Many and the One: Religious and Secular Perspectives on Ethical Pluralism in the Modern World*, ed. Richard Madsen and Tracy B. Strong (Princeton, NJ: Princeton University Press, 2003), 89–114; Joseph Chan, "Confucian Attitudes Toward Ethical Pluralism," in *The Many and the One: Religious and Secular Perspectives on Ethical Pluralism in the Modern World*, ed. Richard Madsen and Tracy B. Strong (Princeton, NJ: Princeton University Press, 2003), 129–53; and Dale F. Eichelman, "Islam and Ethical Pluralism," in *The Many and the One: Religious and Secular Perspectives on Ethical Pluralism in the Modern World*, ed. Richard Madsen and Tracy B. Strong (Princeton, NJ: Princeton University Press, 2003), 161–79.

41. See, for example, essays by Ren Zhiqiang, "Denunciation of Xi Jin-
    ping: Stripping the Clothes of a Clown Who Is Determined to Be
    Emperor," March 6, 2020, translated in chinaheritage.net, September
    29, 2020. Unfortunately, Mr. Ren has now been sentenced to eighteen
    years in prison.

3

COMFORT IN GROUP EXPERIENCE

The Frenzy for Psy-Training

TERESA KUAN

nthropologists look with double vision at the common problems shared by global humanity that stand in the way of making good societies: structural inequality, labor precarity, and existential alienation. Having produced robust accounts that explain how problematic systems intersect and reproduce themselves—a cumulative effect of human actors not knowing what they do does[1]—we cannot help but see the world through a dark lens. At the same time, anthropologists find reason for measured optimism in the contingencies of social process and in the creativity of ordinary people and communities. In the context of immersive fieldwork, we have observed how people develop unique responses to their predicaments that correspond with their own notions of the good life and the common good.

I begin this chapter with the understanding that a common good is necessarily relational, drawing inspiration from Catholic social doctrine. Relationships, in fact, "are themselves key aspects of the common good."[2] Sharing a meal is a relational good; so is friendship, which—following Aristotle—is pregnant with political significance. Friendship constitutes "a relationship that binds people together as a 'we' and leads them to see the good of this 'we' as their own good."[3] In this formulation, an actor experiences a relationship in which the boundary between *I* and *you* dissolves and a *we* emerges in its place.

A workshop paper from the Pontifical Academy of Social Sciences considers "concentric circles" of personal relationships imperative for human flourishing:

> In order for a person to reach fulfillment, the human being needs the web of relations that he establishes with other people. He thus places himself at the centre of a web formed by concentric circles that are the family, his home, his workplace, his neighbours, his nation and, finally, the whole of humanity. A person draws from each of these circles the necessary elements for his growth, at the same time as he contributes to their improvement.[4]

Hollenbach agrees that relational goods are found at multiple levels: family, neighborhood, city, state, country, and the world. Each level is significant to any single person insofar as they "are *all* essential to human well-being."[5] Indeed, there is virtually nothing individuals can obtain truly on their own because humans are fundamentally social beings. Even the most basic of sense perceptions is experienced in relation to others, who help to constitute and confirm one's own sense of reality and self-coherence.[6]

This chapter phenomenologically unpacks what the emergence of "we-ness" might look or feel like, and why the relational good experienced within it is so fundamental to human well-being and flourishing. I focus on two cases of suffering and healing from my research on psychological training in the context of China's "psycho-boom" to show how crucially important other people are to the constitution of a self, whose coherence may be taken for granted until it is lost.

CHINA'S PSYCHO-BOOM

The first two decades of the twenty-first century saw an explosion of popular interest in psychological concepts, discourse, and treatments among ordinary urbanites in China: "the psycho-boom" (*xinli re*).[7] Having developed in tandem with market reform, the appearance of a middle class, the rise of consumer culture, the growth of entrepreneurship, changes in intimate relations, and the emergence of a host of related stresses, China's psycho-boom is best characterized as a blooming "world of multiplicity."[8] Surge of interest does not mean that more and more urbanites are taking to the couch. Rather, the trend may be gleaned from a flurry of activities that include reading self-help books and books about psychology, attending an evening salon in a rented space, following public accounts on the topic in WeChat, and attending a weekend workshop on self-growth (especially if your boss makes you go). Public accounts on WeChat for psychology enthusiasts are numerous, as are the approaches that enthusiasts and practicing counselors may study or train in before hybridizing something of their own.[9]

This recent surge in popular interest is particularly interesting because it has followed a trajectory that is unique to the Chinese context, shaped by a mix of state-led initiatives and market forces. Researchers in the field have identified two major historical reasons for it. The first has to do with the nightly broadcast since 2004 of the CCTV program *Psychological Interviews* (*Xinli fangtan*). Each episode features a session with a real client, selected from a pool of volunteers from all over the country, demonstrating how family problems may be interpreted from a psychological perspective. As Hsuan-ying Huang has put it, the show is engrossing and its therapists masterful: they extract hidden secrets and make penetrating interpretations within the program's short twenty-minute span.[10] The program's success with audiences has helped to popularize psychology, destigmatize help-seeking, and normalize everyday psychological problems.[11] When I was conducting research for my project on popular advice for parenting in the 2000s, informants sometimes named *Psychological Interviews* as a source of information for how to be a better parent.[12]

More significant, China's Ministry of Labor and Social Security played a major role in stimulating popular interest by creating a counseling certification program, which was short-lived (2002–2017). Their interest was not so much the promotion of mental health but labor diversification as a part of its transformation into "China's main regulatory body overseeing the training and certification for an entire range of jobs."[13] "Psychological counselor" was created alongside other new occupations such as anti-erosion worker, auto mechanic, and mushroom gardener, and it was later grouped together with other popular certifications such as money manager, logistics, and human resources.[14]

It is the National Vocational Qualifications system (*Quanguo tongyi jianding*) that certifies various occupations, but training for the counseling exam was offered by private for-profit companies at the local level. Li Zhang likened the program to a "speedy assembly line" because it was possible to become certified as a counselor who may take clients after a few months of studying textbook materials and passing the exam.[15] No specific academic degree (such as in psychology or the humanities) was required, nor minimum hours of clinical experience. According to a report copublished by the popular digital platform Jiandan Xinli (简单心理), which offers one-on-one psychological services, almost 30 percent of their counselors have academic degrees in business, engineering, the sciences, and "other."[16]

The point here is not to raise questions about professionalism. Chinese psychotherapy is a wide and diverse social field, with hobbyists on one end of the continuum and elite academics and psychiatrists on the other. Instead I bring attention to the way this unique trajectory has created opportunities for the curious to explore a novel way of thinking and being in the world, and in some cases to experience a paradigm shift. Professionalization and standardization is a very real concern and a matter for debate among practitioners working in the state sector (*tizhi nei*, hospitals and schools) or running private companies (*shehui jigou*). However, more than 85 percent of certificate holders never intended to become practicing counselors; they enrolled in the program for the sake of personal development.[17] For this reason, Hsuan-ying Huang has argued for seeing the training frenzy created by the certification program as a social form and popular movement, structurally similar to the *qigong* fever of the 1980s and 1990s in its flourishing of activities and networks.[18] Studying for the national exam was only one way among many to learn and train. This phenomenon of intensely taking courses and attending workshops constitutes a defining feature of China's psycho-boom. The certificate phenomenon in general may be likened to the business card boom Yunxiang Yan observed in 1993; it reflects an ethos of personal development and structural change.[19]

Why training to counsel rather than actual counseling sessions has been a defining feature of the psycho-boom stems in part from the challenge of getting clients, not to mention building a caseload to support a career.[20] From the perspective of a potential client, seeing a counselor would not carry the same stigma as going to a hospital psychiatrist, precisely because counseling is considered a commodity one consumes. But this commodity is costly, and to date virtually no insurance policies cover psychological counseling from the private sector because these "companies" (*shehui jigou*) are registered with business bureaus and aren't considered health-care clinics. In 2018, the typical cost of a single session ranged from 200 to 800 RMB, depending on the counselor's credentials, but could be higher.[21] Therefore, a person seeking talk therapy might choose to enroll in training courses and workshops instead. "From the perspective of a psy-enthusiast," Li Zhang relates, "studying (*xuexi*) offers just as good a way to explore the self and collect some tools for dealing with work and family problems."[22]

Nevertheless, studying psychology is also pricey, particularly for the enthusiast who cannot stop. This predicament is well captured in a series of comics posted by Sugar Psychology (糖心理), a public WeChat account. Taking the format of a call-and-response chant, the comics poke fun at the challenges hobbyists and practitioners face, particularly the phenomenon of crazily attending courses even though they are costly and, in the opinion of its creator, "useless"—only to be met by a nonexistent client base. In one panel, a leader shouts, "Who are we?" And the crowd responds, with stick skinny arms and fists in the air, "Psychotherapists!" "What is our goal?" "Take cases!" "How many cases?!" "No cases to take!" As if the demand is not in fact a description. Another panel in the post self-diagnoses therapists as suffering from "learning personality disorder" (*xuexixing renge zhang'ai*) because it is not enough to have clients, one also needs supervision (*dudao*), personal growth (*ziwo chengzhang*), and training (*peixun*).[23]

An essay posted by Lacan Psychology (Lacan 心理) is darker in tone, characterizing the counseling industry as an ouroboros that feeds upon itself: the proverbial serpent ingesting its own tail. Because the cost of training is so high for counselors, the cost of therapy is high for potential clients, who then fail to materialize. Practitioners resort to training their peers to regain their initial investment. "Since there is no way for the counselor population to earn a livelihood from the outside," the article argues, "it has no other alternative but to suck the blood of its fellows."

It compares the industry to a pyramid scheme; as long as the potential for high income (the serpent's head) keeps attracting newcomers to the field, it enjoys a continuous food supply.[24]

In the absence of a comprehensive training system, newcomers must "go it alone" (*danda dudou*), arranging and self-funding course attendance and case supervision and generating opportunities for personal treatment.[25] For this reason, those who carry on with studying psychology beyond the national certificate program tend to have the discretionary funds to do so.[26] But what reasons compel a trainee to expend limited resources—time, money, energy, and attention—on studies that may not necessarily pay off?

One answer to this question relates to a shared human problem that could potentially arise at any time for anyone: social isolation. Psy-training has been taken up as a response to this. Training sessions themselves inadvertently create small circles of "we-ness"—a form of mutuality based neither in kinship nor political belonging, the effects of which outlast the duration of a course or workshop. In the context of class activities and "doing experience" (*zuo tiyan*), a participant may even undergo profound transformation by virtue of cocreating a common space for seeing and listening to other people and being seen and heard oneself. The same model is employed all over the world for the intentional organization of support groups for trauma survivors and recovering addicts. But the variety of "we-ness" I describe in this chapter is not by design. It occurs because psy-training happens to provide the occasion not only for knowledge transmission but for a gathering of perspectives.

The emergence of novel spaces that facilitate a gathering of perspectives has historical precedents as seen, for example, in "speaking bitterness" sessions during the land reform movement of the 1940s in which peasants learned to take a third-person perspective on their first-person suffering.[27] In call-in radio programs from the 1990s, listeners benefited from hearing the stories of callers because they revealed "how Chinese people's lives really are."[28] The recent case of China's psycho-boom in general, and the frenzy for psy-training in particular, provides a new opportunity for revisiting a very basic human question: What is relationality, and why is it important? The Chinese case is particularly good to examine because structural change to society happened so rapidly and generated all sorts of dysphoric experiences for those who failed to live up to social expectations. That training courses are taken by psychology enthusiasts not only for the sake of knowledge acquisition but also for self-healing—in a context rife with estrangement and social isolation—has much to tell us about the fundamental human need to relate.

A WORLD AMONG WORLDS: STUDYING SYSTEMIC THERAPY

At least three major schools of family therapy are popular in China today. Each is distinct in terms of the vision of its founders, as well as how it understands and approaches problems of mental health. Roughly speaking, *systemic* therapy focuses on patterns of interaction between family members; the *Satir* method address problematic communication styles; and *family constellation* therapy (*jiating pailie*) investigates issues in light of a client's ancestral ties.[29] Of the three, systemic therapy is most closely aligned with hospital-based psychiatry. Created in the mid-twentieth century by psychiatrists in the United States to address the problem of relapse among patients discharged from hospital care, it borrows ideas from cybernetics and systems theory to focus on the unintended effects of relational dynamics that have hardened into "systems"; that is, circuitry in which "energies" circulate or get displaced.[30]

Between 2016 and 2019 I conducted a project on the development of family therapy by doing fieldwork at the Institute for Family Therapy in Kangzhou, China.[31] Specializing in systemic methods, the institute is one of many private organizations on China's psycho-boom landscape where a person might seek training. It offers clinical services and public education as well as professional training by way of *supervision groups* (led by senior teachers who give feedback on the clinical work of trainees), *live demonstrations* (live therapy sessions observable from behind a one-way mirror), and *internships* (essentially small peer facilitated study groups). The internship groups are similar to experiences trainees might have had elsewhere, but the use of live demonstrations for training is unique to this site. Common interest in learning family therapy constituted a common space, which was supported by an organizational infrastructure (the institute) and the therapy rooms, into which we squeezed to watch and discuss videotapes.

Having adopted the role of an intern, I was able to do participant observation in weekly study groups, and I came to know other trainees who happened to live close enough to the institute to take advantage of what everyone perceived as a precious learning opportunity. We would regularly eat lunch together, bring snacks to share, and spend long hours sprawled on chairs or on the floor viewing recorded videos, talking excitedly, and sometimes napping. From this group I choose two trainees to explore what group experience could mean because they crystalized a theme for which I had scattered pieces of evidence. These trainee-informants were more candid and articulate about their reasons for studying psychology than others—more so, ironically, than people I am in fact closer to in terms of mutual affinity and frequency of interaction and collaboration. Ever the raconteur, Cao Xi, the informant in the second case, revealed a great deal about the psycho-boom landscape and how her own journey took shape within it in our long interview, just as she had filled our study sessions with riveting stories and anecdotes. The long interview in the first case was a gift. At first Ruan Danting felt ambivalent about agreeing to an interview because the story of why she walked onto the path of psychological counselling is for her "too horrible to look at" (*canbu rendu*). But she thought sharing it would contribute to a greater good, and indeed I hope this chapter honors her wish in some way.

I first met Ruan Danting at an internship meeting. On this particular day, we watched a video of a discussion between a father and a mother, with no mediation by a therapist. They and their adult daughter had come to the institute for therapy, and this parental discussion was the first part of a clinical protocol the institute has adopted for the treatment of family issues. Like many couples who came for help, they were at their wits' end. Their only child had been in and out of psychiatric wards and on and off psychiatric medications. Every parental discussion we witnessed as interns, whether live or recorded, was tense, if not explosive. Often one parent blamed the other for the misfortune of their child's illness. This particular family was recovering from a highly controversial surgery in a last-ditch effort to treat their daughter's condition.

Yang Yu, the young therapist/staff member running the internship group, was interested in the couple's dynamic; she was actively refining her hypothesis as we watched and discussed. Yang Yu thought the father's aggression toward his wife was caused by his anxiety over the decision to have the surgery done, a decision that had been, it seemed, his alone. Danting, who had trained in both family constellation and Satir-style family therapy, disagreed. She alluded to a technique that addresses a client's problem by way of dramatic bodily enactments of inner emotions in her interpretation. Danting pointed out the straight, firm posture of the father, compared to the hunching over of the mother—who was pouring her weight into her elbows, which were perched on her knees: "He is treating her the way a boss treats a subordinate." Later in the video, when a moment of silence fell over the couple followed by the father asking the assisting therapists in the room whether this part of the protocol was over, Danting expressed disgust. "See! He is completely an absentee from the family!"

I was surprised by Danting's strong responses because they did not square with the image I had of systemic family therapy, which idealizes a therapist's coolness and emotional separation from the family unit being observed. This applies both to the method's theoretical orientation and its material set-up (the use of one-way mirrors, for instance). Over time, I began to notice a pattern to Danting's comments and concerns. Her response to many videos was a constant refrain: "pitiful child," she would say tenderly, shaking her head. Until I sat down with her for an interview in 2018, I did not know what it meant for her to witness misery in other families.

One of the older members of the group, Danting belongs to the demographic that attended university after the disruption of education during the Cultural Revolution, which then led her directly into a career in the world of letters. Psychological counseling is her second career, which she discovered by accident in 2004 from a newspaper advertisement. She registered for the national certification course that year and hasn't stopped training since—although her intensity has waned. Initially, Danting emptied out her bank account—her life savings, estimated at 300,000 RMB—to pay for training. "With the money I had at that time, I could have purchased a few homes," she told me. She had not thought to invest in property when property was still cheap. Instead, she invested in "learning psychology."

"IT ISN'T THAT I FAILED. IT WAS THE TIMES"

Wanting to do something interesting and meaningful was the reason some of the trainees worked as counselors, but for Danting learning psychology was a matter of life and death. She discovered psychology at a low point in her life; it gave her a different perspective on family problems she had taken personal responsibility for, problems that caused her so much pain her body and health suffered. "In reality you are coming to an understanding of your own family in the process of learning, an understanding of why things happen the way they happen," Danting explained while recalling early encounters with systemic therapy. Her studies revealed to her that she wasn't to blame for the bad things that had happened in her life: "It wasn't me. It isn't that I failed. It was the times."[32] She began to speak in terms of a first-person plural: "We are very lucky to have caught the tide, actually. No longer were [we] full of sorrow." Who does the "we" refer to here, what "tide" is Danting speaking of, and how did learning family therapy release her from self-blame?

For sixteen years, she and her husband had been admired as a couple, held up as a model in both natal families, and fortune seemed perpetually on their side. "We were God's favored ones," she told me. A classmate before he was a spouse, Danting's husband was really, really good to her in their early years together. "Docile and obedient" is the way she put it, and he was the "cream of the crop." They were two university graduates who did not have to go out looking for work, work came looking for them. Then, after many years of marital bliss, her husband "went off track" (*chugui le*). He started having extramarital affairs.

Danting does not blame her husband for going off track. His circle of associates had become the group known as the "new rich," characterized by sudden wealth, spectacular ways of mixing business with pleasure, and keeping mistresses. As Danting explained, "Those who had a little bit of success, you know, factory bosses, company managers, those kinds of people, it was like a new tide had formed (*fengchao*). That was late 1990s, around the year 2000, it was the beginning of economic development." Since then, Danting explained, it has become normal for a woman to ask about a friend's "fresh little meat" (*xiao xianrou*) as a greeting, referring to a young lover who is not her husband. In *her* generation, though, infidelity was not a matter women could take lightly. The anger and heartache of a husband's infidelity has literally killed other women she has known, including friends and relatives.

Danting does not blame her husband because a good guy could turn bad too—he and his associates went out and enjoyed themselves in bands (*yibang yibang de*)—but the heartbreak nearly killed her.[33] "Back then, if he gave me a certain look, I would be in pain for a few days. Because he had never looked at me like that before and then suddenly he was giving [me] the look of rejection and indifference." Danting kept her suffering to herself: "Precisely because we grew up in poor families," she explained, "divorce is a very shameful matter." In the three generations she knows of in her own family, there was not a single divorce. Her own situation left her painfully confused: "I blamed myself; I felt that I had failed. How could such a thing happen?"

The change in family atmosphere affected her two children as they hit adolescence. They started having problems at school, and Danting started having problems with her health. It wasn't just the infidelity that caused her to suffer; her husband "expelled" her to Kangzhou from their small town in another province so he could be free to enjoy his new lifestyle. First, he took their two teenage children on a supposed "holiday" to Kangzhou without her consent. He showed them such a good time that they did not want to go home, and they were pleased to find out that they did not have to. Their father had purchased and renovated a home, making possible the transfer of their household registration and consequently the children's schooling. Besides, their hometown had already become unlivable due to pollution from the local processing industry. After twenty years of work Danting was at the peak of her career, and she resisted the move, but she had little choice. Her husband had already arranged everything. She was able to keep her job by working remotely, so she went along with his plan.

In this period of family upheaval, Danting had three surgeries to treat three different health problems. The last one required a long convalescence, and she finally had to give up her career altogether. So she rested in a big home in the city of Kangzhou where she knew no one except her two teenagers and their nanny. There was nothing to do but rest. Danting started practicing meditation and studying Buddhist scriptures. Just as she was finding some strength to walk out of her misery, she discovered information in the newspaper about counseling training.

Solace and Solidarity in Group Experience

In outlining the features of what she called the "common world," Hannah Arendt argued against the homogenizing tendency of mass society.[34] According to Arendt, the common world is defined by difference rather than sameness, by a multiplicity of perspectives rather than a "prolongation" of just one. This common world is only possible in the "public realm," she argued, defined in terms of the "appearance" of things seen and heard by everyone, each assuming a new reality in contradistinction to obscurity—leaving no trace as if it never existed. This kind of common world is far from a global political reality, and for Arendt it is already a thing of the past. But I suggest that ordinary people and communities create mini common worlds all the time.

Arendt's common world is specifically an "in-between," something tangible that "relates and separates men at the same time."[35] Arendt illustrates this idea with the example of a table: people around it share in common the intermediary object, but they all relate to the table from different angles and from different locations. Its objective importance is demonstrated by the hypothetical scenario of a table disappearing at a séance, which would be awkward for all who are present.[36] No-table creates a situation of "worldlessness," which for Arendt is the problem with mass society: there is no in-between to gather people in a way that relates and separates at the same time. "Only where things can be seen by many in a variety of aspects without changing their identity," Arendt argues, "can worldly reality truly and reliably appear."[37] This is—in my understanding—Arendt's way of saying that the meaning of a person's experience is realized in the presence of others.

The antithesis of the common world is utter privacy; that is, the complete absence of any other person who can confirm your reality.[38] That prisoners in solitary confinement demonstrate a strikingly consistent cluster of symptoms is telling. They become completely unhinged; their sense of basic reality and of self-coherence unravels.[39] There is even, as Charles Dickens observed, "a complete derangement of the nervous system."[40] Solitary confinement affects people in this way because healthy perception depends *fundamentally* on the constant dialogue between private sensory experiences (e.g., the perception of a cup on a surface) and perceiving the experiences of others (another person seeing the same cup from across the room). In this way we are reassured that we are relating to reality in a way that is shared.[41]

Danting's heartbreak is not equal to solitary confinement in a prison, but her interpretation that anger and heartache could literally kill a woman makes more sense when set next to Guenther's account of how total disconnection and isolation could cause a breakdown in perception and deterioration of bodily systems. I had earlier heard her say that she had become depressed without knowing it was called "depression" at the time. I asked if she thought this was the cause of her illnesses. She corrected me in proposing a line of causality that bypassed depression, linking her physical suffering directly to the relational problem: "What happened was the emotions [*ganqing*] changed. [I] could not take it. You start off great, and then you're not facing the same direction anymore [*bei dui bei*]. [I] could not take this. I would cry all the time, and yet I was too embarrassed to tell anyone." No longer sharing a common world with her husband or anyone else, Danting suffered in utter privacy.

After a doctor gave her the news that led to the convalescence that forced her to end her first career, she exited the hospital, accompanied by others yet feeling alone: "I remember I was one person (*wo yige ren*)—accompanying my children and the nanny, the nanny was still young herself, you see—and then I stood there on the street and watched other people walking so freely. I suddenly envied everyone, all healthy and able to walk." The image of "one person" standing while others moved about is poignant. And it is counterpointed by the way Danting talks about her experiences in training courses, in which the first-person subject is a plural "we" rather than a singular "I."

"We were all experiencing what they were experiencing," Danting said of a live demonstration of an actual therapy session with a volunteer family modeling Satir-style family sculpting. Sculpting is a technique that involves dramatizing modes of communication by using props (e.g., chairs to stand on), postures, and gestures (e.g., finger pointing) to explore the relationship between family dynamics and inner feelings.[42] But the experience of "we-ness" is not unique to being in a live audience; training may also consist of watching a teacher conduct a mock session with trainees who have volunteered to play the role of a client or family member. When we spoke, Danting conflated the experience of watching live demonstrations with watching mock sessions and video recordings, naming for me a series of famous masters and training courses where such modalities were applied—hypnosis, family constellation therapy, and many others, implicitly including the systemic therapy study group in which she and I had met. In these settings, "there would be a stirring [chudong] that is very deep." Lumping together herself with fellow trainees, she recalled, "We were just soaking [jinpao] in that kind of learning environment." Danting quietly cleaned her own wounds as she learned of the "adversities" (huannan) and "wreckages" (cuican) of others. She could never bring herself to volunteer to "do experience" (zuo tiyan) for fear of losing control and falling apart, so she only witnessed as a by-stander, soaking and soaking, until she depleted her savings.

"PSY-SOCIALITY" IN THE CHINESE CONTEXT

Both Hsuan-ying Huang and Sonya Pritzker in their work on group activities in the context of the Sino-German Course and Family Constellation Therapy, respectively, have drawn from

Whitney Duncan's "psy-sociality" to describe the highly social character of therapeutic experiences in the Chinese context.[43] In the former, a term that remains relatively technical in Germany—*Selbsterfahrung*—tends to be used in its translation (*ziwo tiyan*) by Chinese trainees in a much more expansive way to cover "all kinds of deep experiences," which may occur both within the formal curriculum and in the social activities that take place in the evening.[44]

Why the group experience has been a significant feature in China's psycho-boom cannot be reduced to "culture" and collectivist ethos. It is partly the result of multiple historical contingencies that include the development of psy-training's ambiguous status as vocational/adult education and the direction of knowledge transfer.[45] Training courses and workshops have to be squeezed into short time spans of consecutive days to accommodate trainees with full-time jobs and limited leave days, as well as the travel schedules of international teachers. (This is true both at the center of the psycho-boom and at the fringes.[46]) In this sort of arrangement, socializing is intense and multidimensional, occurring not only within the formal curriculum of a given course but also during meals, bathroom breaks, after-hour study sessions, and casual chats—all bookended by chatroom activities such as organizing hotel rooms and group registrations on one side and sharing photos and personal reflections on the other.

Another explanation for the intensity of group experience among psy-enthusiasts in China is more interpretive, although not less considerable. Sonya Pritzker has argued that group therapy practices in China "provide an opportunity for participants to entertain the notion that personal experiences of suffering are embedded in larger-scale cultural, historical, and chronotopal dilemmas that are not, after all, entirely personal."[47] In group settings, a certain kind of *entrainment* occurs between individual participants in the process of taking a "third-person perspective" on one's own life, such that the "I" becomes a "we."[48] For Danting, this sense of a "we" has remained years after witnessing others participate in *tiyan*. Recall her use of the first-person plural in describing a sense of fellowship in her early days of learning psychology: "We are very lucky to have caught the tide, actually. No longer were [we] full of sorrow." She was not the only person to have found a way to forgive herself for a life gone awry, something for which she had previously taken responsibility. She found solace and solidarity in group experience, seeing how others perceive what they too had taken as personal problems, and that she had related to the "personal" in a way that is shared.

Psy-training in the Chinese context has a dark commercial side, and it is politically ambiguous for this reason.[49] Group training is not a public good that is there for all, available to anyone who wishes to have access.[50] It is, however, a novel social space in which the usual norms are suspended, inner secrets make a public appearance, and a dialogue of perspectives can be put into play—offering to women who have failed to live up to social expectations the possibility of healing historical wounds.[51] The common worlds made possible by psy-training are a result of multiple historical contingencies. In them participants cocreate a sense of "we-ness" and reconstitute broken selves.

"MY WOUNDS WERE DISSOLVING AWAY, SO I KEPT ON LEARNING"

Like Danting, Cao Xi was a member of the supervision group the year I did extended fieldwork at the institute. Although there are common themes in their stories of becoming a psy-counselor, they could not be more different in comportment.

Xi's sense of humor, frenzy for learning, knack for imagistic communication, and perceptual skills earned our respect and a nickname we used in the cozy setting of our study group: *Xiao Yao*, or Little Witch Doctor.

One time Xi and I were the only two interns at a study group meeting. We were viewing a video recorded therapy session, and she was interested in how the therapist pulled the couple in the session in the direction she wanted them to go. The couple wanted to talk about their daughter's severe eating disorder (she had once dropped to twenty-something kilograms). But the therapist was taking the misfortune of the child's illness as an occasion to work on the hidden tensions between the couple that had debilitated one person in the family (the daughter) on behalf of the whole system. The couple kept normalizing their own problems and fixating on their daughter, frustrating the therapist's efforts at every turn. Xi began to enumerate the number of times and the different ways the therapist asked the couple the same question, refusing to let them lead the conversation. She was fascinated. Generally speaking, Xi has long been enchanted by the abilities of the great masters in systemic therapy. The senior therapist at the institute in particular used "words like knives," as Xi put it, working with an efficiency to which traditional psychoanalysis could lay no claim. Her intensity in studying the work of masters was as high as her ambition to learn.

Still this vital person has had her own share of pitiable suffering, and it was against such a backdrop that Xi seized every opportunity she could for *tiyan*. Once, in a "group growth circle" led by China's most well-regarded psychoanalyst, Xi volunteered herself so much that he had to pull her aside and ask her to give others a chance. She explained to me the reasons behind her zeal: "I just felt it was too good an opportunity. Everyone else was too timid to share. They were missing out! The teacher needs material for the class, after all." Xi did not disclose to me details about her past traumas because she understood I had publication plans. She withheld not because she is a private person but because she had been *too* public in the past—anyone from the local psychology circle where she lives would recognize her if I were to give an account of her specifics.

Like Danting, Xi's journey began with studying the national certification program in the mid-2000s when it was still new. Unlike the wealthier Danting, Xi continued to work full-time in her primary field, using her "free time" to train and build her client base. Determined to do it all, she saw clients on her lunch breaks and filled her evenings with study activities: "I probably only had nine free evenings per month. I was either taking courses online or I was giving a class online in a study club (*dushu hui*). Sometimes we got together in person. Sometimes I would mentor (*dai*) those who were even more amateur than I was. I would leave myself half an evening for doing laundry; I used the rest to study." Eventually she realized the case load she was carrying—six per week—was too many, "You're hurting other people and you're hurting yourself (*hairen haiji*)." She was not in this for the money—her demanding full-time job already provided enough. She was just *that* eager to learn "because what I want is to polish my craft." So she tapered down to three clients a week.

When her work schedule changed with a promotion to a managerial position, she began working twenty-two consecutive days a month with eleven days off. On her work days, "I would go to work at 6:00 in the morning, get off at 3:00 in the afternoon, and rush over to some other place [*bie de difang*] and study in the evening. Just really crazed in those days [*fengkuang de na jinian*]." On her nonwork days, she said, "I could easily be in a class from 9:30 in the morning to 6:00 in the evening."

We had been drinking tea on her covered balcony when this discussion of her early days prompted her to excuse herself to find something in her bedroom. She came back bearing a large black three-ring binder full of paper certificates, each tucked into a protective plastic sleeve. We went through each and every one, as if the binder was a family photo album. Her certificates triggered memories and stories. "This one is from 2006," she began, "this is my starting point." We thumbed past certificate after certificate. When she stopped at one earned for hypnosis training, she wanted to explain its appearance, as if it were an outlier: "I will learn anything that might be useful, but I don't feel I need to become a professional hypnotist." We came across a letter of appointment for a counseling center associated with her city's local branch of the Women's Federation, and then turning a page, she exclaimed, "Oh! Psychodrama!" as if she had forgotten about this particular course. "I attended 200 hours of this course. I wanted to understand a little of everything." Later, we came across a certificate for a program offered by a major hospital in Kangzhou, which happened to help her fulfill an annual quota of learning credits required by her job. The tour went on and on, ending with a certificate in French psychoanalysis: "I feel lucky I have attended the classes of many international masters."

The intense review of Xi's collection of certificates overwhelmed me; I directly and viscerally confronted the sheer vastness of China's psycho-boom. A part of me longed to shut down even as I tried to catch every piece of her narration. There must have been at least one hundred workshop and training certificates, spanning nearly fifteen years, each reflecting a distinctive system of practice with its own unique history. Xi estimates she has averaged ten trainings per year, with some lasting three to four days and others meeting monthly for one year. How could I understand her frenzy for learning, and how did it fit into the larger web of her life?

The Purchase of Psy-Training

Like Danting, Xi has invested a tremendous amount of time, energy, and money, sustaining high opportunity costs: "I spent 30,000 to 50,000 RMB a year. Everyone else was putting their money into houses and cars."[52] In association with the question of whether one could have spent limited resources elsewhere, both women spoke of intangible, invaluable dividends: "It isn't that this investment has yielded no return (*huibao*)," Danting told me. "This return is too enormous [to calculate]. What I got in exchange is life (*shengming*), a continuation of life (*shengming de yanxu*). What could be more precious than life?" Xi also spoke of life in economic terms, but more as the resource she invested than as the one she reaped: "Psychology is something I used my life (*yong shengming*) to go and study. So when I am studying psychology, I study with all my heart." Xi's commitment to training was a cause for concern for the family members she was closest with, who believed she ought to be investing her attention elsewhere: "When you are thrown into [study], other people will start to wonder, why aren't you trying to date? I feel like in my condition (*wo zhezhong zhuangtai*), dating would mean finding someone to take revenge on (*zhao bieren suanzhang*). It doesn't beat studying more."

Also like Danting, Xi's discovery of the national certification training program was accidental. She had been attending continuing education classes for work when she was drawn to check out the class that was meeting next door, which let out later than hers: "Because mine was a publicly funded class," she explained, "we were dismissed at 10:30 in the morning. Theirs was a self-funded class, so they ended at noon."[53] Even though the attendees next door were spending their own money, they still seemed to be having all the fun. "Our classroom always had very few people. Their classroom always had so many," she said, chuckling at the memory of the contrast.

It turned out to be a training course for the national counseling certificate, and she negotiated with the teacher to sit in each day after her own class dismissed. Once she got a taste, she was hooked: "After that, I began to register [for classes] to learn psychology, and I would tell all my vexations to the teacher, the teacher would comfort me, and care for me (*aihu wo*). During *tiyan* I had a lot of growth, a lot of gain (*shouhuo*). I felt like each of my wounds were dissolving away, so I kept on learning."

Like Danting, Xi found solace and solidarity in the group setting: "[with] my own griefs (*aishang*), tears would start to flow as soon as I heard that others had similar [griefs]. There were opportunities for this in the process of learning, for example, in personal experience (*geren tiyan*). I would always go and do it." Here again is an image of entrainment, in which a self merges with the other, leading to a reconstitution of one's own sense of private reality as something shared.[54] Thinking with Hannah Arendt and Lisa Guenther, if group experience in the world of psy-training provides an alternative social space for seeing and hearing the intimate experiences of others, constituting reality by confirming it, psy-training in Xi's case provided a common world for public appearance *and* a chance to carve out an alternative life plan, beyond existing social constraints, many of which stem from patriarchal culture.

It is worth mentioning here that marital infidelity was also something that destroyed her, although it was not the only thing. Unlike Danting, who is now her husband's caretaker because he is not well, Xi did not stay married. She is proud to be able to support herself and grateful to her sister for caring for their father when he was ill so she could go and study. She is the youngest of a long line of siblings, so studying psychology has always been, as she put it, an expression of her freedom. Like Danting, she feels fortunate to have caught the tide when she did: "I am not a professional by training. I was able to squeeze into the ranks when our country had yet to become strict [in regulating the field]." Xi is also "grateful to the Party" for giving her the income she needed to pursue her own happiness—or as she dreamily put it, to "*da da da da* go and study."[55] But the freedom that has allowed her to study so intensely has always been accompanied by an acute sense of precarity.

Studying is also a matter of survival, specifically, a matter of surviving an "economy of dignity"—which involves emotions that "hint at a deeper mystery, of the meaning of things, of care, and of belonging."[56] An employee in the state sector, Xi will retire at fifty-five, and psy-counseling is her retirement plan—not only for income but for a dignified life: "There is no way society will not change, there is no way society will have no upheaval, and there is no way your life will be smooth (*pintan*). But if you have a craft (*shouyi*), regardless of how society changes, you have a craft that will feed you, only then will you have dignity (*zun-yan*)." It isn't that keeping oneself fed and not having to rely on others (which is indeed a primary concern) confers dignity. What confers dignity, in this particular case of sense- and life-making, is the effort and the vital force one puts into a cultivated practice, the value of which is then constituted and confirmed by others (because the practice is necessarily performed *for* others). With a polished craft, Xi imagines she will not have the smell of spoiled leftovers when she is advanced in age. She tells me about a local expression, "old person smell" (*laoren wei*). "What is old person smell?," she asks rhetorically, "The hair is not washed, the clothes are not laundered." The term encapsulates the state of despair that psy-training has allowed her to transcend. She does not mind having a sense of precarity, but she refuses to live in despair, living instead with gusto and sharing what she has learned with her next of kin and beyond.

The day we did this interview we took a long lunch break at a nearby farm-to-table restaurant. Her favorite older sister, Cao Yun, joined us. The two sisters, equally talkative and humorous, entertained me with many stories about Yun's twenty-something-year-old son, who Xi claims as her son.

One story went like this: When he was in junior middle school, he had a crush on a girl. The family found out. What to do? "Puppy love" (*zaolian*) was normally punished by public shaming. The parents of both parties would be summoned to personally chide and slap the child in front of the entire class. The point, Yun explained, is to rip your face apart (*si po lian*)—total humiliation. In her son's case, the homeroom teacher (*ban-zhuren*) found out and confronted Yun. Yun feigned surprise, "Who could fancy him?!" in an effort to defuse the situation. In the end, the homeroom teacher handled the matter privately because Yun was the class representative to the parent's commit-tee at the school. The family, meanwhile, handled the matter in their own way, in the context of a group experience Xi designed.

They recruited the boy's father and conducted a mock replay of the son's awkward interaction with the girl based on a descrip-tion he provided, with his father playing the boy and his mother playing the girl in the living room of their family home. The mock replay was then followed by a debriefing of every one's experience (*tihui*): the parents in their role as two adolescents and the son as a bystander observing his parents act out his confusions.

The sisters punctuated the end of this story by noting how different "puppy love" could turn out by telling me about a sui-cide that followed a public shaming, widely reported in the media. One party to the relation subsequently jumped to death from a tall building (*tiaolou*). "Their" son, meanwhile, is now in the United States studying in a graduate program for the creative arts, as if to suggest that psychology had something to do with the way the boy was parented, and something to do with why a boy from a "little place" (*xiao difang*) could do what had been unimaginable for them.

CODA

Like parks and libraries that are "there for all if they are there at all," the human propensity to be copresent—related and separated at the same time—is near at hand and near for all.[57] Well-being and flourishing depend on it, and many take it for granted until they lose it. Neither a sum total nor an aggregate, this propensity for copresence is a common pool resource like forests and fisheries insofar as this propensity is "given by nature." It is an expression of the phenomenological fact of an organism having a perspective *on* and an interest *in* its environment. "Life is inherently expressive," Lisa Guenther writes, drawing from ideas first formulated by the German biologist Jakob von Uexküll. All living beings, "from the amoeba to the poetic genius, articulates both a relation to itself and a relation to something other than itself, something that sustains and supports its own life." The living being's interest in its environment, indicated by its comportment toward it—think flower turning toward the sun—contributes to what Guenther calls "living, loving relationality."[58] For our purposes, we may say that the propensity to be copresent, to contribute to something shared and to be sustained by it, is near at hand if one is alive at all.

Whatever its limitations, the psycho-boom in China has created spaces for copresence and a mini common good to thrive.[59] These spaces are flooded by a mutuality based neither on kinship nor political belonging but on common interest and shared suffering. Like Arendt's metaphorical table, psychology training provides an occasion for coming together while differences are still preserved. Whether, when, and to what extent this sort of horizontal mutuality can be scaled up or integrated into larger systems remains to be seen. It is a long way to go from the two cases I present here to an understanding of shared problems and human responses to them, a key theme of this book. I trust the universe of human discourse will continue to expand with every story told.[60]

NOTES

Thanks to the many people who have commented on drafts of this paper, particularly members of our research group: Becky Hsu, Richard Madsen, Gonçalo Santos, Lynn Sun, and Yunxiang Yan; discussants for panels and workshops where I presented earlier versions: Li Zhang, Jonathan Mair, and Lihong Shi; and the fantastic attendees of a Senior Research Seminar at Cambridge, Department of Social Anthropology. Many thanks to Betsy Stokes for masterful editing. All shortcomings are my own.

1. See Dreyfus and Rabinow for more context, particularly their quote of a personal communication with Michel Foucault: "People know what they do; they frequently know why they do what they do; but what they don't know is what what they do does." Hubert L. Dreyfus and Paul Rabinow, *Michel Foucault: Beyond Structuralism and Hermeneutics*, 2nd ed. (Chicago: University of Chicago Press, 1983), 187.
2. David Hollenbach, "The Glory of God and the Global Common Good: Solidarity in a Turbulent World," *Proceedings of the Catholic Theological Society of America* 72 (2017): 56.
3. Hollenbach, "The Glory of God and the Global Common Good," 56.
4. Roland Minnerath, "The Fundamental Principles of Social Doctrine: The Issue of Their Interpretation," in *Pursuing the Common Good: How Solidarity and Subsidiarity Can Work Together*, ed. Margaret S. Archer

and Pierpaolo Donati (Vatican City: Pontifical Academy of Social Sciences, 2008), 48.

5. Hollenbach, "The Glory of God and the Global Common Good," 56, emphasis in the original.

6. Hannah Arendt, *The Human Condition* (1958; repr. Chicago: University of Chicago Press, 1998); and Lisa Guenther, *Solitary Confinement: Social Death and Its Afterlives* (Minneapolis: University of Minnesota Press, 2013).

7. Hsuan-Ying Huang, "The Emergence of the Psycho-Boom in Contemporary Urban China," in *Psychiatry and Chinese History*, ed. Howard Chiang (London: Pickering & Chatto, 2014), 183–204; Hsuan-Ying Huang, "Untamed *Jianghu* or Emerging Profession: Diagnosing the Psycho-Boom Amid China's Mental Health Legislation," *Culture, Medicine, and Psychiatry* 42, no. 2 (June 2018): 371–400; and Arthur Kleinman, "The Art of Medicine: Remaking the Moral Person in China: Implications for Health," *Lancet* 375 (2010):1074–75.

8. Huang, "Untamed *Jianghu* or Emerging Profession," 389.

9. Li Zhang, "Bentuhua: Culturing Psychotherapy in Postsocialist China," *Culture, Medicine and Psychiatry* 38 (2014): 283–305; and Li Zhang, "Cultivating Happiness: Psychotherapy, Spirituality, and Well-Being in a Transforming Urban China," in *Handbook of Religion and the Asian City: Aspiration and Urbanization in the Twenty-First Century*, ed. Peter van der Veer (Oakland: University of California Press, 2015), 315–32.

10. Huang, "The Emergence of the Psycho-Boom," 196–97.

11. See also Zhang, "Bentuhua."

12. Teresa Kuan, *Love's Uncertainty: The Politics and Ethics of Child Rearing in Contemporary China* (Berkeley: University of California Press, 2015).

13. Huang, "The Emergence of the Psycho-Boom," 191.

14. See Huang, "The Emergence of the Psycho-Boom," 191–92. I am grateful to Yichen Rao for gathering posted certificate exam results where available so I could see for myself the grouping of multifarious occupations under a single system.

15. Zhang, "Bentuhua," 288. Counselors passing this exam received the intermediate level certificate (*Guojia erji xinli zixunshi*).

16. Jiandan Xinli and CBNData, "Report on the Psychological Counseling Industry" (*Xinli zixun hangye renqun dongcha baogao*), 2018, 29.

17. See Huang, "The Emergence of the Psycho-Boom"; Huang, "Untamed *Jianghu* or Emerging Profession"; Zhang, "Bentuhua"; and Zhang, "Cultivating Happiness."

18. Huang, "The Emergence of the Psycho-Boom," 201; and Huang, "Untamed *Jianghu* or Emerging Profession," 389.

19. Yunxiang Yan, "Dislocation, Reposition and Restratification: Structural Changes in Chinese Society," *China Review* 15 (1994): 1–24.

20. Huang, "The Emergence of the Psycho-Boom," 195, 202.

21. Jiandan Xinli et al., "Report on the Psychological Counseling Industry."

22. See Li Zhang, "Cultivating the Therapeutic Self in China," *Medical Anthropology* 37, no. 1 (2018): 50.

23. Sugar Psychology, "Who Are We? Psychological Counselors!," August 16, 2017, https://mp.weixin.qq.com/s/BRjXoJVaT97DPmsEX8dC9w.

24. Lacan Psychology, "Ouroborus: The End of the Psychological Counselor?," April 17, 2019, https://mp.weixin.qq.com/s?__biz=MzI1NDcoMDcxNg ==&mid=2247487782&idx=1&sn=77d771a68855fd7c68d7fe687728e47c&chksm =e9c1c0a5deb649b317d1d1a17cb0af2ce9e2101b143ee4ce68632010a1f134dba65a 639aeaeo#rd. Thanks to Barclay Bram for sharing this post with me.

25. Xu Jingjing, "The Self-Cultivation of a Psychological Counselor" (*Xinli zixunshi de ziwo xiuyang*), *Sanlian shenghuo zhoukan* 18, no. 46 (November 2019): 50–54.

26. Huang, "The Emergence of the Psycho-Boom," 202.

27. William Hinton, *Fanshen: A Documentary of Revolution in a Chinese Village* (New York: Vintage, 1966).

28. Kathleen Erwin, "Heart-to-Heart, Phone-to-Phone: Family Values, Sexuality, and the Politics of Shanghai's Advice Hotlines," in *The Consumer Revolution in Urban China*, ed. Deborah Davis (Berkeley: University of California Press, 2000), 164–65.

29. For a study of family constellation therapy, see Sonya E. Pritzker, "New Age with Chinese Characteristics?: Translating Inner Child Emotion Pedagogies in Contemporary China," *Ethos* 44, no. 2 (2017): 150–70; and Sonya E. Pritzker and Whitney L. Duncan, "Technologies of the Social: Family Constellation Therapy and the Remodeling of Relational Selfhood in China and Mexico," *Culture, Medicine, and Psychiatry* 43, no. 3 (2019), 468–95. For a study of Satir-style family therapy, see Wenrui Chen, *Invoking Personhood in Contemporary China: Seeing*

Through the Lens of a Beijing Family Therapy Center (PhD diss., New York University, 2015).

30. Heather Hayes, "A Re-Introduction to Family Therapy: Clarification of Three Schools," *Australian and New Zealand Journal of Family Therapy* 12, no. 1 (1991): 28; Deborah Weinstein, *The Pathological Family: Postwar America and the Rise of Family Therapy* (Ithaca, NY: Cornell University Press, 2013), 27, 188; and Murray Bowen, *Family Therapy in Clinical Practice* (New York: Jason Aronson, 1978).

31. Both the institute and city name are pseudonyms. I was in a major metropolitan city. Names of fellow trainees to appear in this chapter are also pseudonyms.

32. The gendered historical consciousness Danting alludes to here is very much a creative localization of systemic therapy. Systemic therapy, as it was taught at the institute, is strictly focused on the unintended effects of family systems rather than on social systems.

33. For an excellent ethnographic account of how the wealthy and the powerful socialized in the early 2000s, see John Osburg, *Anxious Wealth: Money and Morality Among China's New Rich* (Stanford, CA: Stanford University Press, 2013).

34. Arendt, *The Human Condition*, 50–58.

35. Arendt, *The Human Condition*, 52.

36. Arendt, *The Human Condition*, 53.

37. Arendt, *The Human Condition*, 57.

38. According to Arendt, the experience of pain is the most isolating of human experiences because it is the "least communicable of all" (Arendt, *The Human Condition*, 50–51). It is, as Elaine Scarry has put it, undeniable for the person in pain but not possible for the listener to confirm. See Elaine Scarry, *The Body in Pain: The Making and Unmaking of the World* (New York: Oxford University Press, 1987), 4.

39. Guenther, *Solitary Confinement*, 144.

40. Quoted in Guenther, *Solitary Confinement*, 19.

41. Guenther, *Solitary Confinement*, 146.

42. Chen, *Invoking Personhood in Contemporary China*, 59–61, 85–86.

43. Hsuan-Ying Huang, "Being Together in Shanghai: Self-Experience and Psy-Sociality in a Legendary Psychotherapy Training Course," paper presented at the "Living Well in China" conference, Long U.S.-China

Institute, University of California, Irvine, November 13, 2018; and Pritzker and Duncan, "Technologies of the Social."

44. Huang, "Being Together in Shanghai," 5.

45. Huang, "The Emergence of the Psycho-Boom," 191.

46. Huang, "Being Together in Shanghai," 4; and Pritzker, "New Age with
Chinese Characteristics?," 150.

47. Pritzker coined the term "chronotopal dilemmas" to refer to dilemmas
that stem from conflicting imperatives, past and present. See also Pritzker and Duncan, "Technologies of the Social," 488; and Pritzker, "New
Age with Chinese Characteristics?"

48. Pritzker and Duncan, "Technologies of the Social," 485.

49. Compare with Tomas Matza, *Shock Therapy: Psychology, Precarity, Well-
Being in Postsocialist Russia* (Durham, NC: Duke University Press, 2018).

50. Hollenbach, "The Glory of God and the Global Common Good," 53.

51. Regarding novel social spaces, compare Yunxiang Yan, "Of Hamburger
and Social Space: Consuming McDonald's in Beijing," in *The Consumer
Revolution in Urban China*, ed. Deborah Davis (Berkeley: University
of California Press, 2000), 201–25. For healing wounds, compare Janice
Boddy, "Spirits and Selves in Northern Sudan: The Cultural Therapeutics of Possession and Trance," *American Ethnologist*, 15, no. 1 (1988): 4–27.

52. This section title makes reference to Viviana Zelizer, *The Purchase of
Intimacy* (Princeton, NJ: Princeton University Press, 2007).

53. She was earning credentials as part of a plan for an extended convalescence following a major life event, but she did not disclose the details.

54. Pritzker and Duncan, "Technologies of the Social."

55. The way she said this evoked in my mind an image of a cartoon heroine
floating up a flight of stairs, magically carried by a gust of joy. "Party" in
this sentence refers to the Party-state. Xi works in the state sector.

56. Allison Pugh, *Longing and Belonging: Parents, Children, and Consumer
Culture* (Berkeley: University of California Press, 2009).

57. Hollenbach, "The Glory of God and the Global Common Good," 53.

58. Guenther, *Solitary Confinement*, 120–21.

59. The term "mini common good" is taken from Richard Madsen's bril-
liant comments on an earlier draft of this paper. The question of integration raised later in the paragraph is also inspired by his comments.

60. Clifford Geertz, *The Interpretation of Cultures* (New York: Basic Books,
1973), 14.

4

REBOOTING A FAMILY

Helping Children in Internet Addiction
Treatment Camps

YICHEN RAO

Whenever Dr. Huang, a thirty-five-year-old female psychotherapist, mentioned Chenxing's father in a therapeutic session, the smile on the face of sixteen-year-old Chenxing would disappear instantly. "I can't forgive him!" Chenxing exclaimed as he related his experience of being "kidnapped" by his parents and forced into residential treatment. "My father and uncle came to pick me up from school and said they would take me to a good restaurant for dinner. After entering the car, I saw a 'friend' of my dad also sitting inside—later I realized that he is one of the drillmasters. As soon as the door was closed, the friend and my uncle, sitting on my left and right, took control of me, and my father drove us. . . . I wanted to shout to get people's attention, but they covered my mouth. Tell me, is this something humans would do (to their children)?"

Chenxing is one of the many Chinese adolescents enrolled by their parents for nonvoluntary residential treatment of their "internet addiction" (*wangluo chengyin* or *wangyin*, abbreviated as IA in this chapter), an adolescent issue that has haunted Chinese families for decades. In 2008, when international academia still contended that IA was an invalid concept, Chinese practitioners were already testing various methods to treat it in young people.[1] A nationwide survey by the China Youth Internet Association estimated that twenty-four million young people in China had IA.[2] It presents as an individual problem of impaired self-control over internet use, and various symptoms may be used to identify this illness category.[3] However, in actual practice in China, the term is only meaningful when referenced alongside what treatment programs describe as "abnormal and rebellious behaviors." Experts and parents label and often institutionalize these young gamers for what parents perceive as uncontrollable, excessive gaming that negatively affects their child's normal social functioning, i.e., school success and family normalcy. Many adolescents deemed "internet addicts" spend days and weeks at a time playing video games, often in an internet cafe and against their parents' will.

The scourge of youth misbehavior related to excessive internet use has long been a key concern in Chinese policy circles as well as in public media. As early as the 2000s, Chinese media was highlighting stories of families coming to blows over children's frequent trips to internet cafes. Some children have stolen from their family to pay for gaming, and some have even harmed or killed their parents over gaming-related conflicts. In 2002, after a thirteen-year-old set fire to an internet cafe in Beijing, the government banned minors from entering them. Later a 2006 revision to China's Law on the Protection of Minors added "infatuation with the internet" to the list of negative behaviors for underage children—alongside gambling, alcohol, and prostitution. The law mandates that the school and family must act responsibly to monitor a child's online misbehaviors.[4] I learned of Chenxing's story during my fieldwork in 2014, but institutional interventions against IA have continued and even escalated in today's China. In the summer of 2021, the Chinese government implemented a new step in the state's long-standing campaign to help parents manage their children's academic responsibilities and fight perceived problems like internet addiction: minors are now strictly limited to three hours of online gaming per week. These kinds of state policies often only result in new problem areas in need of further regulation, however, because Chinese children are drawn to less regulated internet cafes and international games that operate outside of state surveillance and parental controls.

This gap between policy language and real-world effect has pushed parents to find their own solutions, fueling the rise of a private industry in IA treatment programs featuring military-style training and psychotherapy. Since the first of these institutions was founded in Beijing in 2005, the sector has been dogged by controversy. Some camps have been accused of physically abusing young people with inhumane training: as early as 2009, reports that one camp was treating addiction with electroshock therapy provoked a public outcry.[5] Yet the demand for such services—and the profound self-discipline they promise to instill in wayward minors—remains sizable, especially among middle-class parents desperate to turn out high-performing kids.

Research over the past couple of decades has traced the development of IA as both institutional discourse and social reality. Bax analyzes the individual struggles of parents and children as represented in their letters to the education expert Tao Hongkai, who advises parents on their children's IA.[6] He argues for a humanistic model that explains the pathology of IA on the basis of the insanity of the broader system (family, consumer society, etc.). Although IA appears to be a universal syndrome of "self-control," I observe that IA has developed in China as an issue of collective social control in my earlier paper.[7] I argue that the special ways internet addicts have been controlled in China demonstrate the term's ontological feature as a "cultural idiom of distress," expressing the collective concerns of Chinese families over the disrupted social-control system during rapid social transition and technological development. "Internet gaming disorder" may be a more accurate clinical term in China although "IA" is commonly used in clinics and by the media. No matter the label, the problem does not change parents' social reality in which children run away from family and schools and play for days and weeks in internet cafes.

Departing from the previous insights on the social implications of IA in China, in this chapter I focus on the intimate encounters of families with IA treatment in China, illustrating how family dynamics might be *rebooted* to the benefit of the adolescent "addict." I underscore the emergence of the issue of internet addiction within the context of China's rapid transition to a digitalized market society, in which conflict arises as diverse forms of communities, characterized by distinct modes of association and communication, collide. In this analysis, I adopt Hsu's framework to conceptualize community not merely as presumed groups sharing common traits or objectives but as manifestations of diverse "associated living" and "conjoined communicated experience."[8] The locus of conflict and resolution lies at the experiential level of these community dynamics. The tensions unfold when parents perceive internet addicts as forsaking family and school to engage in gaming at internet cafes. In reality, these individuals are opting for an alternative lifestyle, communicative style, and association mode, shaped by the designs of the games they engage in and immersed in the life-worlds cultivated by peer-oriented gaming.

Although my fieldwork was based at a major treatment camp of internet addiction in 2014 and follow-up interviews with parents, camp residents, and other gamers in China from 2014 to 2021, my ethnographic study extends beyond the camp's physical and my fieldwork's temporal boundaries. The observed communities, shaped historically and with future implications, encompass paternalistic middle-class families overinvesting in a single child's education, schools oriented toward competitive market values, and gaming communities formed through "addictive" competitions for youth socialization. Conflicting voices regarding competitions and recognitions—described by me as "competition ideologies"—within these communities undergo reorchestration in the camp, a temporary community with a shared challenge and objective.[9] This process introduces a new psychological paradigm to reform moral configurations in Chinese family's existing modes of associations, which emphasize parental authorities and educational disciplines, and to harmonize different community voices that emerge in a rapidly developing China.

I begin with Chenxing's experience, which demonstrates the camp's special paradigm that IA is a result of problematic parenting styles. Then I provide a brief review of how IA has developed as an issue in China, followed by an introduction to the family-based treatment program that seems to help. Then I use ethnographic cases to discuss the therapeutic details of family-based intervention. I conclude with a discussion of the implications of IA treatment in China for a broader institutional and ethical reality faced by Chinese families. The therapeutic success realized through a shifting ethical imaginary of the Chinese family, which is based on new parent subjectivity and healthier communication patterns, reveals a possible approach, focusing on a more ethical "meta-communication" to mitigate the conflict between different modes of associating faced by contemporary Chinese families.

As an intern and an ethnographer, I observed the everyday operations of the residential treatment center and participated in activities; I also interviewed staff, parents, and "trainees" (*xueyuan*, those who had been sent for residential treatment). The treatment program usually lasts for at least six months and consists of life-skills training, psychological counseling, and parent coaching.

Six units cooperate to carry out this comprehensive therapy. The first and most important unit is the psychological group, consisting of psychotherapists from different schools and backgrounds. Their duty is to provide individual and group therapy for trainees and their parents and to help adolescents and parents understand and communicate with each other. Each therapist oversees a group of seven or eight trainees and their parents. The second unit is the drillmaster team (mostly male retired soldiers), who supervise trainees' everyday activities, lead behavior training, and ensure that trainees do not escape the grounds or initiate violence. Through military-style training and diligent supervision, drillmasters teach the trainees group conformity, time rules, and boundaries. The third unit includes clinical experts who oversee trainees' health and prescribe necessary medicines, such as mood-adjusting antidepressants. The fourth unit is the nursing unit, who take care of trainees' hygiene and living conditions and supervise their daily intake of medications and supplements. The fifth unit is the leisure activity group, responsible for all group activities outside the training and psychotherapy realms. The sixth unit is the parents' group, which focuses on the adult accommodations in the camp: parents are expected to reside and "grow" psychologically alongside their children. Psychologists facilitate group presentations on specific topics every weekday night to stimulate conversations between parents and trainees. As the treatment progresses, families are increasingly engaged in joint therapeutic sessions, incorporating "mock interactions" in the final stages. Diverse community dynamics are intentionally

crafted to assist parents and children in nurturing a psychologically resilient self. The aim is to enhance their communication
patterns and address family conflicts effectively.

I stayed with the drillmaster team during my first two weeks
at the center. I then transferred to the psychological team and
worked as a helper for one of the psychotherapists, Dr. Huang.
The therapists do not have medical degrees, but people still call
them "doctors" in respect of their work as healers. The camp had
been associated with a major hospital, so medical protocols are
still influential there: a person's admission is referred to as "hos-
pitalization" (*ruyuan*), and IA is often formally diagnosed with
"comorbidities" such as depression and anxiety, even though
there is no official clinical guideline for IA in China.

Although IA is a major reason for treatment at the camp,
it is only one of the "youth problems" the center aims to treat.
These include medicalized disorders such as mood and conduct
disorders, but issues not formally diagnosed, such as IA, school
refusal, and defiance against family, are also addressed. In short,
the trainees come from families in which parents do not know
how to deal with their child's abnormal or defiant behaviors and
cannot obtain useful support from schoolteachers or outpatient
clinical and psychological professionals. Of the fifty to sixty
trainees present during my stay at the camp, more than half were
(informally) diagnosed with IA.

STARING WITH EMPTY EYES

One Thursday afternoon in early June 2014, Huang asked me
to bring some of the trainees in her group to the counseling
room to join a "compound" therapeutic session with their parents. Huang began the session by inviting trainees to share some

past interactions with their parents. Group therapy sessions normally include parents only or trainees only. So this time the young people remained silent, affected by their parents' presence. But Chenxing, whose father happened to be absent that day, volunteered.

"Great!" Huang said. "Chenxing, can you share an unpleasant experience you had with your father in the past?" Chenxing said, "That day, I went to an internet cafe. I was betrayed by one of my classmates who told my dad where I went. Then my dad came to the cafe and asked me to go home. After I went home, I tried to run out again, and my dad got angry and beat me out in the courtyard of our apartment complex. I felt very shameful. Sure, it is OK for you to beat me at home. But it's really embarrassing that you beat me in front of my neighbors and classmates! So I decided to run away. I ran to the side of the road and stopped a taxi. As soon as I stepped in the car, my dad chased me and pulled me out. I kicked him and tried to close the door but failed, so he continued to beat me. Just then a colleague of his passed by. He took me to his home for that day. The next day my parents came to pick me up and promised they would no longer beat me. Such hypocrites!"

Huang asked Chenxing to pick a parent in the room to act as his father and simulate an interaction that happened between them. Chenxing picked the father of seventeen-year-old Yongtai because he felt Yongtai's father looked the most friendly. Under the guidance of Huang, Chenxing told Yongtai's father to sit upright like his father and put on a serious expression, whereas Chenxing sat on a lower seat, with his head down, just like he used to when communicating with his father.

They simulated a scene in which Chenxing had dropped ten places after a recent school exam and went home expecting criticisms from his father. Yongtai's father and Chenxing sat opposite to each other and stayed silent for a while. Chenxing couldn't bear the silence and commented that he felt embarrassed.

Huang spoke: "This embarrassment shows that Chenxing feels that he and his father should be equal: Why does his father have to preach at him from a higher position?"

Chenxing said, "Yeah! Every time I lowered my head, my dad would say, 'What are you doing with your head down? Look up!' and then I'd look up and my dad would say, 'What are you staring at with your (empty) eyes?'"

Huang asked Yongtai's father to act out these words. Immediately after Yongtai's father spoke these words, Chenxing rolled up his eyes and stared at the man directly without expression. Huang asked, "What do you feel now?" Chenxing replied, "I felt that no matter what I did, my father would still be dissatisfied."

Huang paused their performance and said to the other parents in the room, "Chenxing's eyes express confusion; he just doesn't know what he will face next. After the parent's 'training,' this kind of empty eyes will also appear when the child faces strangers. It becomes a 'daze' that indicates a loss of security and a feeling of hitting the bottom."

"Ai!" Chenxing interjected, "I just feel that my dad preached so much but never solved the problem. What's the use of preaching so much?"

Yongtai's father continued imitating Chenxing's father, lecturing and criticizing Chenxing: "You have no ambition at all. Look at how much I have achieved since I started my career in the countryside when I was a child!"

Hearing this, Chenxing couldn't help laughing. "This is so much like my dad!" he told the group. "That's exactly how he is! He would first brag about his glorious past, and then educate me to be ambitious! There are simply too many 'big principles' (*da daoli*) and 'old stories.' For example, there was once when he fulfilled his promise and bought me a bicycle worth more than two thousand yuan after I got a higher grade. After that, he would repeat this story whenever he tried to preach at me. Very irritating!"

Another father commented, "I found myself having this problem too. I didn't realize that the love for children should be selfless. I would always start by saying, 'I bought certain things for you, so you must do certain things.'"

Huang turned to Chenxing, "So, what do you want your father to be like?"

Chenxing thought for a while and replied, "I just hope that he can respect me at times and stop nagging."

Chenxing's father came of age during China's early economic reforms, marked by the opening of the market and the resurgence of the national college entrance exam, enabling rural/urban mobility. Having transformed his fate from a poor peasant to a respected urban civil servant via the exam, he strongly believed in the transformative power of self-driven academic diligence. As the first generation in his rural community to navigate China's evolving urban economy, he aspired to elevate his status and validate his family's worth in the city. Passing on his knowledge to his son, he employs traditional methods of "preaching" and "disciplining," reflecting an authoritative parenting style prevalent in agriculturally structured communities.

However, the younger generation, growing up in an urban setting and belonging to the middle class, harbors more intricate needs and desires. The path to recognition has become increasingly complex compared to the time when individuals sought to shed their rural identities. The values and identities across generations are entwined with broader conflicts emerging among different forms of communities in contemporary China.

TREATING INTERNET ADDICTION

Sessions like this happen in the camp every day. Surprisingly, those I observed were not about young people's gaming behavior but their feelings of self, their life in camp, and most important, their parents. The shaming and beatings that Chenxing suffered from his father were traumatic, motivating him to stay at internet cafes more often. The intense family communications Chenxing described were common among camp attendees' families. As conflicts escalated, some young people had run away from home and school, staying at internet cafes for as long as they could.

Parents themselves felt helpless, watching online gaming turn their once obedient child into "a bad student who would rather stare at computer screens than spend time working on their study or talking to us," or into "a 'monster' who would shout at us when we told him to stop playing after one to two hours." Most people sent for treatment were adolescents from middle-class families or above, perhaps because the treatment program cost 14,000 yuan ($2,100) a month, which was much higher than China's average disposable income for the urban population (2,400 yuan per month) in 2014. The three most common professions among parents of trainees were teacher, police officer, and doctor. It is interesting to note that these are among the more respected but busiest professionals in China. They tend to have higher expectations for their children's social mobility yet have less time to spend with them and care for their psychological needs. Moreover, as competitors in a market society who witnessed the layoff waves of the 1990s, these parents are keenly aware of the importance of a college degree for their children's security. Therefore, they often push them to study hard so they can earn recognized social positions in an increasingly competitive China.

But it's not just about material success. In her ethnography of middle-class parenting in China, Teresa Kuan borrowed a term from the sociologist Allison Pugh: parents participate in "the economy of dignity," in which they pursue status and social belonging through consumption and other means.[10] When Chinese parents enroll their children in after-school classes and force them to study hard and spend all their free time on homework, it's not just a rational choice in a competitive educational market. Parents feel compelled to save face (for themselves and for their kids) in a society and moral world that is constantly ranking its residents. As the parents often told me, "You know, this is the reality! I don't want to push my child so hard either. But when I saw what the other parents around me did for their child, I felt really pressured." It is through this relational pressuring, bound up with a sociocultural environment that emphasizes a child's academic performance, that such mechanical disciplines are passed to middle-class children from their anxious parents. Here parental aspirations for the sole child's future prosperity intersect with the intensely competitive school milieu, fostering detrimental cycles of social comparisons. These cycles contribute to alienating patterns within Chinese families, leading digitally formed peer communities in gaming to assume greater psychological significance for overworked teenagers than the stress-laden academic reality.

In my study, young students expressed that they use video games to relieve their stress. Also, their primary task at school is to learn rather than to make friends, and gaming builds much-needed social relationships. This outlet is especially important for those who are struggling in class: success in video games becomes a way to satisfy their desire for recognition and respect. In a sense, young people use the internet to create their *own* economy of dignity, giving them an alternative to the stressful reality imposed on them at home. The sheer fact that the majority sent for IA treatment were male adolescents also indicated how the success anxiety is more often experienced by the male in a transforming patriarchal family.[11]

The daily family dynamics scrutinized in the treatment camps are different from the general parenting advice and moral explorations among the ambitious and anxious Chinese parents observed by Kuan and Xu.[12] Rather than being projected onto the uncertain yet hopeful imaginary of a child's future, they are pessimistic and assume a certain broken state accompanied by failures pending rectifications.

In countries with highly developed internet connectivity, excessive online gaming is often an issue. But social reactions to it vary. In the United States, interventions center around individual counseling and self-help. Kimberly Young, an American psychologist who first published seriously on IA, founded the Center for Internet Addiction in 1995, which provided counseling services to addicts.[13] By 1996, small-scale support groups had formed, such as the Internet Addiction Support Group.[14] A few inpatient rehabilitation programs geared specifically toward IA have been founded in the recent decade, which mainly focus on voluntary self-explorations through digital-detox retreats, wilderness therapy camps, talk therapy, and medication.[15] Although ambitious, the IA programs have not focused on social control, which has been customary for drug-abuse treatment, nor have these programs framed excessive online gaming as a national public health threat (with corresponding government interventions). Furthermore, IA treatment in the United States is not geared specifically toward adolescents, although other interventions for troubled youth have long existed in "therapeutic boarding schools," family boot camps, and wilderness programs.[16]

In China, on the other hand, the topic of IA is addressed frequently in family-involved psychological/psychiatric sessions but seldom in the context of individual self-help. Usually, parents pursue treatment for their children to fix an identified issue associated with their excessive gaming. It is the breakdown of parental control that causes distress for parents in China as they seek resources to persuade their child to get out of the games. They might take the child to a psychiatrist or a psychological counselor, read parenting advice books, browse the internet for related knowledge, or even hire "education experts" to visit their homes and converse with the child. Some parents even see doctors and psychotherapists about their own mental suffering resulting from the child's behavior. Seeing no improvement, desperate parents resort to residential treatment for their child, with or without an official diagnosis of IA. In this context, IA treatment camps are specific institutional solutions to the breakdown of parental controls related to the child's excessive gaming.

However, family was not a key treatment focus when the camp was first established in 2005; the founder, a military psychiatrist, designed it to "rectify" a child's mentality and behavior. He told me that it was around 2012, after seven years of exploration, that his team came to realize the importance of formally introducing family-based interventions to help the adolescents cope with IA: "We realized that even if we have trained the children with good enough habits and taught them necessary psychological skills, they could still relapse after going back to a problematic environment with terrible parenting." Since then the camp has worked to reboot the internet addicts' family dynamics. In 2013, the founder told a newspaper that the camp had improved their "success rate" of treatment from 30 percent in 2005 to 80–90 percent in 2013, after having developed comprehensive measures involving family-based interventions.

It should be noted that many other treatment camps featured in the news did not consider family to be their core treatment unit. Also, the introduction of family-based intervention at the camp did not mean that all counselors recruited are well-trained, professional family therapists, like those seen in Kuan's study of China's family therapy institute.[17] Rather, the therapists working in the camp are usually trained in a variety of schools as were those interviewed by Zhang.[18] Many therapists there started their training in individual therapies such as psychoanalysis and cognitive-behavioral therapy, later seeking training through workshops in different schools of family therapy—such as systemic, Satir, and Hellinger—as they realized the need for more family-intervention skills when working with Chinese clients. Therefore, the family program at the camp is not about therapists practicing conventional therapy practices following certain schools but about setting up the entire treatment space with family in mind. Techniques have gradually been developed and are derived from past institutional practices and multiple psychological resources. Consistent beliefs about and protocols for addressing family dynamics are always evolving. Consequently, the program offers individual and group counseling sessions of different styles, parent-training lectures, and the therapists' direct guidance and supervision of parents as they interact with children in words and actions. In a sense, they are like coaches who stay close to the family.

The founder (and then director) of the camp described for me what a successfully treated case would look like: Usually, a cured child will rely less on video games to manage his psychological needs; he will be able to manage his distress through the support of parents and become more confident and less depressive and anxious in school and work. We have a quantitative measurement of those psychological features in our follow-up surveys.

In my fieldwork, I also observed that the involvement of family did seem to help resolve the issue. The more the parent was willing to participate in the training program, the faster the child could complete the camp and return to family and society. Meanwhile, many "relapses" and second or third "hospitalizations" seemed to have happened in families when parents were less devoted to changing themselves. This observation confirms the earlier points that IA is a collective expression of family breakdown.[19] The therapeutic success realized through the family's intimately reformed dynamics reveals a culturally significant paradigm shift of the Chinese ethical imaginary of family. As a foundational social entity, a Chinese family is no longer envisioned solely as a paternalistic community governed by Confucian educational discipline. Instead, it is now conceptualized as a "psychologically healthy" environment in which diverse community ideologies can be harmonized, emphasizing mutual respect for each individual's internal needs on an equitable basis.

BECOMING A COMMUNICATOR-TRAINER PARENT

If a parent could learn to read and respect a child's psychological needs—and communicate with the child at an equal standing regarding each other's expectations and the issues of work-play balance—therapists at the camp believe that online gaming would no longer cause dramatic family conflicts. The emergence of good parenting that attends to a child's inner psyche is, per Kuan's analysis, culturally significant.[20] The Chinese approach to socialization holds the relational sensitivity of the child as its primary goal. Before the introduction of the capitalist economy, psychological interiority did not matter much in a social system that rewarded the ability to read subtle cues and anticipate needs. This historical transformation in parenting methods is comparable to many other spheres of transformation in Chinese society caused by the advent of the market economy, such as "individualization" and the "inner revolution" led by psy-disciplines.[21]

Camp therapists blamed young people's IA on "traditional" Chinese parenting styles: the condescending and coercive way of *guanjiao* (discipline) bound in Confucianist patterns. A more scientific, psychologized way of *guanli* (management) is encouraged to improve parent-child communications. In Chinese, *guan* (管), when used as a verb, refers to a variety of actions that share a common theme of responsibility, care, and management. The word takes on slightly different meanings when used in different contexts. For example, in modern organizations, when people say somebody "*guan*" a group of people, it usually means that the person is in charge of the group or *guanli* (manages) them. In daily conversation, when someone says *buyao guan wo*, it means "stay out of my business" or "don't worry about me."

However, in school and within the family, when *guan* is used between teachers and students or between parents and children, the implied idea is more complicated than management or care. *Guan* can carry both meanings and expand to a distinct category as in the word *guanjiao* (discipline). *Jiao* means "to educate," and the term *guanjiao* refers to a specific culturally and morally imbued discipline and pedagogy. It happens between adults and minors, the powerful and the powerless, the owner and the owned, as influenced by the Confucian ideology of social control. *Guanjiao* rests on the paternalistic notion that "I discipline you for your own good," even if the subject does not appreciate it and resists it. Earlier research had indicated that the traditional Chinese ways of *guanjiao*—through harsh criticisms, moral preaching, and corporal punishments—still prevailed in

Chinese families, and corporal punishment of minors remains an "unacknowledged" problem in China's legal field.[22] Recent studies that focus on Chinese children's moral experience have demonstrated that the tensions regarding whether and how to make such discipline work are complicated by individual habits, values, and power differentials.[23]

In the camp, I observed how such practices of *guanjiao* (discipline) were reconfigured as "problems," "mistakes," and even "pathologies" from a psychological (rather than legal) perspective. Two major features of traditional *guanjiao* were problematized by therapists. One was the loss of communication between parents and children (i.e., the parents failed to delve into their child's psychological interiority). The other was the absence of boundaries and clearly defined rules in the home. The second point seems surprising at first because traditional parenting in China is thought of as strict. There is a famous Chinese saying that resembles the English proverb "spare the rod and spoil the child." It states, "a filial son only comes from under the rods."

To this camp therapists would say that, first of all, beating does not solve problems or help parents and children to better understand each other. Rather, it damages the psychological health of both sides. Second, parents beat their children not for any clearly defined reason but out of uncontrolled emotion. They beat because they are outraged that their parental authority is threatened—not because the child has crossed an expressed boundary or broken a family rule (such as cheating on exams or using foul language).

Parents at the treatment camp had previously maintained rigid lines between the powerful elder and the powerless junior, with the more powerful members' voices as the moral standards of good and bad: e.g., a good child always listens to parents and works diligently at school. However, the psychologized imaginary of a "healthier" Chinese family insists upon communication as equals and mutual agreement between family members, respecting the voice of the child. This echoes what Kuan observes in her ethnography of Chinese family therapy of a suffering adolescent: "the boundaries between persons are by no means a given," and the problem lies "in the entanglement of seemingly discrete persons."[24] To fulfill a healthier imaginary against the previous "instituted fantasy" of a hierarchical family, parents must learn to deal with their child's disobedience in a tactical and psychological way—to become communicator-trainer parents who negotiate necessary boundaries with their child and find different sets of roles and positions for themselves in the family.[25]

First, parents should be self-reflective and capable of withholding their emotions in front of their children. Second, they should listen with their hearts. When a child does something wrong, his parents should encourage him to talk about the incident instead of applying harsh judgments right away. Third, parents should share their own feelings and thoughts, but only after they have listened to the child's perspective, and then communicate with the child on the same level—like a friend, not like a "master." Then parent and child should agree upon the rules based on this incident and refer to this rule as necessary. Parents who have spoiled their children too much also need to learn how to train their children in impulse control, again through communication (discussed in the next section).

In short, a parent is expected to learn a whole new system of knowledge at the camp to become a qualified communicator and trainer. This learning process includes the acquisition of new skills and techniques as well as a renegotiation of the parent identity in general, and a reformation of parent subjectivity. Most parents who went through the program expressed gratitude for having been given the chance to learn something new and convert themselves to more psychologically empowered people in their midlife, which relieved their moral burdens as an authoritative parent. This sentiment was strongly and repeatedly expressed by parents during my interviews and during group sessions and lectures.

However, for most parents, the identity shift is not easy to make. Director Ma and the other therapists expended a lot of emotional labor just to make the parents aware of their own "problems." Most parents came with an expectation that they can have their child fixed by the camp and pick up a "reformed" child a few months later (this was an intentional marketing strategy used to lure parents in the first place). Therapists begin actively persuading parents immediately after their child has been "hospitalized." Many therapists felt uncomfortable with this procedure, which they secretly and jokingly compared to "brainwashing," because they had been trained to work mainly with self-motivated clients seeking help for themselves. But to make their therapies with children more effective and meaningful, they must develop techniques to "activate" the parents' self-motivation and make them want to stay.

Even when parents agree to stay and learn, they may find it difficult to put the knowledge into practice when they are facing their child. Therefore, the training sessions offer plenty of opportunities. Their interactive learning processes facilitate subtle shifts in parenting mindsets and techniques, gradually transforming the parents' words and actions toward their children.

TRAINING DELAYED GRATIFICATIONS

Director Ma, a very experienced psychotherapist, had been with the camp for five years; she had spearheaded the integration of family-based interventions into the program. As director of the psychological group, she supervised the therapists, helping them with their difficulties. And she gave training lessons to newly admitted parents. One Wednesday afternoon, I was invited to sit in for one of those lectures.

Ma used vivid examples derived from her institutional practices to inspire the parents. One such example was used to explain why the children hated it when their parents would preach to them about core principles (*jiang daoli*):

> Actually, your children know those principles very well. They are just against the way you taught them. Every month, a barber is invited to the camp to do haircuts for trainees. Some trainees hate the barber because he would simply press down on their heads and trim their hair into the same "prisoner" style. Though the trainees fully understood why a haircut was needed, they loathed the way it was done. Therefore, the problem of many parents is that you *thought* that your child did not listen and could not understand the right principles you taught. However, the children simply don't like how you "press on their heads" and pour those principles in.

According to therapists, trainees had been immediately turning to computer games to satisfy their psychological needs, partially because they lacked the capability to withhold their desires for "instant gratification" (*yanchi manzu*). This lack of capability was a result of problematic parenting. Ma explained:

> Some parents were used to immediately responding to their children's requests. This immediate response is out of a desire to compensate for their lack of time accompanying their child, due to their busy job. Therefore, when their child requested a bar of

chocolate, they would go ahead and buy him a whole box of chocolates. Next time the child would request an expensive sneaker, because they noticed that their parents were prone to say yes to such requests.

Then, how is this compensation mentality causing your child's problems?

Ma paused for a while to let the parents ponder the question. Then she continued:

By compensating, parents could feel less guilty but never really fulfill the child's spiritual needs. If this pattern continues, the child will be used to using instant material gratifications to satisfy those unmet psychological needs. They would want everything they desired to be immediately available. They cannot self-regulate and will lose the sense of boundary. They will be afraid of being restricted and criticized. Afterward, when they interact with teachers and classmates at school, they will easily feel frustrated, cause troubles, and gradually lose interests in the demanding schoolwork. What makes it worse is that they cannot find sufficient emotional support and guidance from you, as you only tell them to study harder so they could get material rewards.

Therefore, when we hear such requests from the child, we need to learn to put them aside for a while. Don't respond immediately! Of course, it is difficult to overcome our immediate desires to gratify our own need to assuage our guilt."

A father raised his hand: "Director Ma, you just said we should learn to put the child's request aside for a while and not respond immediately. But what if a child repeatedly asks for the same thing? How should I plan my response? Is there a template?"

"There is nothing to be planned," replied Ma:

It is less important to plan for a response than to make sure that you have a comfortable connection with your child. If the feeling is comfortable, it doesn't matter whether you and your child agree or disagree with each other. You just need to make sure that your communication makes them feel that they are seen and accepted. And it doesn't matter how many times your child has made the request. Every person would communicate differently. The way recommended by your therapist may not suit you the best.

A mother asked about another common frustration: "I also tried to cultivate my child's delayed gratification. But the problem is, when he asked for this, I said no. Then he would go on to ask for another one. If I refuse him again, he will change to another request. And sometimes if I said no, he would simply go to his father. If his father said no, he would ask his grandpa. What should we do in this situation?"

"Did your child know why you are doing this?" asked Ma.

"No, he didn't," admitted the mother.

"Then you should let him know why you declined his request," Ma explained. "It was not because you could not afford it, nor any other reason." Then Ma emphasized what she saw as the core problem: "You gave me the impression that you are using this refusal to satisfy your own needs, instead of caring about your communication with the child. You neglected the need for a harmonious relationship."

Parents were trained to work on their communicator role, e.g., to mitigate the negative affects commonly caused by declining the child's request by openly communicating. In that sense, their communicator role could then benefit their role as the child's trainer. Open communication could also become a cybernetic exercise: when parents communicate to their child on an equal basis and listen patiently about their child's feelings—while explaining the reasons for their rules and decisions—the child can absorb these habits and imitate them in the future. Similarly, the capability for delayed gratification could be passed along from parent to child. When parents control their impulse to mitigate their guilt through the instant gratification of material consumption, their child can also be "trained" to respond the same way and more easily resist addictive cycles.

REWORKING COMMUNICATIONS

This communication-based therapeutic mechanism for treating addiction echoes the anthropologist Gregory Bateson's analysis of the methods of Alcoholics Anonymous (AA).[26] It is worth noticing that Bateson is also a founding figure of cybernetic philosophies and systemic family therapy, which had partially influenced the design of family-based intervention in this camp. In Bateson's study, a person's experience in AA is described as a transition from one mode of communication with the world, *symmetry* (a state of mind that focuses on antagonism), to another, *complementarity* (which focuses on integration). In his framework, addiction to drinking is at first a "complementary surrender" to the warmth of alcohol. But when all the relatives and friends of the addicted person keep criticizing the habit, this begins the alcoholic's journey of "fighting against" the environment with a "symmetrical pride" toward the alcohol (a determination to beat it), which usually ends with the person coming back to the "complementary relationship" with the alcohol and finally "hitting bottom." It is after coming to AA that a person realizes that there is a larger system (the community of alcoholics) with which the addicted person can connect. Afterward, the recovering alcoholic develops a "more correct" state of mind (a more sober and harmonious state of control), becoming part of something larger (the group) than the short-circuited connection with alcohol (uncontrolled indulgence). In short, a willing surrender to one's addict identity and to the collective power of community is usually the first step in a person's sobriety.

Bateson's work informs us about the role of systems, community, and communication in the genesis and treatment of addiction. This understanding goes beyond the narrow concept in mainstream psychiatry of addiction as simply a disease of the brain, and it is also reflected in his more influential studies of schizophrenia. Bateson was also part of the research group that produced a foundational publication in the field of marriage and family therapy titled "Toward a Theory of Schizophrenia."[27] The group explained how schizophrenia could develop in a child's otherwise normal brain through a pattern of "double binds"—multiple contradictory injunctions—in the child's communications with his mother. Today, the double-bind theory is still widely appraised as a founding philosophy in family therapy. His work has revolutionized the field of psychotherapy in both theory and pragmatics.

In China, the systems and cybernetic thinking that Bateson and his team have developed found its cultural grounds with psychotherapists after the 1990s. The first batch of contemporary Chinese psychotherapists received trainings of systems family therapy interventions from German experts during the late 1980s.[28] The popularity of the Satir school of family therapy in China was also observed by Zhang as a result of its cultural resonances with Chinese family entanglements.

Another psychology lecturer in the camp explained to the parents how Chinese family habits of teaching children to be obediently respectful of elders may have harmed the parent-child relationship:

> When you command your child to respect elders, you already send him into a meta-communication of disrespect. How can children learn to respect others if they feel disrespected through such commands in the first place? In Chinese families, we care too much about maintaining the harmonious relationships at "face" level without expressing our truthful feelings and making everyone feel comfortable through such truthful expressions.

This lecture also highlighted the importance of a parent's unconditional love for a child, something mentioned previously in Chenxing's story. The speaker critiqued the practice of offering love only with certain conditions. For example, parents may say to the child, "If you have achieved certain exam scores, I will reward you with a laptop." The lecturer offered a more unconditional alternative: A better way of expressing love is not to tell your children that they deserve love only if they do good things. Instead, you could say, "I still love you even if you made mistakes, but as someone who truly cares about you, I must explain to you why your behavior could cause a serious problem."

Parents who attended these courses gradually internalized the techniques, values, and imaginaries regarding how a "healthier" Chinese family can be run and how a child can be positioned comfortably in such dynamics. The therapists also believed that to base their open communications on authentic love, the parents had to learn to first face themselves truthfully at a psychological level. Therefore, they went through a lot of group counseling sessions. They became used to confessing their weaknesses in front of other parents, and finally, in front of their child. This, the therapists claimed, proved to be the most important conversion process in rebooting the family dynamics.

CULTIVATING PARENTAL ENERGY

Director Ma warned newly arrived parents of trainees that talking with their child after the midterm of the program might feel very difficult. They might become afraid of saying the wrong thing and exposing their own weaknesses. But Ma said that this awareness indicates that the parents have begun to have "energy." They just need to let it out by practicing self-exposure.

She gave an example of a parent who had benefited from this energy:

> This mother was a senior manager who worked very hard. She said that at the beginning of the treatment, she felt very tired as she had to travel between the city [where] she worked and the camp, every weekend by night train. But after two months, she realized that though she was catching the same night train back on the weekend, she felt very energized. Her direct reports told her that she seemed livelier than before and treated people more nicely.

Ma said that this energy can be cultivated if parents devote more time to their growth in the camp. "A parent with boosted energy will treat their child's issue with more confidence," she explained. "It is like they have taken the relay baton from the therapist."

But what is this invisible energy? And how did it emerge? In my fieldwork, I observed that parents who had been at the camp for a longer time would be relatively more open in their groups and better at analyzing their own psychological activities. In the group therapy sessions, they would more frankly confessed their mistakes when dealing with their child. Newcomers would be influenced by the honesty of the more seasoned parents and gradually became more open. According to Huang, this cultivated desire to confess helps parents develop energy because a person can use such capabilities of moral reflection to empathize with others and build better family relationships. These in-group confessions, again, reminded me of Alcoholics Anonymous.

In fact, the parents *were* relatively anonymous to each other. They came from cities all over China and were known only as [trainee]'s father/mother. This made it easier for them to forget about their professional identities in "real life" and build a more secure group dynamic with other "anonymous" parents sharing similar issues.

On the other hand, these meetings reminded me of the Al-Anon meetings attended by the wives of Japanese alcoholics.[29] Both the Al-Anon meetings and the parents' groups emphasized that family members of the addicts need psychological growth for themselves before they can "solve" other people's problems. For the Al-Anon participants in Japan, their problems revolved around their codependency with their husbands and children. Under the instruction of modern psychology, the wives were encouraged to unlearn the "good wife" identity and release the moral blame for their husband's alcoholism. However, what Chinese parents are expected to do is a bit more complicated: they must start by recognizing their moral failures in pressuring their child to work so hard while not attending to their child's interior needs. Only after this "complementary surrender" to a "failed" identity (like alcoholics in AA) could they start unlearning the previous "good parent" identity as an authoritative figure fully responsible for the child's academic performance and begin "individuating" from their obsessive "entanglement" with their child. In short, through confessions, parents in the camp's program surrendered their attempts to "correct" their child while learning new ways of relating.

Such energies were also transferred to the parent-child communication. For example, parents were encouraged to write letters to their child (under the supervision of a therapist), and these letters can be edited and improved before being delivered. Letter writing is an initial step in the parents' practice of new communicative patterns with their child, empowered by the boosted energy. Afterward they practiced talking and interacting with their child differently on other occasions, with manners similar to those used in their letters.

I read some letters shared with me by the trainees. One of the letters, written by the mother of fourteen-year-old Jiaming, included her sincere regret:

> First, mama [I] did not know how to give love to you in your childhood. When you were five, you were once hit by a motorbike as you were crossing the street. I was very scared, but I criticized you for not being careful. I now realize that I neglected your need for comfort and care rather than criticism. During primary school, you wanted mama to accompany you in sleep. I hated that your request disrupted my work schedule and asked you to be independent. . . . There are times when you feel uncomfortable, and we simply ask you to go to school. If you didn't obey, we would reprimand you and beat you with belts. . . . When I recall the past, I am filled with guilt and remorse. In the world of love, I am completely retarded. . . . After you became addicted to games, I realized that I could no longer control you. I lost my temper and made our relationship increasingly intense.

I asked Jiaming about his feelings toward his mom's expressions. "I was relieved and moved that she finally admitted her problems," he told me. He expressed a cautious optimism about their future relationship: "I will try to learn how to negotiate with them about my plans, and I am happy to tell them what I felt, but I really need to make sure that they don't press me into their values again."

Jiaming was intending to make a career out of gaming. He claimed that he had already earned 400,000 yuan (about $60,000), simply by selling the virtual weapons and avatars he had gathered and cultivated in online games. But as Jiaming's parents were both highly educated professionals in high-end technology fields, they wanted him to obtain a PhD—perhaps in finance or computer science—from a top university. They wanted a more reliable source of income for him and a higher social status than that of a game-item dealer. Therefore, a key therapeutic goal for this family, according to their therapist, was for Jiaming's parents to hear their child's thoughts and feelings before making paternalistic decisions for him.

THE META COMMUNICATION OF A MORAL CHINA

In Naftali's work on contemporary Chinese conceptualizations of children's rights, she interpreted discourse that treated children as distinct and individual persons as "products of cross-cultural translations of various projects of liberal modernity and of a middle-class civility."[30] The treatment programs of internet addiction are only affordable by middle-class families and higher, demonstrating a paradoxical condition. On one hand, internet addiction treatment camps have emerged in China because Chinese parents have been granted the authoritative power and responsibility to limit their child's physical liberality so they can stay on the right track for social competition. The emergent middle-class pursuit of upward mobility renders these controversial disciplinary-therapeutic programs both necessary and effective. But on the other hand, these camps have also become potential sites to liberate the child, psychologically, from conflictual entanglements between different community ideologies within a family, making it easier for them to withstand the harsh social reality of competition. In this chapter, I also depict a more modern, more complicated picture of child rights in practice: Parents who grew up with the earlier economic ethics of hard work to change their family's fate are now forced to face their children's psychological needs expressed through consumerist desires for online games and through the individualized language of self that their children have learned from popular culture.

As demonstrated, an institutionalized private treatment program helped middle-class children cope with the harsh reality of social competition, less through the fanciful sociality of video games and more through real-world family communication. The notion of a "healthier," more communicative family, although constructed with psychological theories and practices imported from the relatively more modernized and marketized states, is grounded in a cultural history of constantly transforming Chinese family values and imaginaries. For example, the Confucianism-inflected paternalistic disciplines and "educational desires"—after decades of Maoist suppression—may be reemerging in China to help ensure children's success in an increasingly competitive and decollectivizing economy.[31] Cultural resources built on the ethical imaginary of hardworking and well-disciplined children who bear the family's hope in obtaining upward mobility once worked for premodern Chinese families. Yet they conflict with some modernist conditions that emphasize individualities and psychological interiorities.

Therefore, in the family conflicts over children's internet addiction, we witness the collective distress experienced by the family as a system bound to a rapidly changing society with conflicting values, dispositions, and habits.

In this light, the emerging imaginary of the Chinese family made healthier through these training programs could be interpreted as a strategic recentering of family from a paternalistic community filled with abstract moral rules and uprooted principles to a psychological environment of mundane but effective "meta communications"—an ethical reflection on the best modes of associations, recentering on everyday relational details, intersubjective communications, and moral negotiations. This recentering lifts the family out of the battlefield of values to cultivate a more complementary connection within the family as well as between family and society. When families begin to accept the reality that their child does not have to be, and may not ever become, a successful student or an obedient person, parents and children will be more likely to respect one another as full persons. People are more likely to become morally robust at a relational level, treating others not as the carriers of abstract values, uprooted wills, and manipulable means toward a certain goal but as humans with feelings and emotions.

As Zigon argues, when asking ethical questions, it is important to use "how" instead of "what." "What" questions make people inclined to act according to "a predefined measure," whereas "how" questions review ethics as "an ongoing existential process immanent to situations within which we find ourselves ecstatically intertwined."[32] The treatment camp's focus on interpersonal communications rather than ethical guidelines engages the "how" question, and people begin to appreciate the existential process, not the objectified humans, as the core of human ethics. This insight is not limited to the amelioration of family interactions. For example, the ethical failure of treating humans as means based on predefined measures was seen in the implementation of strict lockdown policies in China during the recent epidemic, which negatively affected people's well-being.[33]

In this sense, although therapeutic programs attend only to the "meso-level systems,"[34] they demonstrate an alternative path to the cultivation of a moral China at the broader, meta communicative level. The family reboot programs do not attempt to cultivate moral subjects with desirable moral characters under a perceived moral crisis, as reported in other anthropological work on Chinese moral development.[35] Rather, they reveal the existential crisis of a social system caused by the conflicts between people's varying orientation toward uprooted moral principles. These principles define how a family "should" be run and how one cultivates "a good child," but they do not pay sufficient attention to the experiences of intersubjective attunements, connections, and communications. Instead of forging "good" individuals for an ethical society, the treatment programs suggest that people can "develop" an ethical ecosystem to allow more diverse community voices to coexist peacefully within a family.

NOTES

1. Alecia C. Douglas et al., "Internet Addiction: Meta-Synthesis of Qualitative Research for the Decade 1996–2006," *Computers in Human Behavior* 24, no. 6 (2008): 3027–44.

2. China Youth Internet Association, *2009* 年青少年网瘾调查报告 (Survey of internet addiction of young people in China 2009), accessed July 2019, http://edu.qq.com/edunew/diaocha/2009wybg.htm, 2010.

3. American Psychiatric Association, *Diagnostic and Statistical Manual of Mental Disorders: DSM-5* (Arlington, VA: American Psychiatric Association, 2013); Tao Ran, Xiuqin Huang, Jinan Wang, Huimin Zhang,

Ying Zhang, and Mengchen Li, "Proposed Diagnostic Criteria for Internet Addiction," *Addiction* 105, no. 3 (2010): 556–64; and World Health Organization (WHO), *ICD-11 (Mortality and Mobility Statistics)*, accessed July 2019, https://icd.who.int/browse11/l-m/en 2018.

4. National People's Congress Standing Committee (NPCSC), "Law on Protection of Minors" (未成年人保护法), ed. NPCSC (全国人民代表大会常务委员会) (Beijing: Zhong guo fa zhi chu ban she (中国法制出版社), 2007).

5. Xue Bai, "一个网戒中心的生态系统" (The eco-system of an internet addiction treatment center), *China Youth Daily*, May 5, 2009, http://www.cyol.net/zqb/content/2009-05/07/content_2655346.htm.

6. Trent Bax, *Youth and Internet Addiction in China* (Oxford: Routledge, 2013).

7. Yichen Rao, "From Confucianism to Psychology: Rebooting Internet Addicts in China," *History of Psychology* 22, no. 4 (2019): 328–50.

8. Becky Hsu. "Introduction" in this book; and John Dewey, *The Middle Works of John Dewey, 1899–1924*. Vol. 9, *1916, Democracy and Education*, ed. Jo Ann Boydston (Carbondale: Southern Illinois University Press, 2008), 93.

9. Yichen Rao, "E-sports vs. Exams: Competition Ideologies Among Student Gamers in Neo-Socialist China," *Social Analysis* 66, no. 4 (2022): 69–90.

10. Teresa Kuan, *Love's Uncertainty: The Politics and Ethics of Child Rearing in Contemporary China* (Berkeley: University of California Press, 2015); and Allison Pugh, *Longing and Belonging: Parents, Children, and Consumer Culture* (Berkeley: University of California Press, 2009).

11. Stevan Harrell and Goncalo Santos, eds., introduction to *Transforming Patriarchy: Chinese Families in the Twenty-First Century* (Seattle: University of Washington Press, 2016), 1–36.

12. Kuan, *Love's Uncertainty*; and Jing Xu, *The Good Child: Moral Development in a Chinese Preschool* (Stanford, CA: Stanford University Press, 2017).

13. Kimberly Young, *Caught in the Net* (New York: Wiley, 1998).

14. Michael OReilly, "Internet Addiction: A New Disorder Enters the Medical Lexicon," *Canadian Medical Association Journal* 154, no. 12 (1996): 1882.

15. Claire Foran, "The Rise of the Internet-Addiction Industry," *The Atlantic*, November 8, 2015, https://www.theatlantic.com/technology /archive/2015/11/the-rise-of-the-internet-addiction-industry/414031/.

16. Robert M. Friedman et al., "Unlicensed Residential Programs: The Next Challenge in Protecting Youth," *American Journal of Orthopsychiatry* 76, no. 3 (2006): 295–303.

17. Teresa Kuan, "Feelings Run in the Family: Kin Therapeutics and the Configuration of Cause in China," *Ethnos* 85, no. 4 (2020): 695–716.

18. Li Zhang, *Anxious China: Inner Revolution and Politics of Psychotherapy* (Berkeley: University of California Press, 2020).

19. Rao, "From Confucianism to Psychology."

20. Kuan, *Love's Uncertainty.*

21. Yunxiang Yan, *The Individualization of Chinese Society* (New York: Berg, 2009), xvii–xviii; and Zhang, *Anxious China.*

22. David Y. H. Wu, "Parental Control: Psychocultural Interpretations of Chinese Patterns of Socialization," in *Growing Up the Chinese Way*, ed. Sing Lau (Hong Kong: Chinese University Press, 1996), 1–26; Vanessa L. Fong, *Only Hope: Coming of Age Under China's One-Child Policy* (Stanford, CA: Stanford University Press, 2004.); and Orna Naftali, *Children, Rights, and Modernity in China: Raising Self-Governing Citizens* (New York: Palgrave Macmillan, 2014.), 74.

23. Xu, *The Good Child*, 151.

24. Kuan, "Feelings Run in the Family," 699.

25. Steven P. Sangren, "The Chinese Family as Instituted Fantasy: Or, Rescuing Kinship Imaginaries from the 'Symbolic'," *Journal of Royal Anthropological Institute* 19, no. 2 (2013): 279–99.

26. Gregory Bateson, *Steps to an Ecology of Mind* (Chicago: University of Chicago Press, 1972).

27. Gregory Bateson, Don D. Jackson, Jay Haley, and John Weakland, "Toward a Theory of Schizophrenia," *Behavioral Science* 1, no. 4 (1956): 251–64.

28. Xudong Zhao 赵旭东, "The Sino-German Comparison on the Views of Therapeutic Relationship in Systemic Family Therapy"(系统家庭治疗中有关治疗关系的观点——附中德比较), *Foreign Medicine: Psychiatry* (国外医学: 精神病学分册)22, no. 2 (1995): 65–70; and Hsuan-Ying Huang, "From Psychotherapy to Psycho-Boom: A Historical

Overview of Psychotherapy in China," *Psychoanalysis and Psychotherapy in China* 1, no. 1 (2015): 1–30.

29. Amy Borovoy, *The Too-Good Wife* (Berkeley: University of California Press, 2005).

30. Naftali, *Children, Rights, and Modernity in China*, 4.

31. Andrew Kipnis, *Governing Educational Desire: Culture, Politics, and Schooling in China* (Chicago: University of Chicago Press, 2011).

32. Jarrett Zigon, "How Is It Between Us? Relational Ethics and Transcendence," *Journal of the Royal Anthropological Institute* 27, no. 2 (2021): 389.

33. Charlie Campbell, "As the City's COVID-19 Lockdown Tightens Again, Shanghai Residents Have Been Pushed to Breaking Point," *Time*, May 11, 2022, https://time.com/6175179/shanghai-covid-lockdown-residents/.

34. Kuan, "Feelings Run in the Family," 707.

35. Arthur Kleinman et al., eds., *Deep China: The Moral Life of the Person* (Berkeley: University of California Press, 2011); and Xu, *The Good Child*.

5

DREAMS OF MARRIAGE

Social Media and Disconnect for
Young Married Women

LYNN LIN SUN

When I met Xiaona in Shanghai in 2016, she had been married for eight years. Even so, this thirty-four-year-old Shanghainese could still vividly remember the rather surprising wedding she had experienced in 2008:

> On the morning of that day, I was still at the hospital with my mother, who'd rather I abort the unexpected baby than marry the baby's father, due to his unsatisfactory financial situation [at the time]. In the afternoon, I was sitting in front of the officer at the Marriage Registration Office with that man, who had just flown back from Beijing two hours earlier, ready to say our vows. It was so dramatic! We even forgot to bring money, so my mother gave us nine yuan [approximately $1.30 USD] to pay the registration fee. But we were so happy! I remember that night, we were just staring at our marriage certificate and couldn't stop giggling! It was genuine happiness [*xingfu*], from the bottom of our hearts. I felt so hopeful, and I remember telling myself at that moment, "Now I can have a future where he is also part of it."

As dramatic as her wedding day may sound, the logic under-pinning Xiaona's decision to marry is nonetheless typical of the women of her cohort—although each person's decision to marry might be triggered by different things, and the beginning of her marital life might vary. Among the several dozen young married Chinese I have encountered during my fieldwork since 2015, all have agreed that at the moment of saying "yes" they believed or at least hoped that their life would be *happier* after marrying the person they chose. As another female informant pointed out, "Why on earth do we marry nowadays if not for happiness?"

Apparently, the "we" she referenced is a very particular group of people: mostly singleton daughters born in the 1980s with an urban middle-class background, a tertiary level education, and a well-paid job position.[1] They are also the group on whom this chapter is centered. However, the tendency to associate happi-ness with marriage is no doubt ubiquitous among the younger generations of Chinese today—similar to their counterparts in the United States, as Sara Ahmed described.[2] Various studies conducted by government and commercial agencies in China routinely show marriage as the primary happiness indicator, thus reaffirming the message, "Get married, and you will be hap-pier."[3] Even for those who appear to be against marriage, one prominent logic underpinning such rejections is that marriage today does not guarantee happiness.[4]

Happiness, then, seems to be innately attached to marriage today. The association has become so commonsensical that few people think twice before using the phrase "marital happiness" (*hunyin xingfu*). But what does it actually mean? Why have dis-cussions about marital happiness, nearly obscure only a genera-tion ago, flourished in China in recent decades, especially among young urbanites?[5] And more importantly, what does "marital happiness" *do*? Following Raymond Williams's suggestion of adding to the material and sociocultural analysis an *affective* layer, I explore how a certain hegemonic discourse of marital happiness—which I call the "marital happiness recipe"—"got under [the] skin" of these young middle-class Chinese women, as well as how they are responding to this dominant social imaginary.[6]

In addressing these questions, I first introduce the "marital happiness recipe," a dominant marriage (and family) script conditioned by the specific economic, political, and sociocultural contexts of urban China today. I see its prevalence as responding to a corresponding marriage dilemma faced by the younger generations. Then through detailed portraits of the actual marital experiences of several Shanghainese women, I discuss how my informants have variously responded to this dominant vision of marital bliss, and how their responses are intertwined with Chinese social media. This section calls attention to the affective space generated by my informants' ubiquitous use of "the more private-facing social media platform," WeChat, through which the "recipe" is made highly efficacious.[7] I highlight the dual role of social media in constraining and (to a much lesser extent) emancipating these women's capacity to experience genuine happiness within (or without) marriage. This layer of analysis helps us better understand what made many young women I encountered in Shanghai remain attached to this recipe while being keenly aware of its near unattainability. I argue that compared to traditional media, WeChat, which operates largely among one's existing personal contacts, is more effective in materializing and normalizing the recipe. Complicit with the state-facilitated individualization, which continues to see the individual and the family as a means to broader political and social ends, and the historically unique experience of these urban middle-class women of the first one-child generation, the platform serves as an *affect amplifier*, reinforcing the monopoly of the recipe.[8] Finally, I conclude by deliberating the boundaries of this dominant social imaginary and the possibilities of developing and achieving alternatives. I point out the potential, however limited, of "the more public-facing social media platforms," such as Weibo and Douyin, to inspire new paths to happiness for young urbanite women.[9]

The data presented here are drawn from my fieldwork in Shanghai since 2015, during which I conducted in-depth interviews with thirty married Shanghainese women in their thirties, asking about their marriage experiences. For those who allowed me to follow their lives more closely, I visited their homes from time to time, dined and went grocery shopping with them, met and talked with their spouses, and babysat their young children. I also attended birthday parties and New Year's celebrations when usually the whole family assembled, as well as women-only gatherings in which wives freely complained of their marital distresses. Some informants kept in contact after my fieldwork officially ended in 2018. During my two follow-up visits in 2019 and through social media, many have updated me on bits and pieces of their marital life. In addition to the data I collected from these thirty women, I also gathered information on marriage from government reports, popular media content, and informal chats with locals from all walks of life. All the names that appear in this chapter are pseudonyms. I sometimes took extra measures to disguise details of my informants' age, occupation, and family composition to better protect their identities.

TALK OF MARITAL HAPPINESS: AN AFFECTIVE INTERVENTION TO THE MARRIAGE DILEMMA

A conversation I had with a single woman in her mid-thirties whom I encountered at a friend's gathering in Shanghai still stays on my mind after nearly seven years. Feeling empathetic after hearing my research topic, she began to gripe about, in her own words, "the horrific parental pressure" she was experiencing:

> Whenever I'm at home, my mother will take out a piece of unfinished knitwear and start to knit. I once asked her what she was knitting. She then showed me this tiny sweater and said, "It's nothing. I'm just doing it to kill time, and thinking perhaps one day soon it will be useful." This is so much pressure!

Ironically, after another half hour of her telling me how painful she finds the constant pressure for her to marry (and have children), and how absurd the current marriage institution is, our conversation ended on a rather unexpected note: she sighed and asked me, and maybe herself as well, "Why do you think I can't get married?"

Later on, as my fieldwork in Shanghai deepened, this woman's seemingly peculiar and conflicting remarks began to make more sense to me. I began to see her ambivalent feelings toward marriage as essentially a slice of the personal experiences of Chinese people: living in a society in which the rising individual encounters uncertainty and precarity, brought on by a state-dictated market economy, means that the family (continued through marriage) remains the only reliable safety net against the vicissitudes of life.[10]

Today, one can easily observe two seemingly conflicting scenarios in the urban Chinese marriage-scape. On one hand, there is the deepening breakdown of marriage, marked by delayed marriages, falling birth rates, rising divorce rates, and an increasing number of advocates of singlehood. A brief surf on the internet or skimming through best-selling novels and popular Chinese TV dramas on intimate relationships might give the sense that today's young urban Chinese no longer see marriage in a positive light.

Buzzwords like "daily fear of marriage" (*richang konghun*) and slogans like "losers will end up marrying" (*bu nuli shi yao jiehun de*)
are frequently used by popular media and ordinary people alike.
Meanwhile, statistical data collected by various government agencies and nongovernmental organizations reveal a similar picture,
further validating the sense of crisis beyond the virtual and fictional world. For example, according to a survey jointly conducted
in 2015 by Sun Yat-Sen University, Baidu,[11] and an alcoholic bev-
erage company, among 28,500 respondents from all over China
(half being from the four Chinese megacities: Beijing, Shanghai,
Guangzhou, and Shenzhen), 76 percent confessed to feeling afraid
of marrying, and 91 percent thought about marriage as "very burdensome and troublesome" (*yali henda hen mafan*).[12] The marriage
rate in China has been falling since 2014, especially in eastern
coastal areas such as Shanghai.[13] In 2021, only around 7.6 million
people in China got married, the lowest figure since 1986.[14]

On the other hand, the growing anxiety for individuals, especially women, to marry and marry "well" reveals that marriage is
still seen as not only desirable but very often imperative for a massive number of young Chinese today. As Lynne Nakano points
out, "In Shanghai, marriage is seen as . . . a life requirement . . .
[and] the only way to enter into a successful life."[15] Despite the
declining marriage rate in recent years, most Shanghainese people
today, like those in the rest of China, are still expected to marry
and eventually do. According to the 2015 Shanghai One Percent
Population Sample Survey, released by the Shanghai Bureau of
Statistics, only 17.8 percent of its citizens aged thirty to thirty-
four were still single in 2015, and this number shrank to approximately 7.7 percent in the thirty-five to thirty-nine age group.[16]
The booming matchmaking business and the intense involvement of parents in their adult children's "lifelong event" (*zhong-
shen dashi*) of marriage also point to the enduring desirability of

getting married, as well as pressure to do so, among the majority of young people in China today.[17]

If the majority of young Chinese today still wish to marry, why is there a marriage "crisis" at all—and vice versa? I believe that these seemingly contradictory situations are in fact two sides of the same coin. Although individual backgrounds and lifestyle preferences might play a role here, both are the general signs of ambivalence and struggles young people experience today in the face of the various contradictory expectations coalescing around marriage. On one hand, the institution of marriage continues to be "rigid and narrow in its expectations of heterosexual reproduction, childcare, service to family members including parents and in-laws, and sacrifice of one's career and personal development."[18] So many Chinese women of the younger generations hesitate to enter it—especially those economically independent and well-educated urban middle-class women who have, to various degrees, internalized the neoliberal ethics of individual autonomy, self-enterprise, and self-reliance. On the other hand, the lack of viable alternative paths to obtaining a safety net, social recognition, and conjugal/familial warmth—as well as the lingering risks and burdens of facing parental/familial pressure, social marginalization, and even stigmatization[19]—has made marriage remain not only feasible but even desirable for many.[20] This is the structural dilemma underpinning both the equivocal attitude of that Shanghainese woman I met at the gathering seven years ago and the seeming contradictory scenarios I noted previously—a dilemma no doubt more acutely faced by women than men in China due to its lingering emphasis on the association between womanhood and marriage/family. And as I will argue, one possible and indeed popular reaction to this dilemma is the growing tendency to associate marriage with *happiness*, the magic word of our time.

This association between happiness and marriage can be seen as one consequence of the government's new political project of building a "harmonious society" (*hexie shehui*).[21] As pointed out by Jie Yang, aiming to pacify growing social discontent in China—itself caused by the widened wealth gap and deteriorating upward mobility despite cutthroat competition—state leaders have adopted happiness as a crucial psychologizing governing technology, or an "affective intervention" to conjure "a fantasy of hope and harmony" and cover up deeply rooted structural deficiencies.[22] Similarly, in the specific realm of marriage, the flourishing discourse of marital happiness has been adopted both by the state and by individuals, especially women, to justify asking the question: *Why do you/I still need to marry today?*

In her book *Talk of Love*, Ann Swidler argues that "culture develops capacities for action, and culture proliferates where action is problematic."[23] Therefore, she contends, the root cause behind the proliferation of the culture of love in recent decades among middle-class Americans is the incongruity and thus confusion resulting from "the dual properties of marriage—as relationship and as institution."[24] In other words, for those Americans in Swidler's book, "talk of love" serves as a solution to the ambiguousness caused by the paradoxical expectations of marriage by offering individuals "certain cultural, psychological, and even cognitive equipment" to help them form lines of action to navigate uncertainties.[25] Following her line of thought, I argue that the growing tendency in recent years to associate marriage with happiness, as well as the resulting proliferation of knowledge on marital happiness (what it means, what it constitutes, what one should do in order to achieve it), can be seen as a cultural solution used by social actors at various levels to the previously mentioned marriage dilemma. "Marital happiness" thus becomes shorthand used by individuals, as well as various government and social agencies, pondering how to navigate a rigid institution of marriage with its burdensome obligations, a neoliberal self that longs for self-fulfillment, and a chilly society full of uncertainty and precariousness. Entering marriage remains the most viable way to obtain much-needed protection and connectedness. What does this mean in the context of this particular study?

Throughout this chapter, I perceive "marital happiness" from two different vantage points. In the next section, I first discuss it in terms of a prevailing cultural script conditioned by the economic, political, and sociocultural context of contemporary China. This marital happiness recipe has little to do with inner feelings of pleasure or joy. It is a set of warm-and-fuzzy logic around which young, urban, middle-class Chinese women today organize their own lines of action in marriage. As I show, "marital happiness" in the Chinese context is different from the Western context, which emphasizes the quality of the relationship between spouses. Instead, both popular media and my informants understand the term more as *happiness in the state of being married*, which is often evaluated by means of contemplating the overall family situation.[26] Therefore, it is often used interchangeably with "familial happiness" by my informants and the masses in general. I then go on to explore how this marital happiness recipe enters into the lives of my informants living in Shanghai and how they variously experience and respond to it. Here, I see "marital happiness" as lived/felt experience, which can be essentially idiosyncratic.

THE MARITAL HAPPINESS RECIPE

In her research examining gendered aspirations of a social group similar to my sample, Kailing Xie found that both her unmarried and married participants desire a "beautiful and complete" family (*mei man jiating*), which she elaborated as "the ideal middle-class lifestyle that relies on a solid economic foundation and is displayed through a happy heterosexual family life."[27] My informants' responses about marital happiness to a large extent resonate with Xie's description. When asked, "How do you understand marital happiness? What contributes to your sense of marital happiness?," my informants in Shanghai usually began their answers with one of two seemingly different views. Often drawing on Tolstoy's famous opening line in *Anna Karenina* (1878), some responded that "happy marriages are all alike." Others claimed that "marital happiness is very subjective and a thousand people might have a thousand interpretations," emphasizing that their own understanding of marital happiness is not typical. However, when I went through all the answers, no matter how people began their response, their visions of marital happiness seldom deviated too far from four "happy objects"— namely, companionate love, material comfort, "high-quality" child(ren), and a sense of conjugal equality.[28] Although these elements might be prioritized and combined differently depending on each informant's own life situation, none was dismissed.

When trying to grasp how my informants see this dominant marriage script, I kept thinking of one thirty-eight-year-old informant's casual comment while cooking *hong shao rou* (red braised pork belly), one of the signature dishes of Shanghai:

> Can you still call a dish *hong shao rou* if one uses meat other than pork belly? Or uses no sugar? Or no dark soy sauce? Every cook might have her own style according to how she accents a certain ingredient, and how she improvises from time to time in terms of steps and techniques. However, as long as she is still making *hong shao rou*, she cannot omit these essential ingredients. . . . The key

to the dish's success is the quality of these ingredients and the degree of harmony they can achieve over time.[29]

Similarly, for the majority of my middle-class Shanghainese informants, "authentic" marital bliss means the "completeness" (*yuanman*) and "harmony" (*hexie*) of all four of Ahmed's happy objects—we could call them "ingredients"—in the recipe.

The psychotherapist Esther Perel has vividly expressed how demanding a marriage can be these days, describing it as "asking [one person] to give us what once an entire village used to provide," including economic support, children, sex, romance, friendship, and social status.[30] Although her observation was based on her clinical experience with troubled couples in the United States, it is not too far from the marital happiness recipe pervading urban China today. Perel's observation embodies the anxiety many young people, again especially women, experience when being torn by the previously mentioned marriage dilemma. Fundamentally, what makes this recipe ideal is its seeming promise to solve the dilemma by allowing independence without precariousness and allowing choice without uncertainty. Perel saw such a marriage ideal as mere fantasy and the root cause for her patients' marital unhappiness.[31] Likewise, few women in my study in Shanghai had achieved the marital happiness recipe, and many were clearly burdened by it, keenly aware of its near unattainability. How did they respond to the discrepancy between this dominant modality of marital happiness and their actual marital experiences? The following sections answer these questions by spotlighting certain slices of three Shanghainese women's marital life. By no means am I suggesting that these women's marital experiences are representative of today's urban middle-class Chinese marriages in general. They nonetheless enable us to delve further into the thick of "marital happiness," not merely as public discourse or cultural

188 • DREAMS OF MARRIAGE

norm but also as lived experience. I begin with the story of Xiaona, the thirty-four-year-old woman in the opening vignette, who appeared to have perfectly embodied the marital happiness recipe.

XIAONA: "SO YOU JUST *WORK ON* IT"

Despite her unexpected "naked marriage" (*luohun*) in 2008, Xiaona in 2016 was acclaimed by many of her acquaintances as having the happiest marital life they had ever seen.[32] Judging from the opening vignette, one might easily guess that, indeed, love conquers all. But according to what she told me during our interview, few people around her had been optimistic about her future. She, however, truly believed in "love conquers all" at that time and thus was determined to marry her middle-school sweetheart, her "only true love." Her mother severely objected due to the man's then insufficient financial situation, believing that, as the old Chinese saying goes, "Poverty consumes marital happiness" (*pinjian fuqi baishi ai*). Although the young couple was not "poor" in a strict sense, living in a rented apartment and not owning a home upon marriage was agreed upon by most of my Shanghainese informants as one of the worst scenarios for marriage, one that could seriously impair marital happiness. Even Xiaona herself admitted that, in retrospect, she was probably just "blindly confident": "To be honest, now in my mid-thirties, while looking at my friends who have all become homeowners, if our condition hadn't improved over these years, if we were still renting, I'm not sure if I wouldn't feel regret about my decision to marry this man solely for love." In other words, if love were the only thing Xiaona's marriage possessed—if they were still renting, unable to afford their children's expensive education and extracurricular activities, or even to have children at all, or if Xiaona were helplessly confined to domesticity—not many people in contemporary China, including herself, would consider her marriage "happy." Love adds the vital finishing touch to the marital happiness recipe. However, without the more material ingredients addressed in the previous section, people who marry for love alone can easily be dismissed as imprudent fools.

What made Xiaona's marriage an exemplar of marital happiness among her acquaintances was how well it appeared to fit the marital happiness recipe eight years after she said "I do." The couple now own a mansion near the city center and are raising two well-rounded children, a boy and a girl, who attend one of the best international schools in town, play ukulele in addition to piano, create oil paintings, and have traveled widely. The couple's long-lasting, satisfying conjugal relationship made them decide to hold a "make-up" wedding ceremony on the twenty-fourth anniversary of the day they met in middle school: "to commemorate our lasting 'original heart' [*chuxin*]." Xiaona appeared to be simultaneously a romantic wife who still spoke lovingly about her daily interaction with her husband, a caring mother who spent quality time with her children (hand-making them tasty and nutritious snacks, keeping "baby journals" with numerous photos recording every memorable moment), and a talented and self-reliant woman capable of living a prosperous life on her own if needed. This last role imbued Xiaona with a sense of conjugal equality, which, in addition to material satisfaction, companionate love, and well-rounded child(ren), is also an indispensable element of the marital happiness recipe. Xiaona's prestigious job as a banker has earned her enough assurance, both economically and mentally, to *feel* that she and her husband are complete equals. Thus instead of being compelled, all the seemingly disproportionate devotion she provides in the domestic sphere is a matter of *choice*.

The Ordinary Fantasy

Through our encounter, Xiaona left me with the impression of a real-life version of "the woman with the flying hair" described in Arlie Hochschild's work, who had managed to combine "child and job, frill and suit, female culture and male."[33] Using her own analogy, Xiaona seemed to be able to "dance her partner dance" well—not missing any steps, with ease—and more importantly, she enjoyed it. When I asked her how she had managed to juggle multiple realms and fulfill various roles simultaneously, she stressed only the importance of *individual choice, responsibility*, and *effort* in the process of her pursuit. In her words, "So you just *work on* it." That is to say, whether the recipe can brew happiness depends on whether one can keep up the good work. And so the logic goes: women who fail are merely lacking faith and effort. This is clearly a private manifestation of the state-led individualization endorsed since the early twenty-first century, foregrounding both individual desires and responsibilities.[34]

Moreover, the reason I kept using the word "appear" when describing Xiaona's marital happiness is that so much of my information about her life was gleaned through the rosy lens of meticulously edited photos and captions. I only met her in person once—a ninety-minute interview plus a three-hour visit to her home. An enthusiastic user of WeChat Moments (called *pengyou quan* in Chinese, meaning "friends' circle"), she posted daily about her life, and as her WeChat friend, I was able to follow up on her marriage in this way. As a result, a good portion of my notes about Xiaona are from my observations of her social media displays rather than our direct interactions. Many details depicted here are drawn from those orchestrated photos, videos, and texts: a sophisticatedly decorated living room upon the Chinese New Year; her "squeezed-in" gym time showing

her well-toned body; a pair of silk pillowcases from a luxuri-
ous brand from her husband on their anniversary; her children's
afternoon teatime at their spacious balcony facing Huangpu
River, plates filled with handmade cakes and organic fruits; her
ten-year-old son making progress in Python programming; her
eight-year-old daughter winning a prestigious English speech
contest; family bonding time in Kyoto, Paris, Cape Town, and
Cancún; her status messages thanking her husband and parents for their understanding and support upon receiving a promotion at her job; and so on. All along I was concerned about
the "flatness" and validity of this set of data. However, when I
read through these notes again along with all the other notes
I had taken in Shanghai, I realized that, compared with some
other informants with whom I had followed up more closely
over the past several years, Xiaona's largely social media–medi-
ated marital life—more reality show than reality—provides us
an extra lens to understand how my other social media–savvy
informants experience the recipe. This lens reveals how social
media facilitates an extended affective space through which
abstract ideals like the recipe become extremely "sticky."[35] It is
probably true that Xiaona cooked up a perfectly happy marriage in accordance with the marital happiness recipe through
her WeChat Moments, telling me and other potential specta-
tors more about the dominant ideal of marital happiness than
about her actual marital life situation.[36] However, this "curated
truth" from an ordinary woman[37]—such as a friend, colleague, or
former classmate—can often appear too real for other women of
the same cohort to simply brush aside as mere fantasy, such as
those promoted by idol dramas, high-end women's magazines,
and quixotic self-help advice. As you will see later, it is exactly
such "ordinary" marriage stories like Xiaona's, voluntarily shared
via private, personal spaces such as the WeChat Friends' Circle,

that engender enormous affective effects—optimism and hope, as well as anxiety and guilt—that make the marital happiness recipe strangely addictive, a *fantasy* imbued with *ordinariness*.

As this ideal of marital happiness is individualized (It's one's own responsibility, for instance, and depends on one's own effort) and normalized (It's something every ordinary person can achieve), it has become what I call an "ordinary fantasy," a form of "*affective structure* of an optimistic attachment" that sustains the fantasy with a perpetual sense of possibility and hope.[38] However, rendering the pursuit of this "ordinary fantasy" as feasible as well as a matter of personal responsibility, while downplaying or completely ignoring both the structural conflicts and constraints and the individual privilege and personal luck involved, can become toxic. As you shall see from the marriage experiences of another Shanghainese woman, Ziyan, the happiness promised by the marital happiness recipe is in fact very often impeded by the "happy ingredients" that compose the recipe at the structural level. Although these structural limitations cannot be easily overcome on a personal level, the burden remains on the individual, whose efforts might well lead to more crises than happiness. Yet seeing it as largely a private issue and believing there is always room for its realization (when looking at "successful" cases like that of Xiaona), this "affective structure" entraps many women I studied in Shanghai in a perpetual oscillation between ambition/hope/happiness and anxiety/guilt/pain.[39]

ZIYAN: "IF OTHERS CAN DO IT, WHY CAN'T I?"

I first met Ziyan in early 2014 during my preliminary fieldwork in Shanghai. At the time, she had been married for almost three years and was five months pregnant with her first child. At the end of that first interview, Ziyan reported a score of 7 when I asked her to gauge the happiness of her marriage on a scale of 1 to 10: "Seven means above average. I do consider my marital life so far as happy (*xingfu*). As for the missing points, most importantly, I hope Xie Tong [her husband] and I can spend more time together." She sounded truly happy and hopeful. Over the next two years, I was away from Shanghai and could only get Ziyan's updates sporadically from her text messages and posts on WeChat Moments. Except for one unintended pregnancy, her marriage seemed to largely follow her expectations and mirror the marital happiness recipe. Six years into her marriage she had been blessed with two healthy, handsome boys. Her family's current financial status, having improved over the years, allowed them a typical middle-class lifestyle. Moreover, during one of our casual chats online, Ziyan happily announced that the number of quarrels between her and her husband had decreased in recent years and thus the couple were becoming more harmonious. On the face of it, Ziyan seemed to have a marriage very similar to Xiaona's, both in form and in degree of happiness. In fact, many people who know Ziyan, including me, did assume she was "happily married" at that time. Therefore, when she described her current marital situation as "slavery" at one of our meetings in late 2018, I was genuinely surprised—until I became her sons' Japanese language tutor and thus got closer to her daily life beyond our social media interactions.

Similar to Xiaona, Ziyan had tried her best to "marry for love." As she recounted, "I had studied hard and worked hard, because I hoped one day I could afford to marry someone I truly love, not for his financial ability, or anything else, but for love alone. And my efforts didn't go unrewarded." However, before long, she found herself pressured by mounting household expenditures—mainly the mortgage payments and child-rearing costs. She wanted to focus more on her career so she could either be promoted to a higher position or land a more lucrative job, but her advancement was severely impeded by her motherhood. Her job, following market-oriented neoliberal logic and a gender-neutral stance, demands vigorous, single-minded, efficient, and self-disciplined workers—who are ruthlessly slotted into the categories "valuable" and "valueless," based on their work performance. Her family life, however, following the nonmarket logic of "generalized reciprocity" and a gender-specific stance, demands a loving, devoted, and ever-vigilant mother who prioritizes her children's needs over everything else.[40] The former provides her the income necessary to sustain the family's middle-class lifestyle and to materialize her parental love while also endowing her with a sense of security and self-worth as a woman independent from and equal to her husband. The latter gives her deeper meaning in life and rewards her with irreplaceable joy. Neither would be easily forfeited.

To mediate the tension between the two, Ziyan had to turn to other women for help: first her mother, then her mother-in-law, and finally, nannies. Although the joint effort of these helping hands indeed made her work-life "balance" possible for the time being, their presence further distressed Ziyan's marital life. In addition to the exacerbated financial pressures these helpers brought to the young couple, the complicated interpersonal and intergenerational relationships involved have weighed down their marital quality. I once received a late-night message from Ziyan, complaining about her mother-in-law's interactions with her younger son:

> She is treating Xiao Tao like her own son! During the months when she was here to take care of Xiao Tao, she just wouldn't let him go from her arms for a second even when he was sleeping. Now Gui Hua [a hired helper] is here, and I want to train him

to sleep alone. She [her mother-in-law] just won't let me! [During the nights when her mother-in-law stays over,] whenever she hears Xiao Tao cry, she just rushes into our bedroom and takes him away, and tells everybody I'm abusing my son!

Ziyan then showed me the tense text message conversations she had had with her mother-in-law and her mother in the family chat group. The sides had changed as the conversation turned white-hot, from Ziyan being a shared enemy blamed by both older women, to her serving as a mediator trying to appease the two, who ended up fighting with each other. Although this was not the first time I had heard about such incidents from Ziyan, I noticed something curious this time: This family chat group has six members, including Ziyan's husband, her father, and her father-in-law. However, none of the men had participated at all in this conversation, which concerned the care of their son/grandson and consisted of 283 messages. In other words, Ziyan again was the only one who had been pulled into the whirlpool of this relationship storm. Her "solution" to alleviate the tension between her career and motherhood only led to new problems and further trapped her into the demands of a "happy marital life."

In all this, Ziyan's personal space and quality time with her husband—said to be key to her marital happiness—were often cut back or squeezed out completely, as she once grumbled:

Before we had children, our interactions with our parents were limited to having dinner together once in a while. Our "two-person world" [*erren shijie*] was largely kept intact. So there was little discord. Once the children came, however, since we had to ask for their help, their intervention in our marital life became inevitable. So are the conflicts.

Nonetheless, Ziyan had no intention of getting rid of her helpers, intrusive or not. She admitted feeling grateful for the external support: "At least now I can still keep everything in balance, albeit barely and not without compromising my career. I'd rather spend time dealing with the troubles [caused by the helpers] than being fettered at home myself." The high cost of keeping this indispensable support network in place means that Ziyan has had to work even harder at her job and further cut back on time for herself, her husband, and her children. This sacrifice, in turn, evokes in her a stronger sense of anxiety, guilt, and unfairness but also an increased desire to be a loving and beloved wife and mother.

In a nutshell, compared with Xiaona's seemingly perfect marital life, Ziyan's day-to-day marital experiences were full of minor crises. Her marital life felt like a battleground where she was kept constantly on the run, handling various contingencies as she held her "ordinary happy marriage" together, following the recipe exemplified by "ordinary" women like Xiaona. If all the "happy ingredients" were apparently in harmonious balance in Xiaona's marriage, they certainly looked discordant with each other in Ziyan's marriage. If Xiaona appeared to have not only fully embraced but also mastered the recipe, Ziyan was still an apprentice—eagerly honing her craft—as were most of her peers. In fact, when zooming out and putting Ziyan's and Xiaona's cases into perspective, it is not hard to discern that the turbulent situation entangling Ziyan is actually the common state of life experienced by the majority of married middle-class women in their thirties in urban China today. Twenty-seven out of the thirty women in my Shanghai sample reported having experienced a similar state of chaos, albeit with different complications. Conversely, Xiaona's claim to near-perfect balance is rather rare.

I have offered elsewhere a detailed analysis of the structural causes that have led to the chaos Ziyan and many others have experienced in their marital life.[41] Here it suffices to describe the problem as individual-level evidence of the negative consequences brought on by the "institutionalized individualization" enacted in China in recent decades.[42] Various conflicting components (e.g., the four "happy ingredients" of the recipe), hinging upon different social mechanisms that follow disparate logics (e.g., a good mother vs. a good employee), collide in individual biographies.[43] Each claims its indispensability to one's marital happiness, but meanwhile, as I have shown, the realization of any one of them undermines the realization of the others. As a result, the person involved feels trapped or even "enslaved," according to Ziyan, kept constantly moving around, patching up problems.

More curious, however, even when keenly aware of the arbitrariness and near unattainability of the marital happiness recipe, most of my informants still tended to be attached to this "ordinary fantasy" while blaming themselves for their failure to fulfill its ideal. Even after describing marriage as "slavery," Ziyan nonetheless had little intention of breaking her bonds. She described the institution as a wolf in sheep's clothing, claiming that it "covers up its exploitive essence with beautiful romantic love stories and heartwarming mother's love, and lures us into investing all our energy and time, willingly and unconditionally, for the sake of the child, the family, and eventually, the society." Yet in the end she still blamed herself, concluding our last face-to-face conversation with a bitter laugh: "Oh well, after all, I guess all these frustrations I feel in my marriage come from my incapability. Otherwise, if there are others who can do it, why can't I?"

Similarly, one thirty-one-year-old woman, married for five years with one child, spent nearly an hour complaining about the difficulties she had encountered in her marital life and pointedly criticizing the unreasonable demands of this gendered marital happiness ideal. However, when asked about the happiest marital life she could imagine, she described her cousin's marriage (which she followed mostly through WeChat Moments), and surprisingly, it resembles that of Xiaona—at least as it is revealed to her circle of friends. In other words, the happiest life this wife and mother can imagine still closely mimics the very ideal she has deemed unreasonable. Why do these women still endeavor to stick to the very cultural script they consider problematic and largely unrealistic?

Living the "Chain of Contempt"

In recounting Xiaona's case, I brought up the idea of "ordinary fantasy" to draw attention to the affective structure of the marital happiness recipe facilitated by social media, which endows it with a perpetual sense of promise and "the affects of aspirational normativity."[44] To answer the question I posed, I now return to this affective dimension of the recipe, again highlighting the role social media has played in facilitating its affectivity. I have described the private manifestations of the structural consequences caused by state-led institutionalized individualization—namely the frustration Ziyan and many others have experienced on the ground trying to live up to the marital happiness recipe—in this section I point to its emotional consequences.

As Ulrich Beck points out, to survive the conflicts inherent in the institution-dependent biographies, the individual must develop "an *ego-centered world view* . . . conceiv[ing] of himself or herself as the center of action . . . [and] the social determinants as 'environmental variables' that can be . . . individually manipulated."[45] This quality of inverting the relation between individual and society is evident from the ways my informants in Shanghai talked about their marital lives. The conventional understanding of Chinese selfhood places the individual as secondary to the collective, including the family, and sees the individual as nonexistent without the family.[46] However, the narratives of my Chinese informants very often position "the self" at the center: "*I decided* to marry this man because *I* love him"; "*I chose* to try for a second baby since *I wanted to* experience raising a daughter"; "*I let* my mother-in-law live with us because *we need* her to help us with our son." Everything in their marital life, from important life events to interpersonal relationships to arrangements of daily activities, seems to exist to serve the *individual*.

Meanwhile, these individuals also increasingly see themselves as the solely responsible bearer of their own consequences. This is clearly revealed by my informants' responses to the question, "What has happened in your marital life so far that contributed to your sense of marital happiness?" Seemingly happier moments—a bouquet of flowers arriving unexpectedly on an anniversary, a warm bowl of soup on a sick day, a romantic trip overseas, or the day when the first child was born—were often mentioned only in passing; the more challenging and even miserable episodes were often told in much more detail. Why do the more arduous experiences feel so important to their sense of marital happiness? One informant's words might give us a clue here: "Because these more challenging events were *initiated by me* and represented how *my efforts* had lifted me from the predicaments I had experienced in my marriage" (emphasis added). In other words, coming up with solutions to their own marriage problems indicates to these women that they are taking responsibility for their own happiness. Compared to the relatively effortless and ephemeral cheery moments, the hard-won struggles are deemed more meaningful to their marital happiness because of the personal initiative and diligence involved. In the traditional Chinese context, the institution of marriage has been perceived as a highly collective practice in which the individual was nearly invisible. Now my informants in Shanghai tend to portray their marriages as a touchstone emblemizing their personal pride or shame. As a corollary, a "failure in happiness," in marriage and elsewhere, is easily interpreted as "a failure of the self."[47]

This ego-centered worldview stems from the individualization of life events.[48] It makes marriage—formerly considered largely a social institution in which individual feelings and efforts bear only minor (if any) importance—and its success the sole responsibility of the individuals (especially wives) involved. As a consequence, among the women who have appeared in these pages we see senses of anxiety and guilt bittersweetly mixed with optimism and hope. The former is apparent at the micro level in individuals' self-blame for their own inadequacy, as we saw in Ziyan's narrative. At the macro level, these wives' anxiety manifests in the pervasive "chain of contempt" (*bishi lian*) that places married women in a precarious pecking order according to their proximity to the marital happiness recipe, with "do-it-all women" like Xiaona as the top links in the chain. This invisible hierarchy, largely shaped by mass media, serves as a highly affective "cultural mirror."[49] It constantly reminds the women who strive to climb it of how much success or failure they have demonstrated toward realizing marital happiness when compared to other women on this path.

When Arlie Hochschild brought up the idea of "the cultural mirror," she mentioned magazines, television commercials, advice books, and scientific papers as its main facilitators.[50] Today in urban China these feelings of relative deprivation and anxiety among middle-class women become most compelling with the ubiquitous use of the internet. Social-networking apps, especially those more private-facing platforms such as WeChat, allow individuals to share their everyday life within the circle of their accepted friends, while at the same time compelling them to constantly be aware of what's going on in their friends' lives. This new way of interaction has led to the phenomenon of *shai xingfu* (the public display of happiness). The fact that the heroines of these displayed episodes are neither celebrities nor fictional characters in women-empowering dramas nor constructed role models, but *ordinary* women—perhaps a former classmate, a colleague, or your neighbor—imbues their marriage stories with a degree of power that brings pressure to bear on other women within their circles. Because of the pervasive use of such social-networking mediums, it is not hard to imagine how far this influence can reach today, unfettered as it is by locality.

Certainly, the experience of this post-1980s generation of urbanites is historically unique. As members of China's first one-child generation, Kailing Xie argues that her privileged informants grew up as the only hope of their families, feeling entitled, as well as pressured, to achieve the "best" things in life. Their desire to achieve success and maintain class privilege has prevented them from resisting the mainstream gendered aspiration toward a "complete and happy family."[51] As members of the same cohort, my informants share similar traits with Xie's. The post-Mao reform and opening up since the 1980s drastically broke people's rigid way of life that had characterized the Socialist era; it brought about a nearly twenty-year period of vigorous transformation. Coming of age during these disorderly years, these women either witnessed or experienced firsthand how dreams could really come true, with hard work and dedication. All my informants in Shanghai came from ordinary families, whose parents had been earning an average of 36 yuan per month in the early 1980s. Although most of their parents did what they could to provide them with the best resources possible, everyone's starting line was nearly the same. It was largely through *individual* endeavors, they believe, that some of them were able to succeed in their studies, their career, and their marriage, and to eventually enter the middle class.

But these women are also acutely aware of the arbitrariness of the whole system in which they are embedded, and thus the fragility of the success they have gained. Illness, divorce, unemployment—any one of these could easily drag them down overnight into the lower social strata that they have tried so hard to escape. This happens all too often these days, and there is hardly any "re-embeddedment mechanism" in China to help these women bounce back.[52] The various government policies upon which their livelihoods hinge—including but not limited to those of the housing market, household registration (*hukou*), school enrollment (for their children), marriage/divorce policies, and population (birth) control—can be flip-flopped on a whim, which makes long-term planning in large part infeasible. Therefore, the only sensible thing for them is, again, to rely on themselves. This fierce determination, instilled in them by their "self-reliant" mothers of the "iron-girl" generation, seems to have worked for many of them in the past.[53]

Meanwhile, the economic slowdown and gradual resolidification of social strata that has occurred in the past decade has dampened these women's sense of upward mobility—which further imbues the new middle class not only with the fear of falling down the social ladder but also motivation to keep climbing.[54] When they look up at those "ordinary" role models higher up on the "chain of contempt," they push themselves harder to fulfill the marital happiness recipe. When they look down at the "losers" below them, their fear of slipping down spurs them to strive even harder. However, as we have seen, most of these young women feel stuck where they are. Some, like Ziyan, might even feel "enslaved." Yet the very source of this "enslavement"—the marital happiness recipe—is simultaneously injected with "a *sense* of normality" by these ordinary people's displayed marital happiness on social media.[55] The hope evoked in their followers by these displays makes their stuckness aspirational and thus addictive: "If only I try harder *this* time, arranging my time better/communicating with my husband more/spending more time with my children/being nicer to my in-laws/earning more money, my marriage will become as happy as so-and-so's." Accordingly, I saw these women bound to a perpetual dance between hope and guilt—between "If she can do it, so can I!" and "If she can do it, *why can't* I? What's wrong with me?" This partially explains why Ziyan and many others I came across in Shanghai remain attached to this "ordinary fantasy" of marital happiness while being keenly aware of its near unattainability.

Why don't these women seek and experiment with alternatives? Is there really only one accessible imaginary of marital happiness in urban China today? Certainly not. As mentioned previously, the marriage dilemma faced by the younger generations has proliferated the talk of happiness in general and marital happiness in particular. Modern Chinese individuals face numerous choices about their own happiness: whom to fall in love with, how to love, whether and when to get married, where to live after marriage (and with whom), whether to have children (and how many), how to parent, and so forth.

A brief surf through the various Chinese social media platforms easily reveals a sense of abundance and diversity in the social *imaginaries* of intimate life—including staying single, having an open relationship, living the DINK life (i.e., double income, no kids), same-sex cohabitation, and conceiving through IVF apart from marriage or heterosexual intercourse. One can also readily discover claims online such as "Each of us has the right to define his/her own happiness and live his/her own way" and "Everyone should maintain healthy boundaries and let others do whatever they desire." These claims, first preached by self-proclaimed feminists, self-help gurus, and even government mouthpieces across various social media sites, were soon picked up by their numerous followers and other netizens to defend and justify their own preferred lifestyles. In other words, alternative imaginaries of what happiness or the good life should consist of, with or without marriage, abound. So why do these women in my study seem so blind to other options? The next section explores this question by looking at the account of Qiaoyi, a thirty-seven-year-old Shanghainese woman who was determined to pursue her own version of the recipe by leaving out one conventional ingredient entirely.

QIAOYI: "WHAT ELSE CAN I DO?"

Unlike Xiaona, Ziyan, and the majority of women I interviewed in Shanghai, Qiaoyi initially chose to safeguard her marital happiness by not having any children. However, by the time of our first interview in 2018, she had become the mother of a three-year-old boy. In a rather disheartened tone, she elaborated on this episode of her life as follows:

> While raising my son might have brought me more pain than happiness, staying childless could be even more challenging. Never mind that there are a lot of people advocating being DINK on the internet these days. In reality, it is extremely difficult to realize. Few people can persevere long enough, including myself.

It's hard for me to identify concretely what difficulties I encountered. Since my husband also didn't necessarily want to have children, we never argued over this matter. My mother did push me very hard, calling me in the middle of the night, crying, and even threatening me, but I don't see it as the main reason, either. After all, she had tried to press me to do a lot of things before but without much success. I also felt harassed by people around me, including friends, colleagues, and sometimes relatives. And WeChat just made them [the harassing comments] constant!

Some made sure that I was reminded of the approaching "fertility deadline" [age thirty-five] every time I saw them. Others would not drop the subject of motherhood whenever I met them. Still others subtly introduced me to various infertility treatments. It got annoying sometimes, but mostly I just either kept silent or laughed away their "concerns." . . . I was certainly discriminated against when trying to find a more promising job. Every interviewer questioned why I had remained childless after being married for three years and when I planned to give birth. I told them I had no such plan and never heard from any of them again. [Laughs] But it was still not too big a deal, since I had a stable job at the time. . . . The internet could be a source of strain as well. I sometimes expressed my advocacy toward DINK on social media. While there certainly were people who supported my ideas, criticisms from total strangers could become pretty nasty. Although I blacklisted the trolls [*penzi*] immediately, some kind comments with different views did shake me sometimes, especially those who shared their own negative experiences as DINKs.

So if you ask me what was the last straw, it's very hard to say. I guess it is due to those cumulative moments of weakness [*ruanruo*]. At times I truly felt exhausted from resisting. It indeed felt much easier to just go with the flow. So I told myself, "Just let it be. . . . What else can I do?"

Once Qiaoyi got pregnant, the social pressures eased. She became "filial" and "normal" again in her mother's eyes. Her married friends began to identify her as part of the group, and they no longer acted skeptical when she said that she was happy with her marriage. She even realized her desired career advancement before her son turned two. "It felt like my life was back on the right track," she told me. "Only, I do not feel happy. . . . All the people around me thought I should, but I don't. I feel stuck [*kazhu*]." She concluded with a bitter smile:

> But again . . . what else can I do? If my situation were a lot worse, say, if my husband or my mother-in-law treated me badly, or if we were impoverished, or if I had been born in a less fortunate place where a woman's situation is much bleaker, then perhaps I would be much more motivated to resist or to escape—to, as the old saying goes, "smash a pot to pieces just because it's cracked" [*po guan po shuai*]. But. . . .

But, Qiaoyi admitted, her situation is far from what people might consider "bad." Similar to Ziyan and most other women I talked to in Shanghai, Qiaoyi has a supportive husband according to the male norm in China. Their income sufficiently affords their middle-class lifestyle. Her workplace promotes women-friendly policies. Even her mother-in-law is said to be kind and generous; she voluntarily does the lion's share of childcare. Qiaoyi is privileged. However, it is precisely all these seemingly favorable conditions that have impeded her pursuit of alternatives. After all, it is often much easier to stay in a not-too-bad situation in exchange for a sense of normalcy and security than to fight for precarious alternatives that risk losing what you've gained so far.

Qiaoyi's narrative serves as a vivid illustration of how (mostly tacit) constraints at all levels (including the individual, the familial, and the societal) hinder many Chinese individu-als from actualizing alternative forms of intimate life that they would deem happy. And it further answers why so many women I talked to still choose to stick to the marital happiness recipe while being clearly aware of its pitfalls. Following Swidler, I find that Qiaoyi's experience elucidates how in such unsettled times "structural opportunities for action determine which among competing ideologies survive in the long run."[56] Despite the abundance of personal lifestyle choices one might find presented online today, the actual realization of any alternative lifestyles on the ground, including living a personal life that deviates from the mainstream marital happiness recipe, remains not only structurally arduous but also morally challenging for most Chi-nese individuals. Unlike its overt intervention into the sphere of private life during the Maoist era, the Chinese state today, with a regime of "human technologies" applied at all levels, harnesses its people to a certain way of life it considers appropriate for its effective control and long-term stability.[57] Any attempt to live differently is likely to face (mostly) soft but constant resistance that permeates every layer of a person's social and emotional life. And so the possible realization of an alternative form of private life that a person deems happier is slowly nibbled away. Social media has clearly played a crucial role in enhancing the affectiv-ity of such human technologies at the micro level.

The Boundaries of the Marital Happiness Recipe

So far none of my Shanghainese informants has managed to live according to any marital-happiness script other than the "recipe." This is partly due to the bias inherent in this sample group. For example, the fact that all my informants were married eliminates "staying single" as a possible alternative. Also, at the time of our first meetings, most of them had been married for less than ten years and had one or more young children, and few had engaged any serious thoughts of divorce. Furthermore, as mentioned previously, being highly educated urban middle-class women of the first one-child generation, they are more susceptible to the allure of the marital happiness recipe than are their male counterparts or women from other economic strata and sociocultural backgrounds. However, I still wonder: Where are the boundaries of this dominant social imaginary? Who might be able to resist it?

Indeed, some women in China have managed to define their own happiness and live accordingly. During my recent virtual catch ups with several informants, more than once they brought up the famous single mother Ye Haiyang and admired her way of life as "ideal," "liberating," or "true happiness for women." Ye's story first went viral because of her effort in 2017 to conceive a mix-race girl through IVF using selected high-quality sperm, on which she spent half a million renminbi (approximately $75,000 USD). Earlier this year, she repeated the process and gave birth to her second daughter. Now she raises them, wholeheartedly, on her own.

Ye documented the whole process of her two pregnancies on Douyin and Weibo and has been posting about her daily interactions with her daughters ever since she gave birth to them. Her unconventional pursuit of happiness in womanhood has brought criticisms and even abusive attacks, but she has attracted millions of followers, including some of my informants, who admire her as a lifestyle pioneer. Comments like the following are frequently seen under Ye's posts: "You're living a life that I dream of. [You're] the new role model for independent women in the new era!"; "Your life is indeed like a fairytale, rich, adorable daughters, husbandless, and no in-laws! If this is not happiness, what is?"; "Now I know life can also be lived in this way! If there was a next life, I would choose this way of life." (@叶海洋Gavin). It is clear that Ye has succeeded in resisting the dominant marital happiness recipe, and she leads a life both she and her admirers deem one of the happiest alternatives. But who *is* she? And what has enabled her to achieve the kind of unconventional happiness that many Chinese women of her cohort can only "dream of" or hope for in the "next life"? One commentator's words might provide some hint. Also an admirer of Ye, she concurred that "If you have enough financial ability to provide your children with a prosperous life, full of love for your children, and strong enough heart to resist . . . gossipers, Ye Haiyang's state is undoubtedly the best."[58]

Ye actually started from scratch and built a lucrative cosmetic business before turning thirty, and her wealth is surely pivotal in sustaining her unusual path. Her courageous determination to pursue her own vision of happiness is frequently demonstrated through her tireless defense on social media of her own choices. In other words, what's underpinning Ye's successful resistance against the dominant script are things that few ordinary women in China can attain.

Ye Haiyang's case is somewhat of an outlier, but I collected other examples of "deviant" but happily married women, both from my own encounters and from stories shared anonymously on social media. They all indicate some type of remarkable trait of the women involved. Indeed, to attain such countercultural ways of life in China today, one needs to be somehow *extraordinary*.

For instance, one thirty-six-year-old woman managed to keep the DINK lifestyle that she desires because she purposefully married a man who is infertile. One thirty-nine-year-old woman shared her nontypical marital life with her second husband: "My marriage might not look happy according to the conventional standard. We don't own any property at this age. Our income has barely reached middle class [*xiaokang*]. We didn't hold a wedding ceremony . . . and received nothing from either side of our parents. . . . We don't have children. But what I have is freedom, independence, health, and unconditional support from my husband." According to her description, they are now living abroad, far away from their parents, in a social milieu where more variety of marital and intimate scripts are available at both discursive and structural levels.

Only a handful of women can truly resist the dominant script of marital bliss, and most others, like Ziyan and Qiaoyi, are left with the marital happiness recipe as the most feasible way to obtain a "happy" life. However, "To recognize antihumanist realities does not require giving up humanist aspirations."[59] Such aspirations begin the moment when Ziyan uttered the word "slavery," when Qiaoyi recounted how she had tried to stay childless for as long as possible, and when, as we have seen, women passionately share and discuss the unconventional stories about their personal lives and the happiness they've experienced or heard about. Here, given the almost diminished civic space offline under the current regime, social media, especially those more public-facing platforms such as Weibo and Douyin, remains the most viable space for many, including my informants, to challenge the existing script of marital bliss. Despite heavy government surveillance and censorship, these platforms enhance people's "capacity to aspire" by inspiring and even initiating alternative scripts of what constitutes a happy marriage, and more broadly, a happy life.[60] And the privileges enjoyed by this group of middle-class women of China's first one-child generation, although largely binding them to the marital happiness recipe shown in these cases, also raises the possibility of their substantiating happiness beyond the recipe.

CONCLUSION

In this chapter, I have explored how a group of young middle-class married women I interviewed in Shanghai responded variously to an unfulfillable dream of marriage represented by the marital happiness recipe. The recipe in turn is a particular set of sociocultural constructs born in response to the marriage dilemma inherent in the specific historical conditions of contemporary China. That is, a generation of single daughters has been raised to be "phoenixes" and have only found compulsory wifehood and motherhood awaiting at the end of their ambitious upward path.[61] Here the marital happiness recipe feels sensible because of its apparent potential to simultaneously satisfy their pursuit of self-fulfillment and their need for stability in a society with few adequate social protection mechanisms available other than family (carried on through marriage).

Then what did the recipe *do*? In other words, how did this piece of hegemonic discourse influence these women (and many more)? And how did these women react to it in turn? Adding to the structural analysis an affective dimension, the ethnographic material presented here foregrounded what Sara Ahmed termed "feelings of structure."[62] What might it *feel* like for these women to live under this hegemony of happiness? This layer of analysis helps us better understand how the recipe became internalized and normalized.

As these cases have shown, the privileged status of my informants, including high education levels and career opportunities, provided these women with the seemingly sufficient economic leverage and social capital required to fulfill the marital happiness recipe. But it also reinforced their hopes for achieving self-realization through competitiveness rather than contentment where they are, as well as their fear of losing the progress they had already gained. In the process, they became alienated from the kind of happiness the recipe had promised, whatever that might be. Meanwhile, this near fantasy ironically becomes the only "comfort zone" available, and staying in it becomes the easiest and most sensible "choice." As a result, the recipe has kept most of them moving around and juggling various spheres that bear structural contradictions, struggling on the invisible but highly affective "chain of contempt."

Throughout my analysis, I also highlighted the key role social media played as an affect amplifier and how it simultaneously constrains and emancipates these women's capacity to experience genuine happiness within (or without) marriage. On one hand, relatively closed social media platforms such as WeChat have facilitated an affective space monopolized by the recipe. On the other hand, more open social media platforms like Weibo and Douyin have become the most common (albeit limited) space for Chinese individuals to witness a diversity of cultural scripts beyond the recipe and possibly aspire to these alternatives.

As Hannah Arendt reminded us, every time individuals reflect upon and attempt to interrupt their routine activities by speech and action, even if just with one deed or one word, and no matter how futile the act might appear at the time, there is the possibility to "change every constellation."[63] Each of these women I talked to and observed on social media is weaving her unique felt experience of family life, marriage, and happiness into a web that might eventually reach others of her kind. A woman's chance to see and, more importantly, to realize genuine alternatives to the quagmire of the marital happiness recipe increases with every new thread of idiosyncratic experience woven into the pattern of her social understanding.

NOTES

1. In line with Li Zhang's understanding of the "middle class" as *zhongchan jieceng* (literally, the "middle propertied stratum") instead of *zhongchan jieji* (closer to the Marxist or Maoist understanding of class), I see my informants in Shanghai as belonging to a socioeconomic cohort with a particular way of life. See Li Zhang, "Private Homes, Distinct Lifestyles: Performing a New Middle Class," in *Privatizing China: Socialism from Afar*, ed. Li Zhang and Aihwa Ong (Ithaca, NY: Cornell University Press, 2008), 23–40. The majority of them owned the apartment they were living in, usually with the help of their parents and a twenty- to thirty-year mortgage. Some also owned private cars. But instead of using it for daily commuting, the car was used primarily for brief family trips to nearby cities or country resorts over the weekends and short holidays. In addition to spending on the home mortgage, most of these families invested heavily in any children they had to cultivate them to become well-rounded. In their own words, they had reached the level of "*xiaokang*" and thus were "neither the wealthiest nor the poorest" (*bi shang bu zu, bi xia you yü*), but "in-between."

2. Sara Ahmed, *The Promise of Happiness* (Durham, NC: Duke University Press, 2010).

3. For example, an online survey conducted in July 2011 by the Institute of Population and Labor Economics, the Chinese Academy of Social Sciences, and the China Population Communication Network, concluded that among the 7,729 valid respondents (mostly young middle-class people living in the eastern coastal regions), those with a spouse rated their sense of happiness the highest (7.253 out of 10), and those of a one-person family (including never married, divorced, or widowed) reported the lowest level of happiness (5.618 out of 10). Wang Guangzhou, Zheng Zhenzhen, and Feng Ting, "2011 zhongguo jiating xingfugan yingxiang yinsu fenxi" (Analysis of the factors affecting Chinese families' sense of happiness 2011), *ifeng.com*, December 24, 2011, https://fashion.ifeng.com/emotion/special/2011xingfugan/detail_2011_12/24/11546006_0.shtml. The same survey repeated in 2015 revealed that "being in one's first marriage with a spouse" contributed significantly to a person's sense of happiness. Wu Jiajia, "2015 zhongguo jiating xingfugan redian wenti

diaocha: daduoshu zhongguo jiating ganjue xingfu" (Survey on the key factors influencing Chinese families' sense of happiness: most Chinese families say they feel happy), *China Economic Network*, June 29, 2016, http://www.ce.cn/xwzx/gnsz/gdxw/201606/29/t20160629_13279236 .shtml. Another study published by the Survey and Research Center for China Household Finance covered the population of all the Chinese provinces and four municipalities except Tibet and Xinjiang. It reported that in 2014 married people scored the highest regarding their sense of happiness (131.5 points), closely followed by people who were cohabiting (130.3 points). More telling, the happiness index of never-married people aged between thirty and forty was 119.8 points, significantly lower than the 126 points reported for never-married people aged between twenty and thirty. Survey and Research Center for China Household Finance, *Guomin xinfu baogao 2014* (Chinese people's happiness report 2014), February 13, 2015.

4. For instance, a message repeatedly delivered in one of SK-II's commercial series, SK-II #ChangeDestiny, which went viral in 2016, targeted the issue of "leftover women," (*shengnü*) in China: "I don't want to marry just for the sake of marrying as it won't bring me happiness this way." Numerous viewers expressed their sympathy toward this slogan through their comments online, which to some extent indicates their belief, perhaps unconscious, that marriage should bring happiness or it is not worth pursuing.

5. Today one can locate abundant information related to marital happiness after a brief stroll in any local bookstore or within seconds of surfing the internet. Among the people under forty years old that I talked with in Shanghai, regardless of sex and marital status, most could tell me some "shoulds" and "should-nots" about how to "properly" cultivate marital happiness.

6. This layer of analysis is associated with the notion of "affectivity." There have been various approaches to interpreting affectivity, but in line with Raymond Williams and his followers, I understand it in a broad sense as "the delicate infrastructure regulating our propensities and modes of presence and participation in social situations." Devika Sharma and Frederik Tygstrup, "Introduction," in *Structures of Feeling: Affectivity and the Study of Culture*, ed. Devika Sharma and Frederik Tygstrup (Berlin:

Walter De Gruyter, 2015), 8. It is "a particular quality of social experience and relationship" embedded in a specific historical moment. Raymond Williams, *Marxism and Literature* (Oxford: Oxford University Press, 1978), 131. It is the power that channels the moves of people/things in certain ways. Teresa Kuan, *Love's Uncertainty: The Politics and Ethics of Child Rearing in Contemporary China* (Berkeley, CA: University of California Press, 2015), 9. Compared to "emotion," affect is less consciously perceived and verbally expressible. See Sharma and Tygstrup, "Introduction," 7. On marital happiness, see Ahmed, *The Promise of Happiness*, 216.

7. Daniel Miller et al., *How the World Changed Social Media* (London: UCL Press, 2016); and Yujie Chen, Zhifei Mao, and Jack Linchuan Qiu, *Super-Sticky WeChat and Chinese Society* (Bingley, UK: Emerald, 2018).

8. On individualization, see Yunxiang Yan, "The Chinese Path to Individualization," *British Journal of Sociology* 61, no. 3 (2010): 489–512. And on the one-child generation, see, Venessa L. Fong, "China's One-Child Policy and the Empowerment of Urban Daughters," *American Anthropologist* 104, no. 4 (2002): 1098–1109; Lynne Nakano, "Happiness and Unconventional Life Choices," in *Happiness and the Good Life in Japan*, ed. Wolfram Manzenreiter and Barbara Holthus (New York: Routledge, 2017), 53–66; and Kailing Xie, *Embodying Middle Class Gender Aspirations: Perspective from China's Privileged Young Women* (Singapore: Palgrave Macmillan, 2021).

9. Miller et al., *How the World Changed Social Media*, 7.

10. See Yan, "The Chinese Path to Individualization," 489–512; and Yunxiang Yan, "Intergenerational Intimacy and Descending Familism in Rural North China," *American Anthropologists* 118, no. 2 (2016): 244–57.

11. Baidu services use a format similar to Google but almost exclusively focus on the mainland Chinese market, with 66.35 percent of the mainland market share as of December 2023 (compared to a 2.34 percent share for Google), and are fully compliant with state censorship. "Search Engine Market Share China," Global Stats, accessed February 28, 2024, https://gs.statcounter.com/search-engine-market-share/all/china.

12. Ma Haiyan, "Diaocha xianshi: 76 percent de shihun qingnian you konghun xinli" (The statistics show: 76 percent of the young people at marriageable age have gamophobia), *ChinaNews*, May 20, 2015, https://www.chinanews.com.cn/sh/2015/05-20/7290275.shtml.

13. In 2019, the marriage rate in Shanghai dipped to 4.1 percent, the low-est among all Chinese regions. Ren Zeping et al., "How Chinese Fell Out of Love With Marriage," *Caixin Global*, March 20, 2021, https://www.caixinglobal.com/2021-03-20/weekend-long-read-how-chinese-society-fell-out-of-love-with-marriage-101677550.html.

14. Alexandra Stevenson, "Divorce Is Down in China, but So Are Marriages," *New York Times*, March 23, 2022, https://www.nytimes.com/2022/03/23/business/china-divorce-marriage.html?smid=url-share.

15. Lynne Nakano, "Single Women and the Transition to Marriage in Hong Kong, Shanghai and Tokyo," *Asian Journal of Social Science* 44, no. 3 (2016): 371–72.

16. Shanghai Statistics Bureau, *2015 nian shanghaishi 1 percent renkou chouyang diaocha ziliao* (2015 Shanghai 1 percent population sample survey) (Beijing: China Statistics Press, 2015).

17. According to an online poll conducted in 2015 by matchmaking service *Zhen'ai Wang*, of its eighty million members, Shanghainese women are the group most actively trying to "get rid of the 'single' label (*tuodan*)": 75.9 percent of the female respondents from Shanghai said they had experienced blind-dating, and 24.1 percent of them reported ten or more blind dates. "Zhan'aiwang fabu 2015 danshen diaocha baogao jiedu 'guanggun weiji'" (Zhen'ai.com releases 2015 singles survey report, interpreting the "bachelor crisis"), *KKNews*, November 11, 2015, https://kknews.cc/news/qjr893b.html. For parents' involvement, see Sun Peidong, *Shei lai qü wo de nüer?: shanghai xiangqinjiao yü "baifa xiangqin"* (Who's going to marry my daughter?: Shanghai matchmaking corner and "grey-hair match-making") (Beijing: China Social Sciences Press, 2012).

18. Nakano, "Happiness and Unconventional Life Choices," 64.

19. Nakano, "Happiness and Unconventional Life Choices," 64.

20. For a more detailed discussion of the structural dilemma, see Lynn Lin Sun, "The Happiness Impasse: Exploring Middle-Class Women's Pursuits of Marital Happiness in Urban China and Japan" (PhD diss., Chinese University of Hong Kong, 2021), 17–22.

21. See, for example, Jie Yang, "'Happy Housewives': Gender, Class, and Psychological Self-Help in China," in *Chinese Discourses on Happiness*, ed. Gerda Wielander and Dered Hird (Hong Kong: Hong Kong University Press, 2018), 129–49; and Lang Chen, "The Changing Notion of

Happiness: A History of *Xingfu*," in *The Chinese Pursuit of Happiness: Anxieties, Hopes, and Moral Tensions in Everyday Life*, ed. Becky Yang Hsu and Richard Madsen (Berkeley: University of California Press, 2019), 19–41.

22. Yang, "'Happy Housewives'," 132, 146–47.

23. For Swidler, culture is understood as "a repertoire" of various cultural scripts that individuals can "[pick] up and [put] aside" so as to construct their lines of thought and action as they go about their everyday lives. Ann Swidler, *Talk of Love: How Culture Matters* (2001; repr. Chicago: University of Chicago Press, 2003), 471–72, loc. 2518 of 6930, Kindle.

24. Swidler, *Talk of Love*, loc. 2290 of 6903. See also Swidler, *Talk of Love*, loc. 2497–2556 of 6903.

25. Swidler, *Talk of Love*, loc. 2497–2556 of 6903.

26. It often includes material conditions, living arrangements, care responsibilities, and relationships with children, in-laws, and other kin or non-kin within the household.

27. Xie, *Embodying Middle Class Gender Aspirations*, 250.

28. For happy objects, see Ahmed, *The Promise of Happiness*, 21. "High-quality" children refers to *suzhi* discourse promoted by the Chinese state since the early reform era, which aims to cultivate a new generation of "well-rounded, entrepreneurial human talents" who can be more fit to modernize the nation in the era of the market economy and globalization. Having *suzhi* also became a key indicator of middle classness. Kuan, *Love's Uncertainty*, 45. For more discussion on the *suzhi* discourse in China, see also Ann Anagnost, "The Corporeal Politics of Quality (Suzhi)," *Public Culture* 16, no. 2 (2004): 189–208; Susan Greenhalgh, "Science, Modernity, and the Making of China's One-Child Policy," *Population and Development Review* 29, no. 2 (2003): 163–96; and Susan Greenhalgh, *Cultivating Global Citizens: Population in the Rise of China* (Cambridge, MA: Harvard University Press, 2011).

29. Her words also inspired my labeling of this dominant cultural script of marital happiness as a recipe.

30. Esther Perel, "The Secret to Desire in a Long-Term Relationship," TED Talks, February 14, 2013, https://www.ted.com/talks/esther_perel_the _secret_to_desire_in_a_long_term_relationship?language=en.

31. Perel, "The Secret to Desire in a Long-Term Relationship."

32. *Luohun* is a Chinese phrase denoting a marriage with no house, no ring, and no ceremony.

33. Arlie Hochschild, *The Second Shift* (1989; repr. New York: Avon, 2003), 1.

34. See Yan, "The Chinese Path to Individualization," 489–512; Yunxiang Yan, "The Changing Moral Landscape," in *Deep China: The Moral Life of the Person*, ed. Arthur Kleinman, Yunxiang Yan, Jing Jun, Sing Lee, and Everett Zhang (Berkeley: University of California Press, 2011), 36–77; Yunxiang Yan, "Neo-Familism and the State in Contemporary China," *Urban Anthropology and Studies of Cultural Systems and World Economic Development* 47, no. 3 (2018): 181–224; and Yunxiang Yan, "Introduction: The Inverted Family, Post-Patriarchal Intergenerationality and Neo-Familism," in *Chinese Families Upside Down: Intergenerational Dynamics and Neo-Familism in the Early 21st Century*, ed. Yunxiang Yan (Leiden: Brill, 2021), 1–30.

35. Sara Ahmed, *The Cultural Politics of Emotion* (New York: Routledge, 2004); and Ahmed, *The Promise of Happiness*.

36. By this I do not mean to say that Chen Na was actively ever seeking to tell other than the truth to me. However, it is quite clear that in her social media as well as in her persona she was conveying a certain image by emphasizing some things and underplaying others, which is worth bearing in mind.

37. Miller et al., *How the World Changed Social Media*, 198.

38. Lauren Berlant, *Cruel Optimism* (Durham, NC: Duke University Press, 2011), 2 (italics in the original).

39. Berlant, *Cruel Optimism*, 2.

40. See Marshall Sahlins, *Stone Age Economics* (Chicago: Aldine-Atherton, 1972); and Karl Polanyi, *The Livelihood of Man* (London: Academic, 1977).

41. Sun, "The Happiness Impasse," 220–57.

42. Ulrich Beck and Elisabeth Beck-Gernsheim, *Individualization: Institutionalized Individualism and Its Social and Political Consequences* (London: Sage, 2002); and Yan, "The Chinese Path to Individualization," 489–512.

43. See Ulrich Beck, *Risk Society: Towards a New Modernity* (London: Sage, 1992); and Ulrich Beck and Elisabeth Beck-Gernsheim, *The Normal Chaos of Love* (Cambridge: Polity Press, 1995).

44. Berlant, *Cruel Optimism*, 2, 164.

45. Beck, *Risk Society*, 135–36 (italics in the original).

46. See, for example, Xiaotong Fei, *From the Soil: The Foundations of Chinese Society*, trans. Gary G. Hamilton and Wang Zheng (Berkeley: University of California Press, 1992).

47. Ahmed, *The Promise of Happiness*, 22; and Jason C. Throop, "Ambivalent Happiness and Virtuous Suffering," *HAU: Journal of Ethnographic Theory* 5, no. 3 (2015): 49. See also, Beck, *Risk Society*; and Nikolas Rose, *The Politics of Life Itself* (Princeton, NJ: Princeton University Press, 2006).

48. Beck, *Risk Society*.

49. Hochschild, *The Second Shift*, 282.

50. Hochschild, *The Second Shift*, 33.

51. Xie, *Embodying Middle Class Gender Aspirations*, 255–56.

52. Yan, "Intergenerational Intimacy and Descending Familism in Rural North China," 252.

53. For a more detailed discussion of the mother's generation, see Sun, "The Happiness Impasse," 72–116.

54. This fear of sliding down the economic and social ladder among China's middle class has been discussed in many works. See, for example, Li Zhang, *In Search of Paradise: Middle-Class Living in a Chinese Metropolis* (Ithaca, NY: Cornell University Press, 2010); Kuan, *Love's Uncertainty*; Xie, *Embodying Middle Class Gender Aspirations*; and Wang Qianni and Ge Shifan, "How One Obscure Word Captures Urban China's Unhappiness," *Sixth Tone*, November 4, 2020, https://www.sixthtone.com/news /1006391.

55. Berlant, *Cruel Optimism*, 176 (italics in the original).

56. Ann Swidler, "Culture in Action: Symbols and Strategies," *American Sociological Review* 51, no. 2 (1986): 273.

57. Following Teresa Kuan, I understand "technology" here as "any human-invented means for channeling energy and attention in a certain direction." See Kuan, *Love's Uncertainty*, 41.

58. "Ye Haiyang, Who Bought a Half-Million-Dollar Daughter for a Second Child: She Has Become the Envy of Many Women," iMedia, accessed June 22, 2022, https://min.news/en/news/9158b8aa736ed08007 4fd1b276871667.html.

59. Kuan, *Love's Uncertainty*, 211.

60. Arjun Appadurai, *The Future as Cultural Fact: Essays on the Global Condition* (London: Verso, 2013), 179–96.
61. Associated with the saying *"wang nü cheng feng"* (hope for daughter to become a phoenix), instead of marrying well, today it conveys parents' high expectations for their (usually only) daughter's academic and career success. See Qiong Xu and Wei-Jun Jean Yeung, "Hoping for a Phoenix: Shanghai Fathers and Their Daughters," *Journal of Family Issues* 34, no. 2 (2013): 184–209.
62. Ahmed, *The Promise of Happiness*, 216.
63. Hannah Arendt, *The Human Condition* (1958; repr. Chicago: University of Chicago Press, 1998), 190.

6

GOOD CARE IN CHILDBIRTH

C-Sections as Individual or Collective Decisions

GONÇALO SANTOS

L ike most things related to reproduction in the twenty-first century, giving birth has become highly technologized, and that means it is also increasingly morally divisive. In this chapter, I build upon a well-established feminist tradition of historical and sociological studies of reproductive technologies to reflect on the question of choice in medicalized childbirth procedures—and how this question might be framed in ways that vary cross-culturally. My account privileges the perspectives of women as childbearing subjects, and I seek to understand the technological and moral frictions and negotiations that take place among ordinary women regarding contemporary processes of routinization of cesarean deliveries.[1]

Although this research focuses on China, it has larger theoretical implications. Rates of cesarean section have increased dramatically worldwide in recent decades, particularly in middle- and high-income countries, with many of these procedures considered elective rather than medically necessary.[2] Women around the world are divided over the relative benefits of this hypermedicalization of childbirth. China and the United States offer interesting examples of these techno-moral divisions.

The rise of U.S. cesarean rates began as early as the 1960s; a countermovement questioned the benefits of excessive child-birth medicalization and called for a return to home births or "natural births" with limited medical interventions.[3] These so-called birth wars have created profound moral divisions: some women are embracing mainstream technocratic values promoted by the medical establishment; others are engaging with alternative, nonobstetric models of labor and delivery as a matter of bodily autonomy. Both ethical visions have become publicly acceptable by many, and the choice between the two is increasingly framed as one of informed, individual decision, although not without significant tensions.[4]

These ethical tensions active in the United States are not transposable to contemporary China, however, without an understanding of the significant differences between the "birthing systems" of the two nations.[5] When U.S. cesarean rates surged in the 1960s, most American women were already giving birth at the hospital.[6] The pace of the increase in C-sections accelerated in the 1970s and 1980s with significant improvements in surgical procedures and the increased availability of privatized health care and medicalized childbirth. Cesarean deliveries had reached rates higher than 30 percent by the turn of the millennium, well above the 10 to 15 percent recommended by the World Health Organization (WHO) since 1985.[7]

In China, rates of hospital birth remained low until the 1980s, and the surge in cesarean rates only began in the 1990s. The launching of the Birth Planning Policy in 1979 led to a significant increase in rates of hospital births in urban areas and in some rural areas, but it was only in the 1990s and the 2000s that health-care policies made medically supervised hospital births compulsory. This usually means going to a public hospital or clinic because they are a more economical option than private ones and can be rendered even more so, depending on the quality of one's social welfare benefits. This shift to a hospital-centered "technocratic model of birth" was accompanied by a truly dramatic increase in cesarean rates—from less than 5 percent in 1990 to more than 35 percent between 2008 and 2014.[8] Unlike U.S. women, birthing mothers in China have experienced *two* dramatic shifts in the last three decades: from home to hospital; and with cesareans, from rare emergencies to routine procedures.

Most women in China do not openly question official discourses of childbirth medicalization and feel that giving birth in the hospital under medical guidance is the safest option for women and children. Many view the increasing popularity of cesareans as a positive development that reflects China's scientific and technological progress. Yes, there is increasing nationwide concern over the potential public hazards of so many cesarean deliveries, but this does not involve a radical collective critique of the medical establishment. Debates arise, however, when some claim that rising cesarean rates harm women and subvert the cherished and long held expectation that a good mother must be able to endure the pain of "natural" birth (that is, vaginal and without pain relief).[9] These moral frictions, which affect Chinese women from all social strata and regions, have an important generational dimension—especially in rural areas, where the dramatic shift from low-tech home births to a regime of high-tech hospital births with high rates of cesareans has happened in a single generation (less than twenty years).

Most young-adult mothers in rural areas consider home births dangerous and want to give birth in the hospital under medical supervision. They are aware that hospitals and medical doctors often make decisions that harm women, but they feel lucky as a generation not to have to go through the hardships and the dangers of a home birth assisted by village midwives and female relatives. For them, the shift to the hospital has been a major landmark in the modernization of local childbirth practices, and they find it difficult to imagine how earlier generations of women managed to cope with the uncertainties of low-tech home births. Older mothers and grandmothers agree that the shift to the hospital has brought many benefits to local women, however, they argue that it has also weakened women's control over childbirth, giving too much power to obstetricians and medical authorities. This view echoes the argument put forward by a large body of feminist scholarship on childbirth medicalization in different parts of the world that shows how the growing power of doctors and hospitals in modern societies goes hand in hand with the decline of community-based female-dominated networks of reproductive expertise and childbirth support.[10] The shift to the hospital and obstetric experts has now rendered these networks weaker and increasingly irrelevant.

These local anxieties echo larger national conversations about rising cesarean rates. One 2010 WHO report showed that 46 percent of all Chinese babies born between 2004 and 2008 were delivered by cesarean surgery.[11] The Chinese government was quick to respond to this report with a number of initiatives designed to counter the cesarean surge.[12] However, national rates remain high (well above 30 percent), and there is no sign that the moral anxieties surrounding high cesarean rates are diminishing.[13]

In both China and the United States, medical doctors are obliged to perform emergency cesarean surgery if needed to save lives, but there are significant differences in the way this option is typically exercised. U.S. doctors attend to a code of informed consent based on the principle of individual autonomy. This principle is not just part of a professional code of action; it is enshrined in law and is a key element of American folk culture.[14] Doctors in China also recognize the principle of individual autonomy, but they must also obtain consent from close relatives of the birthing mother, such as the baby's father and grandparents. This concern with familial consent is not just prescribed by medical codes of ethics; it is also enshrined in legal regulations and is a key component of Chinese folk culture.[15]

My analysis focuses on the generational moral frictions and negotiations shaping the childbirth experiences of young women in Chinese rural communities. I draw on the extended case method developed by Max Gluckman and the Manchester School of Social Anthropology to focus on the contemporary conjuncture surrounding rising cesarean rates in China.[16]

My main case study refers to a childbirth incident that took place in 2012 in Yellow Flower, a rural township in Northern Guangdong, South China, where I have conducted longitudinal ethnographic research since the late 1990s. I learned about this incident and other similar incidents through informal conversations, interviews, and group discussions with village women from different generations.

Due to intense labor pains, a young village woman birthing at her local township clinic requested a cesarean delivery. The request was endorsed by the doctor but denied by the woman's mother-in-law, and the woman had no choice but to carry on with a vaginal delivery. At first sight, this incident seems to confirm Orientalist accounts of Chinese ethical life that highlight the primacy of collective interests and hierarchies over personal liberties. But such a simplistic reading neglects the growing importance of individual agency among pregnant women in China's contemporary landscape of reproductive consumerism.

Most comparative studies of ethical life in China and the United States have contrasted their two different unified systems of shared collective values. This approach has the benefit of generating clear-cut, easy-to-understand pictures of national ethical systems, but it tends to exacerbate the significance of national and civilizational differences. I favor an alternative approach that instead prioritizes the study of moral frictions and negotiations in order to highlight the complexities of living in globalized plural societies with multiple value systems. The study of moral frictions and disagreements must be a key part of the larger project—as eloquently described by one of the members of this research group, Richard Madsen—of constructing ethical bridges of cross-cultural communication between countries like China and the United States.[17]

Such an approach shows not only that there are important moral divisions within each country but that these internal divisions are as significant as, if not more so than, the perceived moral divisions between any two countries. This more nuanced understanding of collective frameworks of ethical life is a good starting point for crafting Madsen's ethical bridges in times of increasing political division and misunderstanding. Instead of approaching national frameworks of ethical life as unified wholes, the *intimate choices approach*, which I have explained more thoroughly elsewhere, attends to the messy details of ethics in action, the conflict-ridden, confused twists and turns of real-life situations, which are downplayed in essentialist understandings.[18] This ethnographic approach does not counterpose individuals versus collectives, communal versus individualist societies, or personal liberties versus social responsibilities. As a dialectical framework of analysis, it approaches people's engagement with new technologies from a grounded processual perspective that recognizes the continuing centrality of moral collectives, social obligations, and networks of social support—without neglecting the importance of individual agency and personal autonomy.[19]

That said, being careful not to depict American and Chinese ethical regimes of informed consent in clear-cut, black-and-white terms, the Chinese emphasis on collective consent can be useful in questioning universalistic assumptions of American cultural ideologies regarding the primacy of individual autonomy and individual choice. In some cases, the comingling of personal liberty and social responsibility in China empowers a pregnant woman to make her own individual choice. But this is not the only possible outcome. In a situation like the main case study reported here, the actions of a senior female relative seem to interfere with the personal liberties of the pregnant woman. This "interference" can be conceptualized as an act of suppression of individual autonomy. But it can also be seen as a moral action prioritizing the social connectedness of the pregnant woman to her community through duty and responsibility. Which interpretation is relevant will depend on the details of each case but also on the moral perspective of the one interpreting it.

THE CASE OF LISA AND THE RISE OF CESAREAN BIRTHS IN RURAL CHINA

On September 15, 2012, at around 11:00 a.m., Mou-dai, then a sixty-five-year-old illiterate grandmother, received a call on her mobile phone from Yi-dai, her second daughter. Yi-dai's daughter-in-law, Lisa, was having labor contractions, and Yi-dai wanted Mou-dai's help because of her vast experience as a rural midwife. At the time, Mou-dai was staying at her youngest son's family apartment in the market town of Yellow Flower in northern Guangdong Province, a few hundred kilometers away from the city of Guangzhou.

I have known Mou-dai for two decades now. I first met her during my initial long-term fieldwork (1999–2001) in her village community, and I visit her every few years when I return to

Yellow Flower for catching-up and follow-up research. Although she never obtained a village midwife certificate, Mou-dai had practiced midwifery for many decades and was well respected for her work in the 1980s and 1990s, when it was still common to give birth at home.[20]

As explained previously, the shift to hospital births in rural townships such as Yellow Flower has rapidly accelerated in the twenty-first century. For women of Lisa's generation, giving birth in a hospital setting under the close supervision of medical doctors is the normative model. Midwives like Mou-dai are no longer allowed to practice midwifery at home or in the hospital, and this ban started to be enforced in the 1990s. A policy of mandatory hospital births has defined obstetric professionals as the sole legitimate birth attendants.[21] This increasing emphasis on the importance of hospitals and obstetric expertise has effectively ended rural home births and I had the opportunity to witness quite closely this transformation.

When Mou-dai received the phone call about Lisa, she had already examined Lisa on at least two occasions in the last three months, providing various forms of advice, including diet. Mou-dai had also agreed to provide support to Lisa during the process of birth. This kind of gynocentric support is not uncommon in the local context. Fathers are increasingly expected to be present at the hospital during the birth of their children, but this does not always happen. In Yellow Flower, where marriage practices remain strongly patrilocal, the most important source of informal childbirth support for young mothers like Lisa is the mother-in-law, with the help of other senior female relatives with recognized reproductive expertise.[22] When Lisa started to have contractions that morning, her husband was away in Guangzhou for work, so she had only her mother-in-law, Yi-dai, to help her. Mou-dai's home was not far from the clinic, so the ladies could walk from there.

Lisa and Yi-dai arrived around noon, and Mou-dai checked Lisa for cervix dilation and fetal position. Everything was in order, but it was still too early to go to the clinic.

CESAREAN BIRTH AND THE PROBLEM OF INFORMED CONSENT

At around 1:00 p.m., the three women walked over to the clinic. Lisa had mentally prepared herself to have a vaginal delivery, but when she arrived at the clinic, she started having problems handling the pain of contractions. At 2:00 p.m., Lisa was taken to the maternity ward alone. In most public hospitals in China, no relatives or birth partners are allowed in the maternity ward; women are expected to give birth in isolation, accompanied only by medical staff. Furthermore, mothers-to-be are not entitled to have a birth plan. This means that there is usually no document stating a woman's preferences in terms of her labor and delivery.

After examining Lisa for a few minutes, the young male doctor on duty hurried out of the ward to talk to the mother-in-law, Yi-dai, in the waiting area. Because Lisa's cervix was not sufficiently dilated and she seemed to be feeling too weak to go through the pain of vaginal delivery, he wanted to perform a cesarean section. In cases like this, doctors need to obtain multiple signatures of consent. Lisa initially told the doctor that she did not want a C-section, but after an hour of painful labor, she changed her mind and agreed to sign the consent form. She was also worried about the possibility of something going wrong during vaginal delivery. With a C-section, she would get anesthetic relief, and the doctor would take full responsibility for the birth.

For the doctor, even more important than obtaining consent from Lisa was obtaining consent from her close family members.

There are several reasons for this. The first is ethical: it is generally assumed that a woman in labor may be too stressed to make such a profound decision on her own. The second reason is economic: explicit consent from close family members is needed because doctors have to make sure that the family has enough money to settle the bill immediately after the delivery, and cesarean procedures cost two to three times more than vaginal births. The third reason concerns legality: doctors and hospitals want to protect themselves against possible litigation in case things go wrong medically.[23]

In this case, Yi-dai was going to be paying the bill, and she was the only close family member there with Lisa. The problem was that she was reluctant to go ahead with the procedure. The doctor insisted that Lisa's pain was unbearable, but Yi-dai remained unconvinced. Mou-dai decided to intervene to support her view. She told the doctor that she herself had given birth to six children and had assisted in the "natural birth" of many babies, and that pain was simply part of the process. She had never met a woman, she told him, who had given birth without pain. She said that Lisa was a strong woman, and there was no reason to think that she could not handle a vaginal delivery. Most local women would never dare to openly question a doctor in this manner, but Mou-dai is well known within her circle of relatives and friends for her outspoken personality. The young doctor dismissed Mou-dai's comments with scorn and warned the mother-in-law that the clinic would not take any responsibility if she refused a cesarean section for Lisa. Yi-dai—under the advice of Mou-dai—insisted on vaginal delivery, in part for economic reasons and in part because of the traditional moral conviction that vaginal delivery is best. In the end, Lisa successfully delivered a baby boy "naturally," in less than forty minutes, under the supervision of the young male doctor.

CHANGING GENERATIONAL
FRAMEWORKS OF ETHICAL IMAGINATION

When Mou-dai, Yi-dai, and Lisa each separately told me this birthing story in June 2013 and then again in September 2015, there were significant differences in their narratives. Mou-dai and Yi-dai attributed the idea of the cesarean to the medical doctor, claiming that he recommended it not out of medical necessity but because he wanted to make more money. Lisa, by contrast, was less critical of the doctor's decision to recommend a cesarean. She would have been happy to have a cesarean delivery because she felt unable to cope with the pain of labor and feared that everyone would blame her if something went wrong during vaginal delivery. Lisa had a second vaginal delivery in 2014—this time in a hospital in Guangzhou—and her second childbirth experience confirmed for her that the first one had in fact been particularly difficult. She had required an episiotomy, including the stitching up of her episiotomy wound without any pain relief medication.[24]

Episiotomies are routine procedures in public hospitals in China and are usually performed without pain relief medication.[25] I heard many young mothers like Lisa complain about the physical pain of having an episiotomy, and some told me that this pain has led them to consider having a cesarean section in subsequent pregnancies. These conversations with younger mothers made it clear to me that fear of pain is a major reason for many women to favor having a cesarean delivery. These women are not just concerned with physical pain; there is also the heavy burden of moral responsibility. Having a cesarean section offers pregnant women the possibility of offloading to the medical doctor the moral responsibility of birthing a healthy child without complications. If anything goes wrong during a C-section delivery, the doctor is to be blamed; but if anything goes wrong during a vaginal delivery, most family members will blame the mother.[26] This expectation of mother blaming puts a lot of mental pressure on women, and not all women are able to handle this pressure, especially because the process of vaginal delivery normally takes place in a situation of medical confinement (i.e., without the support of birth partners, relatives, or friends).

In their account of Lisa's birthing story, Mou-dai and Yi-dai also mentioned this pervasive fear of vaginal birthing, blaming it on the dramatic shift in the physical endurance of young adult women in twenty-first-century China. Both Mou-dai and Yi-dai had many children (Mou-dai had six and Yi-dai four), and they had delivered all their children at home under the guidance of village midwives. Young women like Lisa grew up in an age of material abundance (the Reform period after the late 1970s) and have become "too delicate" (taai giu-ching, 太娇情). According to Mou-dai and Yi-dai, they cannot handle the physical hardships of vaginal birth or of agricultural work. This "delicateness" is not just the outcome of changes to the nature of women's daily work activities (for example, the reduction in physical labor); it is also linked to changes in feminine body culture. Women of older generations strove to be self-reliant and to cultivate a strong body capable of enduring the high physicality of their daily work chores. In contrast, many women of Lisa's generation are no longer interested in cultivating a strong physical body and developing a strong sense of physical endurance. They are more interested in cultivating a feminine beauty shaped by new urban cultural ideals: pale, white, and ultra thin. These new urban ideals of feminine beauty are technocratic, depicting women as fragile subjects who require technological and medical mediation to overcome the pain and uncertainties of childbirth.

These changes point to a radical transformation in generational ethical ideals about childbirth. For women of Mou-dai's generation (born in the 1950s) through Yi-dai's generation (born in the 1970s), childbirth is "natural" and takes place at home under the guidance of local midwives. Childbirth does not need medical and technological mediation because women are strong and capable of handling the physical hardships of vaginal birth. In contrast, for women of Lisa's generation (born in the 1990s), childbirth is dangerous and should take place in the hospital under medical supervision. Women need medical support because childbirth entails many risks, and in some cases, it might be necessary to perform a cesarean delivery to save the life of the mother or the baby.

Women of Lisa's generation are very positive about the value of these life-saving cesareans, but there is criticism of the growing trend toward elective cesarean deliveries. Most still favor vaginal delivery in theory and support the "traditional" ideal that a good mother ought to be able to endure the pain of vaginal birth, but some accept a cesarean as equally virtuous. Many women of both persuasions might opt for a cesarean if they encounter too much pain during labor or if doctors convince them that having a vaginal delivery in their situation is too dangerous (for example, by saying that the head of the fetus is too big for the mother's pelvis or that the mother is too tired or too old to handle a vaginal birth). Another important reason leading some young women to favor a cesarean is that vaginal deliveries are said to negatively impact the mother's figure, especially the hips, and this is an important concern in China's increasingly image-conscious consumer culture. For some women, especially those from poor village households, having a C-section is also a good way to get some additional time off from household work or employment because the average recovery time for a cesarean is longer than for a vaginal delivery.

As more and more young women in Yellow Flower choose the practice of cesarean birth, earlier ideals regarding what counts as a good birth are unsettled, and new questions emerge. What should be the right way to give birth in the age of hospitals and techno-science? Should local women insist on celebrating the virtues of vaginal delivery, or should they embrace the new trend toward elective cesarean deliveries? Should women be allowed to choose the way they want to give birth, or should the ultimate power to decide lie in the hands of medical doctors? What should be the role of close family members in this process of decision-making?

Most mothers born in the 1950s through 1970s are fervent opponents of any attempt to turn cesarean deliveries into a con-sumerist common good for women. They argue that cesarean deliveries are not a matter of personal preference but only of medical necessity, and they consider recent trends toward nor-malized cesarean deliveries as beneficial to no one but medical doctors and as harmful to women and local communities. This negative view of cesareans can also be found among mothers of Lisa's generation. Many are critical of their peers who request an elective cesarean delivery. These criticisms are based on a num-ber of arguments: although it is true that cesareans allow moth-ers to escape the fate of labor pain, there is a lot of pain to endure after the surgery; the whole procedure is riskier than a normal vaginal delivery because it involves surgical intervention and the use of anesthetics; cesareans are more expensive than vaginal births, and many consider the expense not worth the family sac-rifice; and cesareans leave a large scar across the abdomen that is not very pleasing aesthetically. Furthermore, these young moth-ers who are strong supporters of vaginal births say that the trend toward elective cesareans is worse among urban (middle-class) women than among rural (working-class) women. In their view, to quote a forty-five-year-old mother of two boys, "Rural women only have C-sections after trying to give birth naturally for a long period of time, not like urban women who plan to have a C-section from early on."[27]

BIRTH CHOICES BEYOND THE PARADIGM OF INDIVIDUAL CHOICE

This analysis suggests that the increasing popularity of cesarean deliveries in the township of Yellow Flower has given rise to complex moral debates about the "good" way to give birth and what kinds of birthing technologies should be considered "tools of virtuous action" for mothers.[28] These moral disagreements between supporters of traditional ideals of vaginal birth and proponents of elective cesarean deliveries are local and familial, but they are also explicitly connected to larger globalized spaces of ethical reflection. In clear contrast to mothers of Mou-dai's or even Yi-dai's generation, young mothers born in the 1990s are literate and have frequent interactions with medical doctors through prenatal checkups. They also have a higher degree of familiarity with biomedical terminology and perspectives because they can access an unprecedented amount of popular advice from medical experts. Giving advice to pregnant women has become a big business, and a flourishing industry of books and magazines on pregnancy and childbirth has emerged.[29] A growing number of internet forums and WeChat social platforms feature expert advice on pregnancy and childbirth.[30] These virtual spaces reflect the increasing importance of the internet in helping the current generation of internet-savvy moms develop their own individualized views of childbirth.

One important point to make about this process of ethical subjectivation is that it does not take place in a vacuum, which is often assumed by contemporary North American ideologies of informed individual choice (more on these ideologies follow). It is true that young women like Lisa now have access to a growing amount of information and expert advice, but these materials have to be significantly selected and subject to processes of cultural translation, conversion and adaptation before becoming useful and meaningful to these women and their larger social and moral communities. This process of "domestication"—as science and technology studies (STS) scholars refer to it—takes place in the context of everyday life interactions and involves complex negotiations and frictions that play a crucial role in shaping young women's ideas about pregnancy and childbirth.[31] In Yellow Flower, this process of domestication takes place primarily within local families and gynocentric networks of childbirth support and maternity care, which have an important generational dimension. Experienced senior female relatives like Mou-dai and Yi-dai play an important role in this process of domestication because they continue to be highly valued locally as sources of practical reproductive advice.

The childbirth incident analyzed in this chapter highlights the important role played by intergenerational moral frictions and negotiations in shaping rural women's ideas and experiences of childbirth. These intergenerational moral frictions and negotiations can be found in other contexts outside China, but they are often neglected by researchers studying childbirth and cesarean deliveries in the North American context. These scholars tend to situate birth outside the context of everyday life social interactions, and they tend to approach childbirth in light of the notion of *informed individual choice*.

First developed in the 1960s and 1970s, the concept of informed individual choice has become one of the most important forces shaping the institutional makeup of the highly privatized American childbirth care system. It is possible in the United States to give birth outside the hospital, but the majority of American women deliver their babies in hospital settings under medical supervision. In the hospital context, health-care professionals are expected to approach human reproduction largely as a matter of individual autonomy, underscoring pregnant women's rights to access the necessary information to make their own decisions. This prioritization of individual reproductive rights is an important component of the organizational framework of U.S. hospitals and other reproductive care institutions. It is also an important component of the research design of most social studies of childbirth and cesarean deliveries in the United States: researchers are either concerned with studying the individual choices made by pregnant women in the context of childbirth or with exposing their lack of power to make those choices.

A particularly influential example of the latter approach has developed from a well-established tradition of feminist studies of North American processes of childbirth medicalization.[32] This scholarship has shown that the rise of an increasingly commodified and technocratic model of childbirth management in the 1970s and 1980s has empowered hospitals and medical doctors to make decisions but has given too little choice to pregnant women. But this critique is itself based on a theory of female agency that gives primacy to individual choice.[33] American society, so goes the argument, has failed to create a birthing system that grants women the power to exercise their right to make truly informed choices. Caught in the reproductive assembly line of hospitals and maternity wards, and lacking the authority and the know-how to contest medical decisions, pregnant women have no choice but to accept the authority of the medical establishment. This dynamic of reproductive mechanization fragments their bodies and alienates their selves.

This feminist approach is very helpful in making sense of the increasing authority of obstetric experts and hospitals in post-1980s China under the Birth Planning Policy and an increasingly commercialized system of public health-care provision. But instead of assuming that women's childbirth experiences are a matter of individual choice or ought to be so, the intimate choices approach assumes that women's childbirth experiences always involve context-specific moral frictions and negotiations among multiple actors, including not just medical professionals and hospitals but also family members, friends and others forms of social support.

The case of Lisa illustrates the value of this approach. Lisa had prepared for a vaginal delivery under the guidance of local doctors and the advice of Yi-dai (her mother-in-law) and Mou-dai (Yi-dai's mother and an experienced doula). Lisa had also read a significant amount of information about vaginal births. However, when she changed her mind after one hour of intense labor pain at the clinic, her request for a cesarean marked the beginning of a new loop of moral frictions and negotiations between multiple actors. The doctor on duty (for good or bad reasons) responded positively to Lisa's request and sought consent from her mother-in-law, but Yi-dai refused. If we hold to the classic feminist approach to childbirth medicalization, we have to consider the mother-in-law's veto an act of oppression that violates Lisa's individual reproductive rights and illustrates the continuing hold in contemporary China of "traditional" patriarchal family values and related gendered generational hierarchies.[34] This approach is not without its merits, but again its primary concern is to show that the pregnant woman is not allowed to exercise her right to individual choice. This tells us very little about the tensions between Lisa and her mother-in-law, the motivations of the mother-in-law to interfere, and the reasons for Lisa to acquiesce.

In contrast to this reductionist theoretical framework, the intimate choices approach assumes that the uncertainties of women's childbirth experiences always involve moral frictions and negotiations among multiple actors and that whether a pregnant woman has the capacity or not to make an informed individual choice depends on the networks and configurations of power shaping the collaborative arrangements of the birthing process.

This approach can be applied to any context, but one needs to take into account the specificities of each context. One important characteristic of the Chinese context is that most women give birth in public hospitals or clinics because this option is more economical than the private sector. Another important characteristic is that childbirth management in Chinese public hospitals is explicitly and institutionally conceptualized as a complex process of negotiation among multiple actors. Informed consent for cesarean surgery, for instance, entails a number of hospital protocols and legal regulations that postulate a process of collective negotiation among the pregnant woman, her close family members, and the medical doctor. In this framework, doctors are considered very powerful actors; they have the capacity to make a unilateral decision for cesarean in an emergency. But most stories of birth involve some degree of triangulation. A birthing mother who wants to have a cesarean delivery needs to have her request approved by the doctor, but her close family members, usually the husband and the mother-in-law, must also formally consent, and the doctor has to collect their signatures.

When Lisa decided on a cesarean delivery at the last minute, the doctor granted consent quickly because he himself had recommended a cesarean. (I don't analyze the motivations of the doctor here because I am primarily interested in the role of close family members, especially the mother-in-law.) Then the doctor tried to obtain formal consent from Lisa's mother-in-law, but she refused—even after several rounds of angry warnings from the doctor. Yi-dai's commitment to her stance makes it quite clear that it was not taken lightly but was the product of strong moral convictions. Still, respect for doctors is substantial; Yi-dai probably would not have challenged the doctor if Mou-dai had not been present to strengthen her determination.

From the point of view of Yi-dai, choosing the "right" childbirth method is not about a matter of safeguarding the birthing mother's right to individual choice and bodily autonomy but rather safeguarding the reputation and welfare of her patrilineal family and community. Rather than framing childbirth as a wholly individual act, the mother-in-law framed childbirth as a question of collectivity, moral responsibility, and shared communal fate. She favored a vaginal delivery because it is two to three times cheaper than having a cesarean, and this means that it is the best option to protect the economic needs of the larger patrilineal family. There is also the fact that vaginal delivery is generally healthier and less intrusive than a cesarean and so presumably the best choice for protecting the well-being of Lisa and the baby. Yi-dai also trusted the wisdom of her own mother, an experienced midwife, who had examined Lisa and saw no need for surgical intervention. Finally, vaginal delivery is more reputable than a cesarean because it protects the good name of Lisa as a virtuous mother and the good name of the family as a virtuous family in the eyes of the local community, family ancestors, and the local gods.

This view of childbirth choices as acts of moral commitment fits nicely with Lisa's own view of what happened. Lisa had initially valued a vaginal birth, but she changed her mind when she judged her pain to be unbearable. When both Yi-dai and Mou-dai pushed back against her decision and her reason for it, Lisa felt compelled to follow the advice of her senior female relatives. Yes, she felt powerless to arrest her suffering, but nothing in our repeated conversations and interviews over the years suggests that she conceptualized this powerlessness as a violation of her rights of individual choice. For Lisa, individual choice is important but not an inalienable right; she does not see herself as an autonomous individual but as an individual member of larger moral collectives. She undoubtedly experienced her mother-in-law's rejection of her cesarean request as a violation of her personal liberties but not necessarily morally offensive because, as a member of larger moral collectives, she has not only personal liberties but also social responsibilities. Lisa agreed to follow the advice of her senior female relatives, which indicates the extent to which she was aware of these social responsibilities. By choosing the "right" technology, Lisa—not unlike Yi-dai—is trying to anchor herself within the moral communities that make up her day-to-day life worlds and she has many reasons to think that these moral communities will be more important for her (and her children's) future as sources of social support than the money-mediated world of hospitals and medical experts.

BIRTH CHOICES BEYOND INDIVIDUAL-COLLECTIVE OPPOSITIONS

Focusing on birth choices as acts of moral commitment joins other recent theoretical efforts to challenge "Euro-American" liberal assumptions of individual choice in studies of reproduction and reproductive technologies.[35] Writing about the moral dilemmas faced by present-day Vietnamese mothers using advanced prenatal-testing technologies, anthropologist Tine Gammeltoft shows how these mothers are confronted with difficult life-and-death decisions about their pregnancies and refuse to conceptualize these decisions in terms of individual choice.[36] For these mothers, the decision to put an end to a pregnancy is a collective decision through which they strive to tie themselves into relations with others and become part of something larger. These decisions—as Gammeltoft puts it—are not "acts of freedom," through which mothers reaffirm their sense of individual freedom and autonomy, but are "acts of belonging," through which mothers (and their families) try to reintegrate themselves into larger moral communities.[37] The story of Lisa's willingness to tolerate the interference of her mother-in-law and accept the reality of having a very painful vaginal delivery can certainly be read as a story of "collective moral belonging" in Gammeltoft's sense.

We must be careful, however, not to overstate the emphasis on "collective moral belonging" because this expression invokes a series of classic social science analytical dichotomies between individuals and collectives and between personal liberties and social responsibilities. These dichotomies are at the heart of modern thought and classic social science theorizations, and they are still very influential in shaping institutions and processes of policy making globally.[38] However, they are not very helpful in making sense of the moral tensions shaping the increasing worldwide popularity of cesarean technologies. My intimate choices approach represents an attempt to overcome such analytical dichotomies as well as related Orientalist narratives setting countries like China and the United States in opposition, along the lines of collectivist society versus individualist society.

When applied to childbirth, the intimate choices approach maintains that the technological choices involved in childbirth are neither solely individual (shaped by an individualist ideology of personal freedom and personal liberties) nor strictly collective (shaped by a collectivist ideology of social responsibilities and communal belonging). Whatever choices are involved in the uncertainties of childbirth are both individual *and* collective, reflecting a larger dynamic of context-specific moral frictions and negotiations among multiple actors.

Although probably present in some form in most contexts, these frictions and negotiations are particularly salient in contemporary societies due to the increasing impact of ideologies of reproductive consumerism in women's ideas and experiences of childbirth.[39] As consumers of reproductive technologies, pregnant women are increasingly expected to make their own childbirth choices and to develop their own moral narratives around these choices, but this process of ethical subjectivation is not as straightforward as it may seem at first.[40] There are often multiple options available—for example, vaginal delivery or elective cesarean—and each option is legitimate and has its own moral community of supporters. Some of these communities reside within the boundaries of one's immediate day-to-day world; others reside outside this immediate world, quite often on the internet in the virtual world of social media. This means that young women like Lisa develop their ideas about childbirth in a larger landscape of moral frictions and disagreements, and they have to engage in complex negotiations with multiple actors.

The intimate choices approach highlights the importance of focusing on the complex moral frictions and negotiations shaping women's childbirth experiences. In contrast to Gammeltoft's emphasis on a unified framework of collective moral belonging, the intimate choices approach does not look at Lisa's willingness to tolerate the interference of her mother-in-law as a story of moral commitment to one's collective because it problematizes the very idea of a unified moral collective and recognizes the existence of significant moral disagreements within the collective. In rural townships like Yellow Flower, senior female relatives continue to play an important role in shaping the childbirth ideals of younger mothers. Sometimes there is a good mutual understanding and convergence of opinions. In these cases, the moral views of the younger mother and the older mothers converge around the "traditional" value that a good mother must be able to endure the physical pain of vaginal birth. The younger mother may support this ideal and view older mothers like Mou-dai as a source of wisdom and reproductive advice but there are also many exceptions to this rule. In the case of Lisa, the convergence of opinions was only partial: Lisa and Yi-dai initially agreed on the importance of having a vaginal delivery, but Lisa changed her mind, and Yi-dai did not. This led to a moral clash, but Lisa ended up agreeing with Yi-dai's decision, and they subsequently came to terms with their differences.

Not all cases are so harmonious. Some involve a much more radical clash of moral positions, and the birthing mother's request for a cesarean is often an attempt to differentiate herself from the old-fashioned views of senior female relatives and to assert her "modern" sense of individual freedom and autonomy.[41] A particularly dramatic example of such a radical clash of moral positions is the case of Mou-dai's youngest daughter-in-law, Kathy, who delivered her two children by means of cesarean procedures that were criticized by Mou-dai as unnecessary. Kathy married Mou-dai's youngest son in 2005 and had their first child in 2010 and their second in 2014. Both children were delivered by cesarean, and Kathy told me in 2012 and again in 2017 that having a vaginal delivery is very risky and physically challenging and may no longer suit the needs of many women in contemporary society. Both her children were delivered in a hospital in the city of Guangzhou, and on both occasions Kathy wanted to plan an elective cesarean but could not do it because of her mother-in-law's insistence that she should have a vaginal delivery. Both births followed a similar sequence of events: Everything was arranged for a vaginal delivery, but Kathy requested a cesarean soon after the beginning of labor on the grounds that she would not be able to endure the pain and the physical demands of a vaginal delivery. Kathy told me that the key to the success of her two cesareans was having strong support from her husband. Her husband was present in the hospital for both births and was the one to sign the cesarean consent form. Her mother-in-law was also present in the hospital, but her husband was the one responsible for paying the hospital bill so his consent was considered sufficient.

Cases like Kathy's—a radical moral clash between young mothers and their mothers-in-law—help expose the limitations of approaches to birth choices that are too focused on the notion of collective moral belonging. When talking about her two birthing experiences, Kathy did not describe her decision to have a cesarean in the language of collective moral belonging but rather of bodily autonomy and individual freedom. She finds no fault with elective cesarean delivery, and she is aware that her view is controversial and clashes with the views of some close family members and the default assumption of her local community in Yellow Flower. But she also notes that a growing number of local women have a positive attitude toward cesareans because they find vaginal delivery to be very risky and not always possible to achieve. Kathy thinks that women should be allowed to have more choice in the process of childbirth, but instead of referencing individual human rights to justify this view, she draws on the language of consumerism: women as reproductive consumers should be allowed to request cesareans if they decide that this is the right choice to protect themselves and their babies. Kathy suspects that older women like her mother-in-law who are critical of elective cesarean procedures are biased toward their own childbirth experiences. From the perspective of women like Kathy, finding ways to handle these moral disagreements without cutting important ties with senior female relatives is a significant component of the ethical life of their village community.

The problem with approaches to reproductive choices that are too focused on the notion of collective moral belonging is that they evoke earlier Orientalist research agendas and their tendency to place too much emphasis on collectives *as opposed to* individuals, on moral obligations *as opposed to* personal liberties. Gammeltoft's emphasis on collective moral belonging was meant to challenge the global purchase of contemporary Silicon Valley ideologies describing engagement with new technologies as a form of empowerment that allows individuals to achieve greater autonomy. I agree with this critique but I think that we should not overstate it to the point of throwing the baby out with the bathwater. The idea that we have to focus on *either* issues of moral responsibility *or* issues of personal liberty is itself an artifact of classic social science antinomies opposing individualistic and collectivist ethical systems. The intimate choices approach proposes a dialectical framework that recognizes the continuing centrality of moral collectives, ties of sociality, and networks of social support—without dismissing women's efforts to detach themselves from larger moral obligations and assert a stronger sense of individual freedom. From the perspective of elderly representatives of "traditional" moral authority like Mou-dai, the reproductive choices of women like Kathy are acts of moral defiance that can only harm the well-being of women, families, and communities. But from Kathy's perspective, her choice of cesarean is an act of liberation from an outdated ideology that no longer attends to the needs of women in contemporary society. This act of liberation does not just result in detachment from "tradition"; it also leads to new moral commitments as part of a growing community of mothers who are challenging "traditional" ideals of childbirth and subsequently creating some new ones.

CONCLUSION

Making sense of this dialectic of detachment and commitment, liberation and obligation, requires a processual approach that is not built around classic social science antinomies between the individual and the collective, and personal liberties and moral responsibilities. One of the advantages of such a processual approach is that it offers an alternative theoretical framework to the more conventional Orientalist narrative setting Chinese and American birthing systems in opposition along the lines of a collectivist society versus an individualist society. Instead of assuming a priori that in the United States childbirth is primarily about personal liberties and in China it is primarily about collective moral responsibilities, the intimate choices approach maintains that childbirth is full of uncertainties and is everywhere shaped by complex moral frictions and negotiations among multiple actors. These frictions and negotiations are context specific, but they are everywhere structured around an important tension between personal liberties and social responsibilities. The tension should not be understood in antithetical terms but in dialectical terms. Rather than being a fatal flaw of some kind, the tension between personal liberties and social responsibilities is necessary to produce workable versions of technology-mediated care and well-being in the context of childbirth.

I have provided several ethnographic illustrations of this dialectic of personal liberties and social responsibilities in rural women's childbirth experiences, drawing particular attention to the tense relations between younger mothers and their senior female relatives. This dialectical approach allows one to interpret a mother-in-law's rejection of a maternal cesarean request as a form of oppression (a denial of the birthing woman's personal liberties.) But it also allows one to interpret this act of "oppression" as a form of *care* (aimed at fulfilling collective social responsibilities). In the same manner, this dialectical approach allows one to interpret a maternal cesarean request as an act of selfishness and irresponsibility (betraying "traditional" collective expectations), but it also allows one to interpret this act of "selfishness" as an act of liberation that gives the mother a stronger sense of individual freedom and personal autonomy. It allows her to connect to other cesarean mothers and thus to participate in the construction of new technocratic visions of childbirth in the context of increasingly globalized local and translocal networks of moral belonging.

NOTES

1. See, for example, Francesca Bray, "Tools of Virtuous Action," in *Ordinary Ethics in China*, ed. Charles Stafford (London: Bloomsbury, 2013); Ruth Cowan, *More Work for Mother: The Ironies of Household Technology from the Open Hearth to the Microwave* (New York: Basic Books, 1983); Sarah Franklin, "Revisiting Reprotech: Firestone and the Question of Technology," in *Further Adventures of the Dialectic of Sex: Critical Essays on Shulamith Firestone*, ed. Mandy Merck and Stella Sandford (New York:

Palgrave Macmillan, 2010), 29–60; Sarah Franklin, *Embodied Progress: A Cultural Account of Assisted Reproduction* (London: Routledge, 2002); Robbie Davis-Floyd, *Birth as an American Rite of Passage*, 2nd ed. (Berkeley: University of California Press, 2004); Marilyn Strathern, *Reproducing the Future: Anthropology, Kinship and the New Reproductive Technologies* (Manchester, UK: Manchester University Press, 1990); Michelle Murphy, *Seizing the Means of Reproduction: Entanglements of Feminism, Health, and Technoscience* (Durham, NC: Duke University Press, 2012); and Tine Gammeltoft, *Haunting Images: A Cultural Account of Selective Reproduction in Vietnam* (Berkeley: University of California Press, 2014). On "technological and moral change" in general, see Bruno Latour, "Morality and Technology: The End of the Means," *Theory, Culture & Society* 19, no. 5–6 (2002): 247–60; Shannon Vallor, *Technology and the Virtues: A Philosophical Guide to a Future Worth Wanting* (Oxford: Oxford University Press, 2016); Peter-Paul Verbeek, "Materializing Morality: Design Ethics and Technological Mediation," *Science, Technology and Human Values* 31, no. 3 (2006): 361–80; and Sheila Jasanoff, "Ordering Knowledge, Ordering Society," in *States of Knowledge: The Co-Production of Science and Social Order* (London: Routledge, 2004), 13–45.

2. For a medically informed overview, see Ana Pilar Betrán et al., "The Increasing Trend in Caesarean Section Rates: Global, Regional and National Estimates: 1990–2014," *PLoS One* 11, no. 2 (2016): e0148343; and Ana Pilar Betrán et al., "Trends and Projections of Caesarean Section Rates: Global and Regional Estimates," *BMJ Global Health* Volume 6, Issue 6 (2021): 1–8 doi:10.1136/bmjgh-2021-005671.

3. Davis-Floyd, *Birth*; Robbie Davis-Floyd, "The Technocratic Body: American Childbirth as Cultural Expression," *Social Science & Medicine* 38 (1994): 1125–40; and Christa Craven, *Pushing for Midwives: Homebirth Mothers and the Reproductive Rights Movement* (Philadelphia, PA: Temple University Press, 2010).

4. Not all North American mothers fit into these two opposing models of childbirth, but the frictions between them are a defining feature of the larger ethical landscape of childbirth and motherhood in contemporary North American society.

5. On "birthing systems," see Brigitte Jordan, *Birth in Four Cultures: A Cross-Cultural Investigation of Childbirth in Yucatan, Holland, Sweden,*

and the United States, 4th ed (1978; repr. Prospect Heights, IL: Waveland, 1993); and Robbie Davis-Floyd and Melissa Cheney, eds., *Birth in Eight Cultures* (Prospect Heights, IL: Waveland, 2019).

6. On the history of rising cesarean deliveries in the United States, see Jacqueline Wolf, *Cesarean Section: An American History of Risk, Technology, and Consequence* (Baltimore, MD: Johns Hopkins University Press, 2018).

7. WHO and HRP, "WHO Statement on Caesarean Section Rates," 2015, http://www.who.int/reproductivehealth/publications/maternal_perinatal _health/cs-statement/en/.

8. On the "technocratic model of birth," see Davis-Floyd, *Birth*; and Davis-Floyd, "The Technocratic Body." For 1990 rates, see Xing Lin Feng, Ling Xu, Yan Guo, and Carine Ronsmans, "Factors Influencing Rising Caesarean Section Rates in China Between 1988 and 2008," *Bulletin of the World Health Organization* 90, no. 1 (2012): 30–39. For 2014 rates, see Hongtian Li et al., "Geographic Variations and Temporal Trends in Cesarean Delivery Rates in China, 2008–2014," *JAMA* 317, no. 1 (2017): 69–76.

9. By "natural," women in China mean vaginal, not analgesic-free vaginal, which "natural childbirth" often means to U.S. women. Unlike the near ubiquitous access to epidurals in U.S. hospitals, most public hospitals in China do not provide pain relief medication during standard vaginal delivery.

10. See, for example, Ann Oakley, *The Captured Womb: A History of the Medical Care of Pregnant Women* (Oxford: Basil Blackwell, 1986); Ann Oakley, *Women Confined: Towards a Sociology of Childbirth* (Oxford: Martin Robertson, 1980); Jean Donnison, *Midwives and Medical Men: A History of Inter-Professional Social Rivalries and Women's Rights* (New York: Schocken, 1977); Barbara Ehrenreich and Deirdre English, *For Her Own Good: Two Centuries of the Experts' Advice to Women*, 2nd ed. (1979; repr. New York: Anchor, 2005); Barbara Ehrenreich and Deirdre English, *Witches, Midwives, and Nurses: A History of Women Healers*, 2nd ed. (1973; repr. New York: Feminist, 2010); Barbara K. Rothman, *In Labor: Women and Power in the Birthplace* (New York: Norton, 1982); Barbara K. Rothman, *A Bun in the Oven: How the Food and Birth Movements Resist Industrialization* (New York: NYU Press, 2016); Judy Wajcman, *Feminism Confronts Technology* (Cambridge: Polity, 1991), chap. 3;

Cecilia Van Hollen, *Birth on the Threshold: Childbirth and Modernity in South India* (Berkeley: University of California Press, 2003); Suzanne Z. Gottschang, "Reproductive Modernities in Policy: Maternal Mortality, Midwives, and Cesarean Sections in China, 1900s–2000s," *Technology and Culture* 61, no. 2 (2020): 617–44; Sheila Cosminsky, *Midwives and Mothers: The Medicalization of Childbirth on a Guatemalan Plantation* (Austin: University of Texas Press, 2016); Gonçalo D. Santos and Suzanne Z. Gottschang, "Rethinking Reproductive Technologies and Modernities in Time and Space," *Technology and Culture* 61, no. 2 (2020): 549–58; Gonçalo Santos, "Birthing Stories and Techno-Moral Change Across Generations. Coping with Hospital Births and High-Tech Medicalization in Rural South China, 1960s-2010s," *Technology and Culture* 61, no. 2 (2020): 581–616; Gonçalo Santos, *Chinese Village Life Today: Building Families in an Age of Transition* (Seattle: University of Washington Press, 2021), chap. 4; Chiaki Shirai, *Umisodateto josan'no rekisi* (History of childbirth: childrearing and midwifery in Japan) (Tokyo: Igakushoin, 2016); and Chiaki Shirai, "Historical Dynamism of Childbirth in Japan: Medicalization and Its Normative Politics, 1868–2017," *Technology and Culture* 61, no. 2 (2020): 559–80.

11. Pisake Lumbiganon et al., "World Health Organization Global Survey on Maternal and Perinatal Health Research Group. Method of Delivery and Pregnancy Outcomes in Asia: The WHO Global Survey on Maternal and Perinatal Health 2007–08," *Lancet* 375, no. 9713 (2010): 490–99.

12. Juan Liang et al., "Relaxation of the One Child Policy and Trends in Caesarean Section Rates and Birth Outcomes in China Between 2012 and 2016: Observational Study of Nearly Seven Million Health Facility Births," *BMJ* 360 (2018): k817; Lara Owen and Aidila Razak, "Why Chinese Mothers Turned Away from C-Sections," BBC World Service, March 2, 2019, https://www.bbc.com/news/world-asia-china-46265808; and Ming Die, "Guojia wei jian wei: 900 yu jia yiyuan jiang kaizhan wutong fenmian shidian" (National Health and Medical Commission: More than 900 hospitals will launch pilot programs for painless delivery), News.China.com.cn., August 22, 2019, http://news.china.cn/2019-08/22/content_75125715.htm.

13. There is some evidence of a slight decline in urban areas since 2014. See Liang et al., "Relaxation of the One Child Policy and Trends." But the

significance of this decline is debatable. My colleague Jun Zhang has gained access to a large database from a major public hospital in the city of Guangzhou that points to an average cesarean rate of 38.5 percent between 2015 and 2017. This database includes detailed information on more than 30,000 deliveries taking place between January 2015 and April 2017 (except for May 2015). The parents of these babies are not necessarily Guangzhou natives, but at least one of the four addresses provided to the hospital (including contact address and address of household registration of both parents) is located in one of the city's ten administrative districts. The cesarean rate of this hospital between January 2015 and April 2017 oscillated between a minimum rate of 29 percent and a maximum rate of 39.7 percent. In April 2017, the cesarean rate was still as high as 39.6 percent. See Gonçalo D. Santos and Jun Zhang, "The Rise in Cesarean Births and the Technocratic Medicalization of Childbirth in Late-Reform China." *Modern China: An International Journal of History and Social Science*, first published online February 20, 2024.

14. Jennifer M. Torres and Raymond G. De Vries, "Birthing Ethics: What Mothers, Families, Childbirth Educators, Nurses, and Physicians Should Know About the Ethics of Childbirth," *Journal of Perinatal Education* 18, no. 1 (2009): 12–24.

15. For an account of the Chinese medical tradition of informed consent, see Yali Cong, "Doctor-Family-Patient Relationship. The Chinese Paradigm of Informed Consent," *Journal of Medical Philosophy* 29, no. 2 (2004): 149–78.

16. On the extended case method, see Max Gluckman, "Ethnographic Data in British Social Anthropology," *Sociological Review* 9, no. 1 (1961): 5–17; and Michael Burawoy, "The Extended Case Method," *Sociological Theory* 16, no. 1 (1998): 4–33. This account also draws on Santos, "Birthing Stories"; and Santos, *Chinese Village Life Today*, chap. 4.

17. Richard Madsen, "Beyond the Clash of Civilizations: Seeking the Common Good Through East-West Dialogue," paper presented at the Research Workshop on Culture and Society, Initiative for U.S.-China Dialogue on Global Issues, Georgetown University, Unpublished Manuscript, 2019. See also chapter 2 this volume.

18. On the "intimate choices approach," see Gonçalo Santos, "On Intimate Choices and Troubles in Rural South China," *Modern Asian Studies* 50,

no. 4 (2016): 1298–1326; Gonçalo Santos, "Multiple Mothering and Labor Migration in Rural South China," in *Transforming Patriarchy: Chinese Families in the Twenty-First Century*, ed. Gonçalo Santos and Stevan Harrell (Seattle: University of Washington Press, 2017), 31–65; Gonçalo Santos, "Love, Family, and Gender in 21st Century China," in *Socialism with Neoliberal Characteristics*, ed. K. W. Endres and C. Hann (New York: Max Planck Institute for Social Anthropology, 2017); Santos, "Birthing Stories"; and Santos, *Chinese Village Life Today*. See also Charles Stafford, ed., *Ordinary Ethics in China* (London: Routledge, 2013); and Yunxiang Yan, *The Individualization of Chinese Society* (New York: Berg, 2009).

19. Elsewhere I draw on the work of Karl Polanyi to conceptualize this dialectical framework as a synthesis of personal and social freedom. See Gonçalo D. Santos, Yichen Rao, Jack L. Xing, and Jun Zhang, "Capitalism, Overwork, and Polanyi's Dialectics of Freedom. Emerging Visions of Work-Life Balance in Contemporary Urban China," in *Work, Ethics and Freedom: Chimeras of Freedom in the Neoliberal Era*, ed. Chris Hann (Oxford: Berghahn, 2021), 132–57.

20. For more details on home births, see Santos, *Chinese Village Life Today*, chap. 4; and Santos, "Birthing Stories."

21. Ngai Fen Cheung and Rosemary Mander, *Midwifery in China* (London: Routledge, 2018).

22. In rural Northern Guangdong, mothers are not expected to provide childbirth and childcare support to their daughters because their primary care responsibilities are towards their daughters-in-law. Marriage practices in this part of China remain strongly patrilocal and this means that a daughter is expected to marry out and move into her husband's family and community upon marriage. In this context, there remains a clear-cut patrilineal bias in local household patterns of division of labor when it comes to maternity care support.

23. For a moving documentary film account of some of these tensions in a public hospital in Wuhan, see Weijun Chen, dir., "This Is Life" (*Shengmen*), 2016, China documentary film.

24. An episiotomy is a surgical incision made at the opening of the vagina during childbirth to aid a difficult delivery and prevent rupture of tissues. The episiotomy is usually performed during the second stage of labor to quickly enlarge the opening for the baby to pass through. The

surgical cut is often repaired after delivery with stitches (sutures). There is no agreement on the medical benefits of the routine use of episiotomies, but it remains one of the most common medical procedures performed on women. In many countries, the stitching after delivery involves the use of local anesthetic.

25. Santos, "Birthing Stories"; and Eileen Wang, "Requests for Cesarean Deliveries: The Politics of Labor Pain and Pain Relief in Shanghai, China," *Social Science & Medicine* 173, suppl. C (2017): 1–8.

26. On blaming mothers for the outcome of childbearing, see Gammeltoft, *Haunting Images*, 134–35.

27. Here is the original quotation in local Cantonese: "nung-chyun fu-neui saang-ng-cheut sin hoi-dou, ng-chi sing-si fu-neui jou jau gai-waak hoi-dou" (农村妇女生唔出先开刀,唔似城市妇女早就计划开刀).

28. Bray, "Tools of Virtuous Action," 13–45.

29. See, for example, Qi Wang, *Huaiyun, Anchan, Yuezi: Yi Ji Shen* (Pregnancy, safe birth, postnatal confinement: do's and don'ts) (Beijing: Zhongguo Renkou Chubanshe, 2011); Yongmei Chen, *Anchan, Zuo Yuezi, Xinshenger Huli Yibentong* (Safe birth, postnatal confinement, infant care comprehensive manual) (Beijing: Zhongguo Nongye Chubanshe, 2013); Yuqiao Zheng, *Zheng Yuqiao Yu'er Baihuo* (Zheng Yuqiao's encyclopedia of childcare) (Beijing: Huaxue Gongye Chubanshe, 2015); Zouyan Lin and Yuru Zhou, *Huaren Yu'er Baike* (Encyclopedia of child care for Chinese people) (Beijing: Beijing Lianhe Chubanshe, 2016); Shuqing Jiang, *Hao Xin Qing Bei Yun* (Good mood for pregnancy). (Nanjing: Yilin Chubanshe, 2016); Liangkun Ma, ed., *Xie he Zhuanjia + Xie he Mama Quan Ganhuo Fenxiang: Chan Jian* (Cooperate with experts, cooperate with circle of moms' substantial sharing: antenatal examination) (Beijing: Zhongguo Qinggongye Chubanshe, 2016); Liangkun Ma, ed., *Xie he Zhuanjia + Xie he Mamaquan Ganhuo Fenxiang: Huaiyun* (Cooperate with experts, cooperate with circle of moms' substantial sharing: pregnancy) (Beijing: Zhongguo Qinggongye Chubanshe, 2016); and Xiaoyu Pan, *Quan Huli: Hao Yun an Chan Bai Ke* (Complete nursing: good pregnancy and safe birth) (Beijing: Beijing Llianhe Chubanshe, 2017).

30. Examples of popular internet forums and WeChat public accounts include Mom Help (mama bang), Baby Tree (baobao shu), Craddle

Net (yaolan wang), Good Pregnancy Mother (haoyun mama), Number One Gynaecology (diyi fuchan), Little Home Bean (dian dian jia de tu xiao dou), Clove Mother (ding xiang mama), Six Mamas Luo Luo (liu ma luo luo), Dr. Pei (pei yisheng), and Snowball Mama (xueqiu mama).

31. Domestication theory is a well-known theoretical framework in science and technology studies and media studies that describes the process by which technology is "tamed" by its users. Domestication theory draws on qualitative methodologies such as long interviews and ethnography to highlight the role of users in innovation—the work of appropriation, translation and conversion done by individuals and communities to make a technology from the outside do practical work, and to make sense within that community. Here I am arguing that expert medical advice, like technology, needs to be appropriated and domesticated by users in the context of everyday social interactions to be evaluated, adapted, translated, and converted into something useful and meaningful.

32. See, for example, Ehrenreich and English, *Witches, Midwives, and Nurses*; Rothman, *In Labor*; Rothman, *A Bun in the Oven*; Emily Martin, *The Woman in the Body: A Cultural Analysis of Reproduction* (Boston: Beacon, 1987); Gena Corea, *The Mother Machine: Reproductive Technologies from Artificial Insemination to Artificial Wombs* (New York: Harper Collins, 1985); Oakley, *Women Confined*; and Oakley, *The Captured Womb*.

33. For a similar critique of the primacy of individual choice in Euro-American feminist approaches, see Marilyn Strathern, *The Gender of the Gift: Problems with Women and Problems with Society in Melanesia* (Berkeley: University of California Press, 1988).

34. For a detailed critical discussion of this argument and its limitations, see Stevan Harrell and Gonçalo Santos, eds., introduction to *Transforming Patriarchy: Chinese Families in the Twenty-First Century* (Seattle: University of Washington Press, 2016), 1–36.

35. See Gammeltoft, *Haunting Images*; and Lynn Marie Morgan and Meredith W. Michaels, eds., *Fetal Subjects, Feminist Positions* (Philadelphia: University of Pennsylvania Press, 1999).

36. Gammeltoft, *Haunting Images*.

37. This argument is in line with ancient Chinese traditions about the role of techniques and tools, or what we today call "technology," in society.

Writing about the period prior to nineteenth-century modernization, the philosopher of technology Yuk Hui shows that most Neo-Confucian, Daoist, and Buddhist writings about techniques and tools were less concerned with questions of mastery of natural processes than with questions of moral virtue and harmony. See Yuk Hui, *The Question Concerning Technology in China* (Cambridge: MIT Press, 2016). This way of thinking about "technology" as a philosophy of virtue (as opposed to a philosophy of nature) is useful in making sense of present-day moral tensions in China regarding the increasing popularity of cesarean technologies. Chinese women do not agree on the value of new cesarean technologies because they have different understandings of the right way to give birth, and these different "philosophical" conceptualizations of birthing methods and technologies reflect the existence of different local and translocal networks of moral belonging.

38. Bruno Latour, *We Have Never Been Modern* (Cambridge, MA: Harvard University Press, 1991); and Gammeltoft, *Haunting Images*.

39. See, for example, Davis-Floyd and Cheney, *Birth in Eight Cultures*.

40. See Zhang on the role of consumerism in gendered processes of ethical subjectivation in urban China. Jun Zhang, "(Extended) Family Car, Filial Consumer-Citizens: Becoming Properly Middle Class in Post-Socialist South China," *Modern China* 43, no. 1 (2017): 36–65.

41. This criticism of the "backwardness" of older women echoes widespread public discourses on the backwardness of elders and their incapacity to cope with the new realities of contemporary technological society. These discourses are particularly strong in debates on the education of rural "left-behind children." See Santos, "Multiple Mothering."

7

REPAIRED REFLECTIONS

The Associative Act of Preparing Burial Clothing

BECKY YANG HSU

It's a happy thing. Everybody does it.
I've had mine for more than ten years!

—Woman in Fujian (age seventy)

One sunny April afternoon Zhang Lanfen, whom I call auntie (Zhang *ayi*), brought out a box she had carefully stored away and showed me and some of her friends its contents.[1] The box contained burial clothing she had prepared for herself, along with a purse, hat, shoes, earrings, and a small laminated color portrait of herself. As she began passing the items around, her friends did not protest or reassure her that she was still healthy. One friend said, "These shoes are really nice. This kind of shoe is very pretty." And she proudly replied, "They were 10 yuan" (about $1.50 USD).

Within a couple of minutes it became clear that this group did not consider this a somber moment. Instead, her friends admired the items as she took them out of the box. She was asked about costs—especially when she took out a pair of sparkly drop earrings fit for a ball. (The earrings cost 500 yuan, about $83.) Zhang *ayi*, a vivacious woman in her seventies, a ballroom dancer, and a grandmother who volunteers at the temple, told us, "I'm going to put these on for you to see." Then she took the earrings out of the cellophane pouch one at a time and put them on, becoming suddenly shy for just a moment before laughing and pretending to slap someone.

One may wonder what put this group, Zhang *ayi*'s fellow volunteers at the temple, in such good humor. Perhaps, after toiling in this life, they were celebrating at the prospect of a friend having nice things upon exiting the world. Or perhaps they appreciated her future position, in the status of an ancestor, a part of the natural progression in life in which individuals continue to be visited and given gifts long after they have taken their last breath. "Death has been banished," writes Philippe Aries, a cultural historian of Western Europe.[2] "A new system of constraints and controls . . . has led society to be ashamed of death": but this "invisible death"—a milieu in which death has become a private and isolated event, mourning is hidden, and reminders of mortality are erased—did not seem to govern the attitudes of the individuals looking at Zhang *ayi*'s burial clothing that afternoon. Instead, these individuals were aging and addressing their mortality in a social context where death is understood in relation to the family, in that the individual has a future social identity of ancestor to the descendants that follow.

From the start, individuals in China are familiar with graves. The yearly calendar is organized around a few important holidays, one of which is Qingming, or Tomb Sweeping Day, a time to go visit the graves of parents and grandparents. People address the departed and present paper gifts. Mourning practices address death collectively, recurrently, and regularly throughout the lifetime in China.[3] When our national survey asked adults over age 18 whether they had gone grave sweeping in the previous year, 78 percent responded in the affirmative (and 73 percent did so on or around Tomb Sweeping Day in April, which is an official holiday; many also go on death anniversaries and other occasions). "Life is as beautiful as flowers," posted a young woman on social media with a photograph of herself wearing sunglasses and posing with her three stylishly dressed sisters at their father's grave. "Although the people and years of the past have left forever, they are still the unforgettable warmth in our lives. Another year has passed, and it's the day to visit my father's grave."[4]

As Fei Xiaotong's model of the self in differential modes of association depicts, individuals in China see themselves as the center in a network of social relationships with the closest family and friends near them, then acquaintances, and the rest of the world, like rings fanning out from a stone cast into a pond.[5] Every year when they visit the grave they reaffirm their ties to the departed, they are also confronted with the fact that one day they will be in the ground. Individuals occupy the center of their network and see themselves continuing to do so after passing away, remaining in the networks of their descendants as others still interact with them.

Preparing burial clothing is a "mode of associated living," or in John Dewey's terms, a "conjoint communicated experience."[6] It handily knits together a basic activity of life—getting dressed to meet people—with the status that will follow one's death: being an ancestor in the family lineage. It's during the mundane acts of choosing between textiles that a social fabric composed of both the dead and the living comes into existence as individuals anticipate being seen (after their death) by the living (their descendants). Self-presentation is a generative activity—as people present themselves to others through their choices, they are also weaving social material by interlacing strands of interaction between the living and the dead.[7] As much as they don't look forward to passing away, being seen by others is motivating;

imagining the funeral prompts self-presentation and image-building labor because there will be people present from their work unit, friendship circles, and family. A woman told me that preparing burial clothing is "a happy thing." A father of five received burial clothing and coffins as a thoughtful gift from his children, who want to look after him. The definition of the clothing as a way to cherish someone is shared by several women who buy their own burial clothing as an act of self-care. By procuring these tangible objects, they address death both as a normal occurrence and one that warrants special care.

Beginning with our own acquaintances, one research assistant and I identified thirty-one individuals (fifteen men and sixteen women) who prepared their burial clothing while healthy, or had their children prepare them, and who were willing to talk to us about it. Four of them lived in Yunnan, fourteen in Hunan, and thirteen in Fujian. All of them were from small towns rather than major cities, but they were not necessarily in remote areas. Most interviewees were in their fifties or sixties: the youngest was forty-four and the oldest was eighty-six. We viewed six sets of burial clothing people had prepared for themselves. Fieldwork was conducted from 2014 through 2016 and included spending time in a small funerary boutique in Xiamen.

SOCIAL ACKNOWLEDGMENT AS REPAIR

Paul Lichterman and Nina Eliasoph define civic action by three features: (1) participants coordinate interaction around a mission of problem-solving according to participants' sense of what a shared problem is, (2) participants coordinate ongoing interaction, and (3) participants act as members of a larger, imagined society.[8] The preparation of burial clothing meets the first and third characteristics of civic action, but it stretches the second characteristic.

The first quality of preparing burial clothing is like preemptive repair. It involves conceptualizing in a tangible way one's social representation after death. Around middle age, people realize that death is somewhere on the horizon, but are not used to thinking or talking about their own death. (Whether there is a particular Chinese taboo on talking about death is a subject of debate.[9]) As one ages, one's own death remains interiorly known but unacknowledged—leaving an important part of an individual's story out of the picture, and a fissure in the reflection of self that becomes increasingly obvious over time. This creates a growing sense of dissonance as people refrain from acknowledging aspects of themselves. If participants' sense of self is centered on their web of relationships, then one of the scariest things about death is the ending of those relationships. But if there are things people can do to continue those relationships—now between descendant and ancestor—then there is comfort in that continuity.

It would be difficult to overemphasize the importance of culture in how one approaches death: the symbols, meanings, and principles existing prior to individuals, the habits and norms of interaction (or lack thereof) revolving around this question, and the items that facilitate relationships. Individuals organized their ties to family and friends when they asked them to select or purchase it or showed them the clothing because these actions classified others by how close they were, and what role they played in their lives. Moreover, Erving Goffman's dramaturgical theory suggests that individuals employ gestures to manage the impressions that others have of them.[10] The audience's response, whether affirmative or disconfirming, becomes a vital part of how self-perception is constructed by an individual. The process of preparing burial clothing presents opportunities for individuals to receive acknowledgment from others—that they will die, but that they will remain socially important. The acknowledgment seems to provide relief from dissonance, reducing the discomfort felt when there is something important about us that is not acknowledged by others. A part of one's identity is recognized, reversing the distortion of self that had been occurring and mending the reflection of the self in others' eyes.[11] Like an ad hoc committee, the group coordinates interaction—the second aspect of Lichterman and Eliasoph's definition—for as long as needed to complete the task of preparing burial clothing, then dissolves when the task is complete.

That the preparation of burial clothing gestures at an ongoing community of living and deceased family members is remarkable. The third characteristic of civic action, that participants act as members of a larger, imagined society, is the most striking one here, because the community includes the living and the dead. When they imagine the individual being viewed by the living, it is done with an understanding that the relationship between the ancestor and the descendant continues on. Preparing burial clothing is an organized social interaction that repairs an individual's aging self while symbolically and creatively weaving together the mundane activities of the living with the realm of the afterlife. In China's historical and economic context, society is understood to be composed of many family lineages, each of which incorporate the living and the dead into ongoing communities. For an individual, the passage of time means dropping old statuses and taking up new roles in the community of the family. Young adults begin taking up responsibilities for taking care of elders when they get older. Elders become ancestors in this society of the living and the dead.

HISTORICAL AND ECONOMIC CONTEXT
OF BURIAL CLOTHING

Burial clothing as tangible objects embodying meaning has been a topic of discussion in old Chinese texts since at least 200 BCE. Then, as now, clothing had social significance. "Fashion is merely a product of social demands," Georg Simmel wrote, "even though the individual object which it creates or recreates may represent a more or less individual need."[12] Within the act of preparing clothing, an individual anticipates presenting one's self to an audience. Simmel noted that clothing is rarely about practical considerations. People select clothing to identify with a group—signal membership in it—while distinguishing their own place in it. Those who prepare their burial clothing are getting ready for their future place in the family and the larger community.

Interest in burial clothing in China is visible in family rituals going back to the Warring States period (471–221 BCE). The *Huainanzi*, a text of Chinese political philosophy compiled by scholars of the king's court in early Han China, includes a debate between intellectuals about whether it was better to have a lavish or a thrifty burial.[13] One member of the Han literati under Emperor Wu, a scholar-official named Yang Wang-sun, wished to avoid the excess, so he gave his son clear instructions:

> I wish to be buried naked so that I may return to my true home. You must not go against my wishes! When I am dead, put my corpse in a hemp bag, dig a hole in the ground seven feet deep, and lower me into it. Then take hold of the bag at the end where my feet are and pull it off so that my body will rest directly on the ground.

His son was not sure what to do, so he sought advice from an old friend of his father's, who sent a response directly back to Yang Wang-sun:

> Do you intend to appear naked in front of your ancestors? Personally I don't think you should do so. Moreover, the *Classic of Filial Piety* says: "Let clothes, coverlets, and inner and outer coffins be provided for the dead," and these after all represent the rules handed down from the sages. Why must you alone be different?

The debate continued, but evidence suggests that through late imperial China the standard for a good burial consistently included having a high-quality coffin, burial clothing, and funerary gifts.

This standard has persisted, at least for some, into the twenty-first century.[14] Things have changed since the 1940s, when Francis Hsu observed an old man happily standing on his future grave and chatting "with pleasure and satisfaction" with his guests on Tomb Sweeping Day, in a small town in Yunnan province.[15] Yet the reflection of a long history of mourning practices—in which there is a notion of the self that remains connected to the family in death, just as in life—is still visible. The meaning of old age as a time to enjoy one's authority has existed since dynastic times, when people lived "under the ancestors' shadow" and prepared tombstones and graves early, speaking of them with pride as if they were a family residence for the living.[16] His life had turned out well, which was reflected in the large red square paper with the word "blessing" (*fu*) pasted on his tomb, and having a beautiful grave affirmed that he was prepared for what came next. "We all have to be prepared for it," a young man in another family said about his father's future funeral.[17]

During the Mao era, the funeral as a socialist memorial ceremony was created that highlighted the relationship of the deceased to the state and "grievability," or deservingness to be mourned, defined by what the individual had done for the state.[18] For most people, the state provided funeral benefits according to old customs. "At the same time that the new communist leaders vehemently favored favored simple, secular burials, they failed systematically to alter actual funeral practices," according to Deborah Davis-Friedmann.[19]

After reforms in 1979 the family structure in China underwent changes, including the implementation of the one-child policy from 1980 to 2016, which produced the "4-2-1 structure" whereby one child receives abundant attention from four grandparents and two parents.[20] Reflecting the importance of workplace and kinship, typical funerals today include a eulogy given by a work unit representative (usually describing the deceased as a model socialist citizen) along with a family eulogy, and sometimes with Buddhist elements.[21]

Preparing burial clothing requires stability—a place to store them, and friends and family nearby to know where they are—as well as some disposable income. Over the past few decades of rapid urbanization and marketization, most people in China have enjoyed a substantial increase in disposable income despite fluctuations in the national economy and increased inequality. According to the Chinese National Bureau of Statistics, the annual per capita disposable income of urban households increased more than threefold in fifteen years, from 11,619 yuan in 2006 to 35,128 yuan in 2021.[22] That's an additional 23,509 yuan (almost $4,000 USD). This generation of elders has a material life that is much better than what they had growing up (through the 1940s and 1950s), so they consider themselves fairly comfortable.

Burial clothing is not tightly regulated by the government today, and clothing sets bought and made specifically for burial have a recognizable style: "the eight-piece suit" or "the nine-piece suit" (which adds a cloak). Most are styled as a Tang dynasty (618–907) suit or a Chinese tunic suit, with layers of undergarments. This clothing style evokes a kind of timelessness by referring to a historical past and a representation of an immutable China. A complete burial set adds accessories such as bedding, a hat, shoes and socks, a handkerchief, and jewelry.

Burial clothing can be purchased online or in person. In 2019, a search on *Taobao* (the online marketplace where most internet shopping happens in China) revealed about eight hundred shops offering burial clothing in a diversity of styles. It is also possible to purchase burial clothing for much less, around 500–600 yuan ($83–$100), at funerary shops that also sell paper items for offerings and provide services for ceremonies. These shops are often strategically located near hospitals or cemeteries. Handmade pieces are available at some boutique-style shops. I interviewed one shop owner who produced burial clothing as a mother-daughter enterprise: the daughter owned and managed the shop, which sold both ready-to-wear and handmade clothing (made by her mother).

Ruifuxiang is one of the largest providers of ready-to-wear, having made burial clothing since the mid-1970s. The two thousand employees in Tianjin (northeast China) who work in Ruifuxiang's factories and in sales produce five thousand pieces of burial clothing per day, with annual sales of over 50 million yuan ($8.3 million).[23] A typical full set of burial clothing from Ruifuxiang costs the consumer about 2,000 yuan (about $330) if the suit is cotton. A package with a silk suit can cost 4,000 yuan ($660) or more.

ONE'S PLACE IN
THE IMAGINED COMMUNITY:
FAMILY AND THE ART OF MOURNING

As a symbolic system and a way of ordering reality, family rela-tionships provide organizing principles in the event of death, with specific roles designated by generation and relationship to the deceased. In one recent study, rural Chinese elderly articu-lated an ideal scenario of having their children gathered around their death bed.[24] At the parent's last breath, the oldest son would lift the deceased parent while other siblings change the parent into burial clothes before the onset of rigor mortis. Then the son would lead the burial activities of putting the body of his deceased parent into the coffin, holding as big a funeral as pos-sible, and bearing the coffin to the family grave.

The task of managing one's various connections, of associ-ating appropriately, continues in death, and parents like having their adult children assist with it. For Yang Guanghong, it had to be that his children buy burial clothing and coffins for him and his wife. A retired party cadre in Yunnan, and a member of the Dai, one of the fifty-six officially recognized ethnic groups in China, he had enough money to buy everything himself, but he wanted to make sure he could bless his children, grandchildren, and other descendants after he died. If they helped him, it would be an expression of filial piety, of helping him get ready.

Yang Guanghong began to think about his coffin. He sported a short buzzcut for his salt-and-pepper hair, and on the day we interviewed him, he wore gray dress slacks and light-yellow plas-tic slippers. When the weather was warm, he liked to sit shirtless in a well-worn bamboo-and-wicker chair in his courtyard. He had handled administrative work in the county. Typically, vil-lage cadres are competent individuals who are respected by other villagers enough so that they can get tasks done that require villagers' cooperation. Some tasks are easier, such as managing the sale of crops, distributing subsidies, and taking care of public security issues such as fights or theft; but other tasks are more difficult, such as collecting taxes and government fees.

Guanghong was busy with this work for decades, but that changed when he retired. He was a bit bored and had "nothing to do" after he retired. Having extra time and energy, he started doing some carpentry work. In the meantime, he began dropping hints to his children that he wanted coffins and burial clothes for himself and his wife, to whom he had been married for fifty years.

He got a tremendous response from his six adult children, five daughters and a son. His children were somewhat scattered by location, but they came home during the lunar New Year. Their oldest daughter married and moved to Sichuan province, the furthest from home of all their children. The rest stayed in Yunnan province: one lived in the big city of Kunming, another in a nearby town, and the last two daughters stayed in the county. Their youngest, now married, lives in the same village with them. Their son works in the county government. All but one became involved in the preparations.

During the lunar New Year, when everyone was back home visiting, four of his daughters discussed and coordinated the efforts to buy their parents' coffins. The coffins cost 8,000 RMB together (about $1,300). Being a carpenter, Guanghong was particular about what he wanted. The dimensions of the coffins needed to be exact: 65 cm wide by 63 cm deep at the head, 50 cm deep and 53 cm wide at the foot, with a total length of 222 cm.

Seeing his sisters' contribution to their parents' preparations, Guanghong's son set about getting Dai burial clothes custom-made for them by tailors in town, costing 1,200 RMB ($200). The burial clothes were all in black, consisting of a top and pants for him, and a top with a skirt for his wife.

Within a year of his hint-dropping, Guanghong got the coffins and burial clothing that he wanted. His son brought the clothes home and showed them to his parents. They showed the whole village. To protect the coffins, he built a shed next to the house with just enough space for both coffins to protect them from the sun and rain damage. They kept the burial clothes in the coffins on the side of the house. "Although I have money to buy coffins and clothes to wear after death, I feel like if the clothes weren't purchased and prepared by my children for me, after I die, I won't protect my descendants," Guanghong said. "So it has to be that my children come to do these tasks."

The adult children came together to prepare for their parents' aging, with their father's retirement serving as a catalyst for organizing social relations. His hinting brought individuals to assume specific roles; his daughters collaborated to buy two coffins, prompting their brother to purchase burial clothes during the holidays. They had a shared task. The high-quality burial clothing, stored inside the coffins that were made just-so, were preparing a parent for death, and an act of love. For Guanghong and his wife, seeing the shed on the side of the house reminded them of their children's enduring support. Getting organized for the transition to the next stage, the final steps of life, was a way to create order. When Guanghong started to feel the urge to prepare, he hinted to his children that he wanted burial clothing and a coffin. Once these things were ready, he found relief. For him, preparing the burial clothing got his adult children involved in his transition to old age and his preparation for a place in the imagined community of the living and the dead.

MEMBERSHIP IN A LARGER, IMAGINED SOCIETY: BURIAL CLOTHING AND COFFIN PARTIES

Zhang Lanfen and Wang *shifu* (expert or master), the founder of a temple in a coastal city in Fujian province and a funeral-rites master, live in a world where aging is celebrated.[25] This point of view—a celebration of aging and the social roles that come with it—is what the historian Judith Farquhar and the ethicist Qicheng Zhang evoke for their readers in writing that "old age is a self-evident good." Upon encountering an octogenarian in their neighborhood, they describe what one of their graduate students said, "Having such old people in our neighborhoods is a good thing, it speaks well for the nation and our culture."[26] In this environment, there is value in aging.

The celebration of aging also extends to the inclusion of death in the narrative of one's life.[27] One October afternoon in 2015 Wang *shifu* told me that a year after the fiftieth birthday celebration was the time to start thinking about preparing for your own burial, which would be cause for another social gathering of friends and family, a burial-clothes-and-coffin party. "People with money buy their coffin [and are] proud of it. It means, 'My child has money. I have money. I can buy my coffin.'" One would prepare burial clothes, and then have a party to have friends and family over to show them the coffin and the burial clothes. They would say, "After I die, I have clothes to wear." It's comforting. "Buy the coffin and put up red lights. You put the coffin in the house for everybody to see." These were celebratory red lights. The reason for the party, according to Wang *shifu*, is "because you're not sure if you'll have another ten years, twenty years, thirty years."

Since cremation was mandated to save land space, with a rollout starting in 2003 and mostly in place by 2014, coffins have become of less interest.²⁸ "The coffins are just paper now." Instead, many people buy expensive burial plots in which to place the urn holding the ashes. A middle range plot costs 20,000 RMB (about $3,300), and the asking price for a good one is more than 100,000 RMB (about $16,600). At these parties, the guests view the grave site, then go back to the individual's home to eat. In the current era, marked by abundant food resources and the availability of most desired items, hosting such gatherings involves serving specific foods. "Here, in this generation, you have to have at least two dishes for people. Chives represent longevity, because they grow faster than other vegetables. Fried noodles, too," because noodles are long, "and then the other dishes are up to you." Regarding this time when everybody comes over to see the grave plot and eat, Wang *shifu* said, "It's a happy time."

People who buy their burial clothes and arrange their grave details are deemed happy because they had done well enough in life to afford them. But these celebrations are also a moral statement. When people prepare their burial arrangements, it means that they are okay with putting the spotlight on themselves, that they are proud of their life: "I'm born, I do a lot of good things, and then I have to prepare for myself after I die. If you usually are really good to people, good to society, when you get to fifty years old, you buy your coffin, and people say your *ming* [fate] is good. They bless you." To bless is an active word. When people bless you, they contribute to your trajectory, sending you onto your path. Doing good things includes giving money to the poor and being filial to parents. It was the rare person who had the gall to hold a party to celebrate preparation for death when he hadn't lived this kind of life. Wang *shifu* said, "If that person usually does bad things, he is afraid to do those things related to burial. He's afraid people will say bad things about him." In that case, he should just lie low and not draw attention to his arrangements:

If you are a bad person [and you try to display your burial items], people will criticize you. Even if he has money, everybody will reprimand him. If I have been contributing to society, then I can buy this coffin. The bad person, even his descendants will say bad things about him. . . . So bad people don't dare to do this. Everybody knows this.

Wang *shifu* noted that some people are afraid to die. But his view is that people realize that they will die, so they prepare for it: "Even if you're afraid to die, you're going to die." Do those friends who are afraid of death go to those celebrations for burial clothes and coffins? Yes, they do. "You can't *not* go," Wang *shifu* told me. It would be more than rude to refuse to go to "see him out of this world"; it would be very unkind. The social dimension is a compelling factor. Even those who harbor personal fears about death or wish to deny its inevitability must extend well-wishes to individuals in their death preparations to avoid conveying ill intent or making enemies.

Against this backdrop of burial clothing and coffin parties, the interaction described at the beginning of this chapter in which Zhang Lanfen showed us her burial clothing—a show in the receiving room of the temple complex that unfolded cheerfully and in good spirits—made sense and can be reexamined. Along with Wang *shifu* and some other temple regulars, we viewed her package, which included clothing, shoes, a pillowcase, and a pair of earrings. "Artifacts" are components of an "identity kit" in which personal identities and feelings about oneself are located, invested, and stored in material possessions, in Erving Goffman's terms.[29] Zhang *ayi* had put together a package of objects that expressed herself.

The topic of burial clothes came up when I was chatting with Wang *shifu*'s apprentice who was learning how to facilitate funeral rites while he had a day job making a living working shifts at a glass factory. Was there a taboo on talking about death? No, he said, sometimes people prepare their burial clothes. Wang *shifu* nodded toward Zhang *ayi*: "She has her clothes all prepared."

"I've got them in my room," she said. (The temple provided a few regular volunteers who are frequently there early in the morning with a room in which to sleep and keep things.) "We don't buy coffins as much now, because we are cremated. So why buy a nice coffin?" One of the other women nodded in agreement. "Can I see them?" I asked hopefully. She nodded, indicating for me to wait one moment, and left the room. I grabbed my phone to capture this on video.[30]

Zhang *ayi* brought out a cardboard box full of items. After carefully untying the string that kept it closed and taking off the yellow plastic she had wrapped it with, she began passing around each item for everyone to see. First, she showed us a brown knitted winter hat. Then came a yellow satin pillowcase with embroidery on it, and a matching yellow blanket, both still wrapped in plastic from the store. She held the pillowcase up to her tilted head and shortly mimicked resting upon it (as would, presumably, her corpse). Everybody looked on with interest, smiling and commenting. Then came out a pair of olive-green pants, which she unfolded so I could see, and a matching top. There was a white inner outfit as well as other inner pieces to be worn under the clothes. There was also a pair of soft, black, cloth shoes, of the style that Buddhist nuns wear. Wang *shifu* said, passing around the shoes, "These shoes are really nice. This kind of shoe is very pretty." "They were 10 yuan," she informed him (about $1.50 USD).

During the show, Zhang *ayi* demonstrated her look by draping a blue cloth money purse on herself and swinging one hip outward to emphasize the purse while miming a swagger. She was enjoying showing off a little, proud of what she had put together, and we were an eager audience. Also in the box was a color photograph of herself for display at her funeral, about three by five inches and laminated. The photo could also be placed next to her *paiwei* (a small tablet with her name on it placed in a temple or home that family and friends can visit). As is typical of these photo portraits, her visage was calm and unsmiling.

Zhang *ayi* didn't mind the scrutiny, or the occasional criticism. She had saved the best for last: silver diamond drop earrings fit for a formal ball. A temple regular said, "Oh, you're going to wear earrings?" "I spent 500 yuan," she answered (about $83), as if to say, of course I'm going to wear them. Her friend protested, saying that's too much to spend on a pair of earrings. Wang *shifu* gave her a playful slap on the arm. Zhang *ayi* put the earrings on anyway, one at a time. She was unfazed by the possibility of being judged for her extravagance. Suddenly she was shy for just a moment, hiding her face behind her hand. Then she started laughing, pretending to slap back, and then returned everything to the box.

Wang *shifu's* apprentice was impressed with Zhang *ayi's* preparations and said to me, "Doesn't this have so much value, preparing this stuff? The clothes you're going to wear when you die, you have it all prepared." I agreed and noted the celebratory atmosphere that had arisen while we looked at our friend's burial clothes. We were all collectively anticipating an event: her funeral.

Most of the time, one's death is socially *invisible*—blurred, disguised, displaced, or moved into the background of awareness, obscured by everyday life. Because people do not routinely talk about their own death for most of their lifespan, these interactions revolving around the burial clothes were liberating, releasing Zhang *ayi* to divulge her thoughts and plans for the event that would memorialize her death. As we looked at the items, commenting and asking questions, her death became socially *visible* and acknowledged through the interactions. The objects, when viewed by her friends, provided social acknowledgment of an important future event for a significant person.

On a practical level, Zhang *ayi*'s death is associated for her with new clothes that she can look forward to wearing, so to speak. Wang *shifu*'s apprentice continued, now talking about his own preparations: "I've been working hard my whole life, so at the end, I want to have nice, new clothes. I prepared [my clothes] more than ten years ago."

MODE OF ASSOCIATION

Preparing burial clothing may seem like an individual act, but, like other clothing choices, it is a social act that anticipates encountering others. My fieldwork suggests that people in these small towns plan their burial clothing in a way that is socially meaningful and joins people together. The burial clothing and coffin parties described by Wang *shifu* and Yang Guanghong's summoning of his adult children to the task of preparing his burial clothing are examples of individuals who do not face death alone, but consider the living and the dead as still connected in the family lineage.

The examples discussed in this chapter are geographically diverse, spanning Hunan, Yunnan, and Fujian provinces, and predominantly from small towns. This mode of association occurred more often in the past, according to the people with whom I spoke, and a systematic inquiry into the prevalence of this mode of association is yet to be conducted. There is evidence that many people in China use other means to cope with the awareness of their own mortality. For example, Hand in Hand, a Shanghai-based nonprofit organization, takes a different approach by addressing this issue with the provision of psychological counseling for cancer patients and their families.[31] Wang Ying, the founder, was inspired to become a counselor during her mother's battle with cancer when she was upset and uncertain about how to cope. Her response was to pursue studies in psychology, similar to the training in psychotherapy described by Teresa Kuan in this book.

The sense of community in this act of association does not emerge from a durable or stable collection of individuals similar to a civic group organized to do a task, but it does connect individuals to one another in a significant way. Amid the choices and limitations in the decades after reform in China, this practice of preparing burial clothes stands as an aspect of "unofficial China" that reflects descending familism and an emphasis on internal life.[32]

THE REALITIES OF THE TIES: DESCENDING FAMILISM AND BURIAL CLOTHING

On January 1, 2016, the government announced the end of the one-child policy by signing a bill into law allowing couples to have two children. Thirty-seven years of the policy changed family dynamics, and intergenerational bonds have become intense in new ways. The emphasis of family life has shifted from glorifying ancestors to prioritizing the well-being and development of grandchildren. The mobility of the population, urbanization, and an achievement-based occupational structure have increased the need for young adults to rely on their elders. After rising social inequality and the emergence of a very challenging job

market, adult children rely on parents to provide childcare, housing, and daily assistance. This has fostered a new level of intimacy between parents and their adult children in China, but it
is one in which the older generation does a lot of work—taking
the load off the young people, who must focus on school, then
jobs, in an intensely competitive environment.

The grandchildren are the focus of family attention, and the
elders worry about how their adult children may suffer in the
event of their own serious illness or death. People age sixty and
over contrast what they did for their own parents with what
they expect their own children to do for them when it comes
to care and grave sweeping. For example, they visit their own
parents' graves but don't necessarily expect their own children to
do so as much, and they don't want to burden them financially
or with demands on their time. The older generation believe the
young adults are busy, and when talking about a good death, they
emphasize "going" quickly so as not to be too much trouble for
their children.

Many of the older generation are willing to prepare their
own burial clothes rather than give their children more to
do. But some have a lingering desire for their children to be
involved. Near the temple where I stayed, there was a neighborhood elderly association that holds two luncheons per year
for the elderly women in the community. One of these luncheons was held at a reasonably priced restaurant serving fresh
seafood. Downstairs the restaurant displayed the catches of the
day; we were seated upstairs at six tables of eight retirees and
guests (like me). While we ate, I chatted with three women
about their burial clothing and why they prepared it for themselves. One woman considered it "a happy thing." Another
described preparing one's burial clothes as a way to alleviate
the burden on one's children. By doing it themselves, they can

ensure that they get what they like and save their children the trouble of doing it.

When the adult children are not the ones who picked out the clothing, sometimes individuals nevertheless try to attribute their involvement. Chen Zhi, a sixty-nine-year-old father of a son and two daughters living in Hunan province, began to want to prepare his burial clothing after his parents passed away and he retired about ten years ago. He wanted to prepare, but he and his wife lived far away from his three adult children, who only visited their village home during holidays. He and his wife shopped for their burial clothes on their own, and when he talked about it, he had an explanation: Their children regularly send them money, and it was with this financial support that they were able to purchase their burial clothes. By his reckoning, it was his children who had provided their burial clothes; he and his wife had just picked them out. During the Dragon Boat Festival in June, they bought four outfits each, taking advantage of the good deals and festive atmosphere in town.

THE SOCIAL SITUATION TO PREPARE FOR

Jin Wenmei, a fifty-four-year-old entrepreneur in Fujian province, thought about what she could take with her, so to speak, and decided that she was going to invest in herself. She saw preparing burial clothing as an action of looking after herself, and she felt good about having her burial collection started. Seeing a set that she liked and could afford she told me that she thought, why not get it? For her, the situation of anticipating her funeral is a case of a social situation to be prepared for.

In her middle age, Wenmei underwent a personal renaissance. She decided to take care of herself, learn, and grow. She began putting together her burial package. On a Friday evening, she took me for a spin on the back of her yellow scooter.

"Well, I saw some that I liked, so I bought them," she said about her burial clothes. In response to the expression on my face (I was surprised because I thought she was relatively young; she was only fifty-four), she said, "Yeah, people do that. I don't have everything, though, just the blanket and the outer outfit." Musing to herself, she remarked that she should get everything else and put it in a box: "So that when the day comes, you just open up the box, and everything's there." She liked being organized. A self-made entrepreneur who had humble beginnings as a motorcycle rickshaw driver, she had subsequently made some good money in real estate, buying and renovating apartments and offices to rent out. She had gotten in at the right time: one place used to be 1,000 RMB per month, and now was 4,000 RMB, for example.

But money wasn't everything. Wenmei took me to an apartment unit she kept for herself rather than renting out. In addition to her four-story home where she lived with her husband and son, this additional two-bedroom apartment was her own space where she could learn and grow without interruption. She could rent it for 1,000 RMB per month, she told me, but she chooses instead to pay 200 RMB for the utilities and have some extra space. In her apartment, she has a computer on which she is teaching herself Microsoft Excel. She has also been learning calligraphy through online instructional videos.

"You can't bring money with you after you die, but you can bring your mind," she said. "If you culture yourself"—she meant "culture" as a verb to denote bettering herself by learning—"it's good for you, and you can bring that with you. You'll recognize it in the next life." Her participation in the temple scripture readings was a way to cultivate herself: "Reading scriptures is for cleansing your mind. So when you chant *amituofu*, it means in the west, east, north, south—there are Buddhas in those places." "You have culture"—now she meant "culture" as a noun to refer to erudition. "So you look at your computer, and you understand what's happening all over the world," she said.

Like her calligraphy, computer learning, and temple activities, her burial clothing tells the story of Wenmei treating herself right. Preparing burial clothing was a way that she focused on herself. Just like she had set aside this space to educate herself, she was also keeping some items for herself. Why not have something nice? After working hard to raise her two children who are now grown, it's her time to be healthy, set priorities, and be connected to her friends.

She had not always felt this way. A turning point came when her husband had had an affair, eventually apologizing and deciding to "return home," but she had taken on a new outlook. She dealt with the fallout from her husband's infidelity by taking time for herself, learning new skills, and becoming educated. Her sense of self-cultivation concerned becoming a person of intellectual and spiritual value. Life is short, she emphasized. So invest in what lasts forever—experience and knowledge. Burial clothing is for a temporary body, but having something nice is part of her broader attitude of self-care: take care of what you have and treat yourself as a person of value.

WHEN BURIAL CLOTHING IS NOT "A HAPPY THING"

Those who prepare burial clothing are a self-selected group, since it is a voluntary thing, so most do it because they want to. However, I spoke with a few people were not happy about their burial clothing. One morning, as I was doing fieldwork and interviews, I talked to a man in Fujian who had a positive view of preparing burial clothing but felt a bit doleful about it, unlike others. He had begun to prepare his package and found that he didn't have enough financial means to set things aside without using them. He had already prepared a few things, he said, but did not want to show them to me.

This man in his early seventies repaired fishnets by hand for a living, a low-income occupation. He lived on the brink of poverty. Another woman I spoke to was in her early eighties and had described burial clothes as a "happy" thing [Minnan: hoaⁿ-hí, Mandarin: *huanxi*], but she perceived her own collection as basic. When I showed her the video of Zhang *ayi*, she said, "Mine aren't as nice as hers."

BURIAL CLOTHING AND THE COMMON GOOD

An act that reflects important ties and creates a feeling of connection to others when contemplating one's own future death seems to have a positive effect on people in small towns across China. The objects and items are for only one individual, but the items facilitate the process of knitting together family and friends—around a subject that is normally avoided—while binding together the living and the dead. Friends confer with one another, exchanging helpful information and helping each other store the packages, and adults are buying them for their parents and taking part in their parents' transition to old age in a positive way. "I'm not afraid of death now," said Yang Guanghong, the party cadre in Yunnan who built the shed on the side of his house to store the coffins and burial clothes his adult children had prepared for him and his wife. "The things I need are ready!"

Did the coordinated action of preparing Yang Guanghong's burial clothing contribute to a common good? Guanghong and his family's efforts were meant to benefit the family, but the cultural practice seems to have the effect of alleviating death anxiety in the population that participates—something good for collective well-being. I saw Zhang *ayi* at the temple again about a week after her "show." In her room she showed me two burial clothing sets for two of her friends, which included outer pieces, shoes, blankets, hats, and various inner pieces. She stored them at the temple because her friends felt having them there for safe-keeping was a good idea for the good vibes.

Zhang *ayi* asked if I wanted to come in, gesturing toward the packages she had laid out. It all seemed painstakingly done. Looking at the light gray outer piece with elegantly embroidered shoes to go with it, the blanket, a hat, and all the shirts and pants that served as underclothing, I had to remind myself that these were going to be for a funeral for her friend. At that time, she would wear this set. A second friend had a beautiful purple outfit that suggested verbena flowers. We admired her friend's great taste. It was energizing; her friends took initiative to beautify their own funerals.

Zhang *ayi*'s preparations for her own funeral facilitated acts of association that improved her own well-being and, in my view, is a practice that contributes to a greater pattern of well-being. In that way, the practice of preparing burial clothing is a kind of social and cultural asset, a shared good that helps people address important challenges. Unlike, say, public radio and national parks, this historically specific approach to preparing for death is not provided by the state. However, like the oceans and the air, it is readily available to (and made use of by) the people described in this chapter. Preparing burial clothing is an example of how ordinary people in China have innovated solutions for universal problems people face. Zhang *ayi* and others I spoke with about their burial clothing exuded a sense of calm regarding their future death. The act of preparing burial clothes summons people's attention to a person's upcoming death, transforming what is socially invisible into a distinctly satisfying recognition, while affirming their place in a community that includes ancestors and descendants.

NOTES

This study received support from the John Templeton Foundation (ID #40148).

1. All names are pseudonyms.
2. Philippe Aries, *Western Attitudes Toward Death: From the Middle Ages to the Present* (Baltimore, MD: Johns Hopkins University Press, 1981), 114.
3. Becky Yang Hsu and Joseline Lu, "Happiness and Grieving Well: Family Bonds and Mourning Practices in China," in *The Routledge History of Happiness*, ed. Katie Barclay, Darrin M. McMahon, and Peter N. Stearns (New York: Routledge, 2024), 35–53.
4. Xiao Qiu, "Grave Sweeping" (Sao mu), *Little Red Book*, April 2, 2023, https://www.xiaohongshu.com/explore/6429427900000000001300f817? app_platform=ios&app_version=8.5&author_share=2&share_from _user_hidden=true&type=normal&xhsshare=CopyLink&appuid =5b4bd84 a4eacab7e7ede6f09&apptime=1694472015.
5. Fei Xiaotong, *From the Soil: The Foundations of Chinese Society*, trans. Gary G. Hamilton and Wang Zheng (1947; repr. Berkeley: University of California Press, 1992). See also Philip J. Ivanhoe, *Oneness: East Asian Conceptions of Virtue, Happiness, and How We Are All Connected* (New York: Oxford University Press, 2017).
6. John Dewey, *The Middle Works of John Dewey, 1899–1924*. Vol. 9, *1916, Democracy and Education*, ed. Jo Ann Boydston (Carbondale: Southern Illinois University Press, 2008), 93.

7. Claudio Benzecry and Daniel Winchester, "Varieties of Microsociology," in *Social Theory Now*, ed. Claudio Benzecry, Monika Krause, and Isaac Ariail Reed (Chicago: University of Chicago Press, 2017), 50.

8. Paul Lichterman and Nina Eliasoph, "Civic Action," *American Journal of Sociology* 120, no. 3 (2014), 810.

9. Weiguo Zhang, "Is Death Taboo for Older Chinese Immigrants?," *OMEGA–Journal of Death and Dying* 84, no. 4 (2022): 1061–80.

10. Erving Goffman, *The Presentation of Self in Everyday Life* (New York: Doubleday, 1959).

11. Ann Rawls and Waverly Duck, *Tacit Racism* (Chicago: University of Chicago Press, 2020); and W. E. B. Du Bois, *The Souls of Black Folk* (New York: Bantam Classic, 1903).

12. Georg Simmel, "Fashion," *The American Journal of Sociology* 62, no. 6 (1904): 541–58.

13. Mu-Chou Poo, "Ideas Concerning Death and Burial in Pre-Han and Han China," *Asia Major* 3, no. 2 (1990): 25–62.

14. Rubie Watson, "Remembering the Dead: Graves and Politics in Southeastern China," in *Death Ritual in Late Imperial and Modern China*, ed. James Watson and Evelyn Rawski (Berkeley: University of California Press, 1988), 203–27.

15. Francis L. K. Hsu, *Under the Ancestors' Shadow: Kinship, Personality, and Social Mobility in Village China* (1948; repr. New York: Doubleday, 1967), 131–32.

16. Hsu, *Under the Ancestors' Shadow*, 132.

17. Hsu, *Under the Ancestors' Shadow*, 133.

18. Everett Zhang, "Grieving at Chongqing's Red Guard Graveyard: In the Name of Life Itself," *China Journal* 70 (2013), 35.

19. Deborah Davis-Friedmann, *Long Lives: Chinese Elderly and the Communist Revolution* (Stanford University Press, 1983), 67.

20. Teresa Kuan, *Love's Uncertainty: The Politics and Ethics of Child Rearing in Contemporary China* (Berkeley: University of California Press, 2015).

21. Huwy-Min Lucia Liu, *Governing Death, Making Persons: The New Chinese Way of Death* (Ithaca, NY: Cornell University Press, 2022), 144.

22. National Bureau of Statistics of China, "Households' Income and Consumption Expenditure in 2021," accessed April 18, 2022, http://www.stats .gov.cn/english/PressRelease/202201/t20220118_1826649.html#:~:text

=In%202021%2C%20the%20median%20per,85.3%20percent%20of%20
the%20average.

23. "Visit the First Village of the Shroud Industry," *Xinhua Daily Telegraph*,
April 12, 2019, http://www.xinhuanet.com/politics/2019-04/12/c_1124356290
.htm.

24. Yanping Liu and Gertina van Schalkwyk, "Death Preparation of Chinese Rural Elders," *Death Studies* 43, no. 4 (2019), 275.

25. Temples like this one are often associated with death and funerary rites
because it focuses on the idea of a heaven-like place where people can be
reborn, which has no sorrow. For Lang Chen's description of "Pure Land,"
see Lang Chen, "Buddhism and Happiness: A Modern Romance or Tale
as Old as Time?," in *Routledge History of Happiness*, ed. Katie Barclay, Darrin McMahon, and Peter Stearns (New York: Routledge, 2024), 27.

26. Judith Farquhar and Qicheng Zhang, *Ten Thousand Things: Nurturing
Life in Contemporary Beijing* (Cambridge, MA: Zone, 2012), 145.

27. Philip J. Ivanhoe characterizes ideas about death in early Confucian-
ism as the "final act in the greater narrative of their lives." See Philip J.
Ivanhoe, "Death and Dying in the Analects," in *Mortality in Traditional
Chinese Thought*, ed. Amy Olberding and Philip J. Ivanhoe (Albany:
State University of New York Press, 2011), 140.

28. Jonathan Kaiman, "In China, a Cremation Order Has Driven Some
Elderly to Desperate Acts," *Los Angeles Times*, November 6, 2015, https://
www.latimes.com/world/asia/la-fg-china-suicides-20151106-story.html.

29. Erving Goffman, *Asylums: Essays on the Condition of the Social Situation
of Mental Patients and Other Inmates* (New York: Doubleday, 1961).

30. Edited footage is available of someone showing me burial clothing in
a *Washington Post* Wonkblog article. See Ana Swanson, "What People
Around the World Mean When They Say They Are Happy," *Washington Post*, accessed August 24, 2018, https://www.washingtonpost.com
/news/wonk/wp/2016/02/03/what-english-speakers-dont-get-about-the
-meaning-of-happiness.

31. Fan Yiying, "Dealing with Death, China's Biggest Taboo," *Sixth Tone*,
April 3, 2018, https://www.sixthtone.com/news/1002031/dealing-with
-death%2C-chinas-biggest-taboo.

32. Perry Link, Richard Madsen, and Paul Pickowicz, eds., introduction
to *Unofficial China: Popular Culture and Thought in the People's Republic*
(Boulder, CO: Westview, 1990).

ACKNOWLEDGMENTS

This book was written under the auspices of the Initiative for U.S.-China Dialogue of the Office of Global Engagement at Georgetown University. Teresa Kuan, Yunxiang Yan, Richard Madsen, Gonçalo Santos, Lynn Sun, and I formed the Research Group on Culture and Society. We carefully selected common challenges faced by individuals in both China and the United States and used our ethnographic fieldwork to explore unique ways that people in China respond to these challenges. Later on Yichen Rao joined our team and made valuable contributions to the book.

In May 2019, when the U.S.-China relationship was fraught with increasing antagonism, our group convened to explore the idea of a common good for both countries, and even for the world at large, drawing inspiration from an essay written by Richard Madsen.[1]

We planned to reconvene at the Chinese University of Hong Kong (CUHK) seven months later, but we could not have foreseen the unprecedented circumstances that would come to shape the rest of our project and, indeed, the world.

As protests in Hong Kong intensified during the summer and fall of 2019, our group faced uncertainty about whether to proceed with our plans. Despite the turmoil, two members of our group who had witnessed some of China's most chaotic decades believed we could carry on. We held our second meeting in December 2019 at CUHK, shortly after the protests had reached university campuses. Over the course of two days, we discussed the various forms of community we had observed in our fieldwork in China. We had observed people dealing with their individual issues, but in the process they had also developed unique forms of association in various domains, from activism to mental health to medicine. These ordinary actions were compelling responses that, in some cases, promoted the common good.

Two months later in early 2020 the COVID-19 pandemic swept across the United States, and the world was plunged into a state of quarantine. In April of 2020 I engaged in an email conversation with Teresa Kuan. In our correspondence and exchange of drafts, we both keenly felt the urgency of finding the common good. The pandemic was raging, and tensions between China and the United States were escalating. It was within this context that Teresa's eloquent words captivated me, and I am compelled to share them here:

> Immersive field research has kept us from falling into despair because small communities, however composed, are always coming up with innovative solutions to the problems they face. Even if they are not perfect, they are innovations nonetheless—a property of a process commonly known but poorly understood as "culture."

Her words illuminated the connection between culture and the small social interactions that give rise to diverse forms of community and copresence. As we all adjusted to new modes of living, the importance of community in the face of various constraints became increasingly apparent.

Instead of holding our third meeting in person at Georgetown, we conducted a virtual meeting in July of 2020, exchanging comments and suggestions. On January 29, 2021, we presented our findings in a virtual event open to the public titled "China, Unseen: Solving Problems in the New Era."[2]

I have been deeply moved by the authors who contributed to this book. They blend their extensive knowledge of Chinese society with empathy for the individuals they encountered during their fieldwork, and this has inspired me. Their approach is characterized by a strong spirit of inquiry and composed perseverance.

I am also grateful to Thomas Banchoff for his unwavering support, Tuoya Wulan for her efficiency and thoughtfulness, Leann Deckert for her help with our meeting in Hong Kong, and to Elizabeth Stokes for her exceptional editing skills.

NOTES

1. Richard Madsen, "Beyond the Clash of Civilizations: Seeking the Common Good Through East-West Dialogue," manuscript, 2019.
2. A video recording of the event is available at https://uschinadialogue .georgetown.edu/events/china-unseen-solving-problems-in-the-new-era.

BIBLIOGRAPHY

Ahmed, Sara. *The Cultural Politics of Emotion*. New York: Routledge, 2004.

——. *The Promise of Happiness*. Durham, NC: Duke University Press, 2010.

American Psychiatric Association. *Diagnostic and Statistical Manual of Mental Disorders: DSM-5*. Arlington, VA: American Psychiatric Association, 2013.

Anagnost, Ann. "The Corporeal Politics of Quality (*Suzhi*)." *Public Culture* 16, no. 2 (2004): 189–208.

Anderson, Benedict. *Imagined Communities*. New York: Verso, 1991.

Appadurai, Arjun. *The Future as Cultural Fact: Essays on the Global Condition*. London: Verso, 2013.

Arendt, Hannah. *The Human Condition*. Chicago: University of Chicago Press, 1998. First published in 1958.

Aries, Philippe. *Western Attitudes Toward Death: From the Middle Ages to the Present*. Baltimore, MD: Johns Hopkins University Press, 1981.

Autor, David H., David Dorn, and Gordon H. Hanson. "The China Shock: Learning from Labor-Market Adjustment to Large Changes in Trade." *Annual Review of Economics* 8, no. 1 (October 2016): 205–40.

Banfield, Edward L. *The Moral Basis of a Backward Society*. New York: Free Press, 1958.

Barboza, David. "Billions in Hidden Riches for Family of Chinese Leader." *New York Times*, October 25, 2012.

Bateson, Gregory. *Steps to an Ecology of Mind*. Chicago: University of Chicago Press, 1972.

Bateson, Gregory, Don D. Jackson, Jay Haley, and John Weakland. "Toward a Theory of Schizophrenia." *Behavioral Science* 1, no. 4 (1956): 251–64.

Bax, Trent. *Youth and Internet Addiction in China*. Oxford: Routledge, 2013.

Beck, Ulrich. *The Metamorphosis of the World*. Cambridge: Polity, 2016.

——. *Risk Society: Towards a New Modernity*. London: Sage, 1992.

Beck, Ulrich, and Elisabeth Beck-Gernsheim. *Individualization: Institution-alized Individualism and Its Social and Political Consequences*. London: Sage, 2002.

——. *The Normal Chaos of Love*. Cambridge: Polity, 1995.

Bellah, Robert N., Richard Madsen, William M. Sullivan, Ann Swidler, and Steven M. Tipton. *Habits of the Heart: Individualism and Commitment in American Life*. Berkeley: University of California Press, 1985.

Benzecry, Claudio, and Daniel Winchester. "Varieties of Microsociology." In *Social Theory Now*, ed. Claudio Benzecry, Monika Krause, and Isaac Ariail Reed, 42–74. Chicago: University of Chicago Press, 2017.

Berlant, Lauren. *Cruel Optimism*. Durham, NC: Duke University Press, 2011.

Betrán, Ana Pilar, Jianfeng Ye, Anne-Beth Moller, Jun Zhang, A. Metin Gül-mezoglue, and Maria Regina Torloni. "The Increasing Trend in Caesar-ean Section Rates: Global, Regional and National Estimates: 1990–2014." *PLoS One* 11, no. 2 (2016): e0148343.

Boddy, Janice. "Spirits and Selves in Northern Sudan: The Cultural Thera-peutics of Possession and Trance." *American Ethnologist* 15, no. 1 (1988): 4–27.

Borovoy, Amy. *The Too-Good Wife*. Berkeley: University of California Press, 2005.

Bowen, Murray. *Family Therapy in Clinical Practice*. New York: Jason Aron-son, 1978.

Bray, Francesca. *Technology and Gender: Fabrics of Power in Late Imperial China*. Berkeley: University of California Press, 1997.

——. "Tools of Virtuous Action." In *Ordinary Ethics in China*, ed. Charles Stafford, 13–45. London: Bloomsbury, 2013.

Burawoy, Michael. "The Extended Case Method." *Sociological Theory* 16, no. 1 (1998): 4–33.

Byler, Darren. "Spirit Breaking: Uyghur Dispossession, Culture Work, and Terror Capitalism in a Chinese Global City." PhD diss., University of Washington, 2018.

Case, Anne, and Angus Deaton. *Deaths of Despair and the Future of Capital-ism*. Princeton, NJ: Princeton University Press, 2020.

Chan, Joseph. "Confucian Attitudes Toward Ethical Pluralism." In *The Many and the One: Religious and Secular Perspectives on Ethical Pluralism in the*

Modern World, ed. Richard Madsen and Tracy B. Strong, 129–53. Princeton, NJ: Princeton University Press, 2003.

Chang, Heng-hao. "From Housewives to Activists: Lived Experiences of Mothers for Disability Rights in Taiwan." *Asian Journal of Women's Studies* 15, no. 3 (2009): 34–59.

Chang, Leslie T. *Factory Girls: From Village to City in a Changing China.* New York: Spiegel and Grau, 2008.

Chen, Chih-Jou Jay. "Deriving Happiness from Making Society Better: Chinese Activists as Warring Gods." In *The Chinese Pursuit of Happiness: Anxieties, Hopes, and Moral Tensions in Everyday Life*, ed. Becky Yang Hsu and Richard Madsen, 131–54. Berkeley: University of California Press, 2019.

Chen, Lang. "Buddhism and Happiness: A Modern Romance or Tale as Old as Time?" In *Routledge History of Happiness*, ed. Katie Barclay, Darrin McMahon, and Peter Stearns, chap. 2. New York: Routledge, 2024.

——. "The Changing Notion of Happiness: A History of *Xingfu*." In *The Chinese Pursuit of Happiness: Anxieties, Hopes, and Moral Tensions in Everyday Life*, ed. Becky Yang Hsu and Richard Madsen, 19–41. Berkeley: University of California Press, 2019.

Chen, Weijun, dir. *This Is Life (Sheng-men)*. 2016. China, documentary film.

Chen, Wenrui. *Invoking Personhood in Contemporary China: Seeing Through the Lens of a Beijing Family Therapy Center*. PhD diss., New York University, 2015.

Chen, Ying, and Chih-Jou Jay Chen. "The State Owes Us: Social Exclusion and Collective Actions of China's Bereaved Parents." *Modern China* 47, no. 6 (2021): 740–64.

Chen, Yongmei. *Anchan, Zuo Yuezi, Xinshenger Huli Yibentong* (Safe birth, postnatal confinement, infant care comprehensive manual). Beijing: Zhongguo Nongye Chubanshe, 2013.

Chen, Yujie, Zhifei Mao, and Jack Linchuan Qiu. *Super-Sticky WeChat and Chinese Society*. Bingley, UK: Emerald, 2018.

Cheung, Ngai Fen, and Rosemary Mander. *Midwifery in China*. London: Routledge, 2018.

Chou, Wah-Shan. "Homosexuality and the Cultural Politics of *Tongzhi* in Chinese Societies." *Journal of Homosexuality* 40, no. 3–4 (2001): 27–46.

Cong, Yali. "Doctor-Family-Patient Relationship. The Chinese Paradigm of Informed Consent." *Journal of Medical Philosophy* 29, no. 2 (2004): 149–78.

Corea, Gena. *The Mother Machine: Reproductive Technologies from Artificial Insemination to Artificial Wombs.* New York: Harper Collins, 1985.

Cosminsky, Sheila. *Midwives and Mothers: The Medicalization of Childbirth on a Guatemalan Plantation.* Austin: University of Texas Press, 2016.

Cowan, Ruth. *More Work for Mother: The Ironies of Household Technology from the Open Hearth to the Microwave.* New York: Basic Books, 1983.

Craven, Christa. *Pushing for Midwives: Homebirth Mothers and the Reproductive Rights Movement.* Philadelphia, PA: Temple University Press, 2010.

Davis, Deborah. "Performing Happiness for Self and Others." In *The Chinese Pursuit of Happiness: Anxieties, Hopes, and Moral Tensions in Everyday Life,* ed. Becky Yang Hsu and Richard Madsen, 66–83. Berkeley: University of California Press, 2019.

Davis-Floyd, Robbie. *Birth as an American Rite of Passage,* 2nd ed. Berkeley: University of California Press, 2004.

——. "The Technocratic Body: American Childbirth as Cultural Expression." *Social Science & Medicine* 38 (1994): 1125–40.

Davis-Floyd, Robbie, and Melissa Cheney, eds. *Birth in Eight Cultures.* Prospect Heights, IL: Waveland, 2019.

Dewey, John. *The Middle Works of John Dewey, 1899–1924.* Vol. 9, *1916, Democracy and Education,* ed. Jo Ann Boydston. Carbondale: Southern Illinois University Press, 2008.

Die, Ming. "Guojia wei jian wei: 900 yu jia yiyuan jiang kaizhan wutong fenmian shidian" (National Health and Medical Commission: More than 900 hospitals will launch pilot programs for painless delivery). News.China. com.cn, August 22, 2019. http://news.china.com.cn/2019-08/22/content _75125715.htm.

Ding, X. L. "'The Only Reliability Is That These Guys Aren't Reliable': The Business Culture of Red Capitalism." In *Restless China,* ed. Perry Link, Richard Madsen, and Paul Pickowicz, 37–57. Lanham, MD: Rowman and Littlefield, 2013.

Donnison, Jean. *Midwives and Medical Men: A History of Inter-Professional Social Rivalries and Women's Rights.* New York: Schocken, 1977.

Douglas, Alecia C., Juline E. Mills, Mamadou Niang, Svetlana Stepchenkova, Sookeun Byun, Celestino Ruffini, Seul Ki Lee, et al. "Internet Addiction: Meta-Synthesis of Qualitative Research for the Decade 1996–2006." *Computers in Human Behavior* 24, no. 6 (2008): 3027–44.

Douglas, Mary. *Natural Symbols: Explorations in Cosmology.* New York: Vintage, 1973.

Dreyfus, Hubert L., and Paul Rabinow. *Michel Foucault: Beyond Structuralism and Hermeneutics,* 2nd ed. Chicago: University of Chicago Press, 1983.

Du, Yue. *State and Family in China: Filial Piety and Its Modern Reform.* Cambridge: Cambridge University Press, 2021.

Du Bois, W. E. B. *The Souls of Black Folk.* New York: Bantam Classic, 1903.

Ehrenreich, Barbara, and Deirdre English. *For Her Own Good: Two Centuries of the Experts' Advice to Women,* 2nd ed. New York: Anchor, 2005. First published in 1979.

——. *Witches, Midwives, and Nurses: A History of Women Healers,* 2nd ed. New York: Feminist, 2010. First published in 1973.

Eichelman, Dale F. "Islam and Ethical Pluralism." In *The Many and the One: Religious and Secular Perspectives on Ethical Pluralism in the Modern World,* ed. Richard Madsen and Tracy B. Strong, 161–79. Princeton, NJ: Princeton University Press, 2003.

Engebretsen, Elisabeth Lund. "'As Long as My Daughter Is Happy': 'Familial Happiness' and Parental Support-Narratives for LGBTQ Children." In *Chinese Discourses on Happiness,* ed. Gerda Wielander and Derek Hird, 86–106. Hong Kong: Hong Kong University Press, 2019.

Erwin, Kathleen. "Heart-to-Heart, Phone-to-Phone: Family Values, Sexuality, and the Politics of Shanghai's Advice Hotlines." In *The Consumer Revolution in Urban China,* ed. Deborah Davis, 145–70. Berkeley: University of California Press, 2000.

Evans, Harriet. "The Intimate Individual: Perspectives from the Mother-Daughter Relationship in Urban China." In *Chinese Modernity and the Individual Psyche,* ed. Andrew Kipnis, 119–47. New York: Palgrave, 2012.

Farquhar, Judith, and Qicheng Zhang. *Ten Thousand Things: Nurturing Life in Contemporary Beijing.* Cambridge, MA: Zone, 2012.

Fei, Xiaotong. *From the Soil: The Foundations of Chinese Society,* trans. Gary Hamilton and Wang Zheng. Berkeley: University of California Press, 1992. First published in 1948.

Fei, Xiaotong. *Xiangtu Zhongguo (Shanghai, 1948).* Translation from "Chinese Social Structure and Its Values." In *Changing China: Reading in the History of China from the Opium War to the Present,* ed. J. Mason Gentzler, 211–13. New York: Praeger, 1977.

Feng, Xing Lin, Ling Xu, Yan Guo, and Carine Ronsmans. "Factors Influencing Rising Caesarean Section Rates in China Between 1988 and 2008." *Bulletin of the World Health Organization* 90, no. 1 (2012): 30–39.

Fong, Vanessa L. "China's One-Child Policy and the Empowerment of Urban Daughters." *American Anthropologist* 104, no. 4 (2002): 1098–1109.

——. *Only Hope: Coming of Age Under China's One-Child Policy.* Stanford, CA: Stanford University Press, 2004.

Ford, Joselyn, dir. *Nowhere to Call Home: A Tibetan in Beijing.* 2014. China, documentary film.

Franceschini, Ivan, and Elisa Nesossi. "State Repression of Chinese Labor NGOs: A Chilling Effect?" *China Journal*, no. 80 (2018): 111–29.

Franklin, Sarah. *Embodied Progress: A Cultural Account of Assisted Reproduction.* London: Routledge, 2002.

——. "Revisiting Reprotech: Firestone and the Question of Technology." In *Further Adventures of the Dialectic of Sex: Critical Essays on Shulamith Firestone*, ed. Mandy Merck and Stella Sandford, 29–60. New York: Palgrave Macmillan, 2010.

Friedman, Robert M., Allison Pinto, Lenore Behar, Nicki Bush, Amberly Chirolla, Monica Epstein, Amy Green, et al. "Unlicensed Residential Programs: The Next Challenge in Protecting Youth." *American Journal of Orthopsychiatry* 76, no. 3 (2006): 295–303.

Friedman, Sara. "Opting Out of the City: Lifestyle Migrations, Alternative Education, and the Pursuit of Happiness Among Chinese Middle-Class Families." *Journal of the Royal Anthropological Institute* 29, no. 2 (2023): 383–401.

Galston, William A. "Liberal Egalitarian Attitudes Towards Ethical Pluralism." In *The Many and the One: Religious and Secular Perspectives on Ethical Pluralism in the Modern World*, ed. Richard Madsen and Tracy B. Strong, 25–41. Princeton, NJ: Princeton University Press, 2003.

Gammeltoft, Tine. *Haunting Images: A Cultural Account of Selective Reproduction in Vietnam.* Berkeley: University of California Press, 2014.

Garzón, Adela. "Cultural Change and Familism." *Psicothema* 12, suppl. (2000): 45–54.

Ginsborg, Paul. "Uncharted Territories: Individuals, Families, Civil Society and the Democratic State." In *The Golden Chain: Family, Civil Society, and the State*, ed. Jürgen Nautz, Paul Ginsborg, and Ton Nijhuis, 17–39. New York: Berghahn, 2013.

Glosser, Susan L. *Chinese Versions of Family and State, 1915–1953.* Berkeley: University of California Press, 2003.

Gluckman, Max. "Ethnographic Data in British Social Anthropology." *Sociological Review* 9, no. 1 (1961): 5–17.

Goffman, Erving. *Asylums: Essays on the Condition of the Social Situation of Mental Patients and Other Inmates.* New York: Doubleday, 1961.

——. *The Presentation of Self in Everyday Life.* New York: Doubleday, 1959.

——. *Stigma: Notes on the Management of Spoiled Identity.* Englewood Cliffs, NJ: Prentice-Hall, 1963.

Goossaert, Vincent, and David A. Palmer. *The Religious Question in Modern China.* Chicago: University of Chicago Press, 2011.

Gottschang, Suzanne Z. "Reproductive Modernities in Policy: Maternal Mortality, Midwives, and Cesarean Sections in China, 1900s–2000s." *Technology and Culture* 61, no. 2 (2020): 617–44.

Gray, David E. "Perceptions of Stigma: The Parents of Autistic Children." *Sociology of Health & Illness* 15, no. 1 (1993): 102–20.

Greenhalgh, Susan. *Cultivating Global Citizens: Population in the Rise of China.* Cambridge, MA: Harvard University Press, 2011.

——. "Science, Modernity, and the Making of China's One-Child Policy." *Population and Development Review* 29, no. 2 (2003): 163–96.

Guenther, Lisa. *Solitary Confinement: Social Death and Its Afterlives.* Minneapolis: University of Minnesota Press, 2013.

Guo, Jinhua, and Arthur Kleinman. "Stigma: HIV/AIDS, Mental Illness, and China's Nonperson." In *Deep China: The Moral Life of the Person, What Anthropology and Psychiatry Tell Us About China Today*, ed. Arthur Kleinman, Yunxiang Yan, Jing Jun, Sing Lee, Everett Zhang, Pan Tianshu, Wu Fei, and Guo Jinhua, 237–62. Berkeley: University of California Press, 2011.

Hagemann, Karen. "Gendered Boundaries: Civil Society, the Public/Private Divide and the Family." In *The Golden Chain: Family, Civil Society, and the State*, ed. Jürgen Nautz, Paul Ginsborg, and Ton Nijhuis, 43–65. New York: Berghahn, 2013.

Haldane, John H. "Natural Law and Ethical Pluralism." In *The Many and the One: Religious and Secular Perspectives on Ethical Pluralism in the Modern*

World, ed. Richard Madsen and Tracy B. Strong, 89–114. Princeton, NJ: Princeton University Press, 2003.

Harrell, Stevan, and Gonçalo Santos, eds. Introduction to *Transforming Patriarchy: Chinese Families in the Twenty-First Century*, 1–36. Seattle: University of Washington Press, 2016.

Hayes, Heather. "A Re-Introduction to Family Therapy: Clarification of Three Schools." *Australian and New Zealand Journal of Family Therapy* 12, no. 1 (1991): 27–43.

Hinton, William. *Fanshen: A Documentary of Revolution in a Chinese Village*. New York: Vintage, 1966.

Hochschild, Arlie. *The Second Shift*. New York: Avon, 2003. First published in 1989.

Hollenbach, David. "The Glory of God and the Global Common Good: Solidarity in a Turbulent World." *Proceedings of the Catholic Theological Society of America* 72 (2017): 51–60.

Hsu, Becky Yang. *Happy Mourning: Relationship Change and Grave Sweeping in China*. Chicago: University of Chicago Press, forthcoming.

——. "Having It All: Filial Piety, Moral Weighting, and Anxiety Among Young Adults." In *The Chinese Pursuit of Happiness: Anxieties, Hopes, and Moral Tensions in Everyday Life*, ed. Becky Yang Hsu and Richard Madsen, 42–65. Berkeley: University of California Press, 2019.

Hsu, Francis L. K. *Under the Ancestors' Shadow: Kinship, Personality, and Social Mobility in Village China*. New York: Doubleday, 1967. First published in 1948.

Huang, Hsuan-Ying. "Being Together in Shanghai: Self-Experience and Psy-Sociality in a Legendary Psychotherapy Training Course." Paper presented at the "Living Well in China" conference, Long US-China Institute, University of California, Irvine, November 13, 2018.

——. "The Emergence of the Psycho-Boom in Contemporary Urban China." In *Psychiatry and Chinese History*, ed. Howard Chiang, 183–204. London: Pickering & Chatto, 2014.

——. "From Psychotherapy to Psycho-Boom: A Historical Overview of Psychotherapy in China." *Psychoanalysis and Psychotherapy in China* 1, no. 1 (2015): 1–30.

——. "Untamed *Jianghu* or Emerging Profession: Diagnosing the Psycho-Boom Amid China's Mental Health Legislation." *Culture, Medicine, and Psychiatry* 42, no. 2 (June 2018): 371–400.

Hui, Yuk. *The Question Concerning Technology in China*. Cambridge, MA: MIT Press, 2016.

Ivanhoe, Philip J. "Death and Dying in the Analects." In *Mortality in Traditional Chinese Thought*, ed. Amy Olberding and Philip J. Ivanhoe, 137–52. Albany: State University of New York Press, 2011.

——. *Oneness: East Asian Conceptions of Virtue, Happiness, and How We Are All Connected*. New York: Oxford University Press, 2017.

Jankowiak, William R., and Robert L. Moore. *Family Life in China*. Cambridge: Polity, 2017.

Jasanoff, Sheila. *The Ethics of Invention: Technology and the Human Future*. New York: Norton, 2016.

——. "Ordering Knowledge, Ordering Society." In *States of Knowledge: The Co-Production of Science and Social Order*, ed. Sheila Jasanoff, 13–45. London: Routledge, 2004.

Jiang, Shuqing. *Hao Xin Qing Bei Yun*. Nanjing: Yilin Chubanshe, 2016.

Johnson, Ian. *The Souls of China: The Return of Religion After Mao*. New York: Pantheon, 2017.

Jordan, Brigitte. *Birth in Four Cultures: A Cross-Cultural Investigation of Childbirth in Yucatan, Holland, Sweden, and the United States*, 4th ed. Prospect Heights, IL: Waveland, 1993. First published in 1978.

Kipnis, Andrew. *Governing Educational Desire: Culture, Politics, and Schooling in China*. Chicago: University of Chicago Press, 2011.

Kleinman, Arthur. "The Art of Medicine: Remaking the Moral Person in China: Implications for Health." *Lancet* 375 (2010): 1074–75.

Kleinman, Arthur, Yunxiang Yan, Jing Jun, Sing Lee, Everett Zhang, Pan Tianshu, Wu Fei, and Guo Jinhua, eds. "Introduction: Remaking the Moral Person in a New China." In *Deep China: The Moral Life of the Person*, 1–35. Berkeley: University of California Press, 2011.

——. eds. *Deep China: The Moral Life of the Person*. Berkeley: University of California Press, 2011.

Kong, Xiangli. "风险社会视角下失独家庭的政策支持机制" (The policy-support mechanism for *shidu* families from the perspective of a risk society). 《北京行政学院学报》 (Journal of Beijing Administration Institute), no. 5 (2018): 101–9.

Korolczuk, Elżbieta. "When Parents Become Activists: Exploring the Intersection of Civil Society and Family." In *Civil Society Revisited*, ed. Kerstin Jacobsson and Elżbieta Korolczuk, 129–52. New York: Berghahn, 2017.

Kuan, Teresa. "Feelings Run in the Family: Kin Therapeutics and the Configuration of Cause in China." *Ethnos* 85, no. 4 (2020): 695–716.

——. *Love's Uncertainty: The Politics and Ethics of Child Rearing in Contemporary China.* Berkeley: University of California Press, 2015.

Kukathis, Chandran. "Ethical Pluralism from a Classical Liberal Perspective." In *The Many and the One: Religious and Secular Perspectives on Ethical Pluralism in the Modern World*, ed. Richard Madsen and Tracy B. Strong, 55–77. Princeton, NJ: Princeton University Press, 2003.

Latour, Bruno. "Morality and Technology: The End of the Means." *Theory, Culture & Society* 19, no. 5–6 (2002): 247–60.

——. *We Have Never Been Modern.* Cambridge, MA: Harvard University Press, 1991.

Lee, Ching Kwan, and Yonghong Zhang. "The Power of Instability: Unraveling the Microfoundations of Bargained Authoritarianism in China." *American Journal of Sociology* 118, no. 6 (2013): 1475–1508.

Li, Hongtian, Shusheng Luo, Leonardo Trasande, Susan Hellerstein, Chuyun Kang, Jia-Xin Li, Yali Zhang, Jian-Meng Liu, and Jan Blustein. "Geographic Variations and Temporal Trends in Cesarean Delivery Rates in China, 2008–2014." *JAMA* 317, no. 1 (2017): 69–76.

Liang, Juan, Yi Mu, Xiaohong Li, Wen Tang, Yanping Wang, Zheng Liu, Xiaona Huang, et al. "Relaxation of the One Child Policy and Trends in Caesarean Section Rates and Birth Outcomes in China Between 2012 and 2016: Observational Study of Nearly Seven Million Health Facility Births." *BMJ* 360 (2018): k817.

Lin, Jean. *A Spark in the Smokestacks.* New York: Columbia University Press, 2023.

Lin, Zouyan, and Yuru Zhou. *Huaren Yu'er Baike* (Encyclopedia of child care for Chinese people). Beijing: Beijing Lianhe Chubanshe, 2016.

Link, Perry, Richard Madsen, and Paul Pickowicz, eds. Introduction to *Unofficial China: Popular Culture and Thought in the People's Republic.* Boulder, CO: Westview, 1990.

——. eds. "Restless China: An Introduction." In *Restless China*, 1–9. Washington: Rowman & Littlefield, 2013.

Liu, Haiyi Monica. "Cyberspace Romance in Translation: The Case of China's Email Order Brides." PhD diss., University of California, San Diego, 2015.

Liu, Huwy-min Lucia. *Governing Death, Making Persons: The New Chinese Way of Death.* Ithaca, NY: Cornell University Press, 2022.

Liu, Wenrong. "转型期的家庭代际情感与团结" (Intergenerational affection and solidarity in families during social transition). 《社会学研究》 (Sociological Studies), no. 4 (2016): 145–68.

Liu, Yanping, and Gertina van Schalkwyk. "Death Preparation of Chinese Rural Elders." *Death Studies* 43, no. 4 (2019): 270–79.

Longji, Sun. "The Deep Structure of Chinese Culture." In *Seeds of Fire: Chinese Voices of Conscience*, trans. Geremie Barme and John Minford, 30–35. New York: Farrar, Straus, and Giroux, 1988.

Lumbiganon, Pisake, et al. "World Health Organization Global Survey on Maternal and Perinatal Health Research Group. Method of Delivery and Pregnancy Outcomes in Asia: The WHO Global Survey on Maternal and Perinatal Health 2007–08." *Lancet* 375, no. 9713 (2010): 490–99.

Ma, Liangkun, ed. *Xie he Zhuanjia + Xie he Mama Quan Ganhuo Fenxiang: Chan Jian* (Cooperate with experts, cooperate with circle of moms' substantial sharing: antenatal examination). Beijing: Zhongguo Qinggongye Chubanshe, 2016.

——. ed. *Xie he Zhuanjia + Xie he Mamaquan Ganhuo Fenxiang: Huaiyun* (Cooperate with experts, cooperate with circle of moms' substantial sharing: pregnancy). Beijing: Zhongguo Qinggongye Chubanshe, 2016.

MacIntyre, Alasdair. *After Virtue*. South Bend, IN: University of Notre Dame Press, 1984.

Madsen, Richard. "Beyond the Clash of Civilizations: Seeking the Common Good Through East-West Dialogue." Manuscript, 2019.

——. "Making the People or the Government Happy? Dilemmas of Social Workers in a Morally Pluralistic Society." In *The Chinese Pursuit of Happiness: Anxieties, Hopes, and Moral Tensions in Everyday Life*, ed. Becky Yang Hsu and Richard Madsen, 110–30. Berkeley: University of California Press, 2019.

——. ed. *The Sinicization of Chinese Religions*. Leiden: Brill, 2021.

Martin, Emily. *The Woman in the Body: A Cultural Analysis of Reproduction*. Boston: Beacon, 1987.

Matza, Tomas. *Shock Therapy: Psychology, Precarity, Well-Being in Postsocialist Russia*. Durham, NC: Duke University Press, 2018.

McBrayer, Kim. "Plotting Confucian and Disability Rights Paradigms on the Advocacy-Activism Continuum: Experiences of Chinese Parents of Children with Dyslexia in Hong Kong." *Cambridge Journal of Education* 44, no. 1 (2014): 93–111.

McCabe, Helen. "Parent Advocacy in the Face of Adversity: Autism and Families in the People's Republic of China." *Focus on Autism and Other Developmental Disabilities* 22, no. 1 (2007): 39–50.

McCabe, Helen, and Guosheng Deng. "'So They'll Have Somewhere to Go': Establishing Non-Governmental Organizations (NGOs) for Children with Autism in the People's Republic of China." *Voluntas* 29, no. 5 (2018): 1019–32.

Miller, Daniel, Elisabetta Costa, Nell Haynes, Tom McDonald, Razvan Nicolescu, Jolynna Sinanan, Juliano Spyer, Shriram Venkatraman, and Xinyuan Wang. *How the World Changed Social Media*. London: UCL Press, 2016.

Minnerath, Roland. "The Fundamental Principles of Social Doctrine: The Issue of Their Interpretation." In *Pursuing the Common Good: How Solidarity and Subsidiarity Can Work Together*, ed. Margaret S. Archer and Pierpaolo Donati, 45–56. Vatican City: Pontifical Academy of Social Sciences, 2008.

Morgan, Lynn Marie, and Meredith W. Michaels, eds. *Fetal Subjects, Feminist Positions*. Philadelphia: University of Pennsylvania Press, 1999.

Mu, Guangzong. "失独父母的自我拯救和社会拯救" (Self-help and social rescue of *shidu* parents). 《中国农业大学学报社会科学版》 (China Agricultural University Journal: Social Science Edition) 32, no. 3 (2015): 117–21.

Murphy, Michelle. *Seizing the Means of Reproduction: Entanglements of Feminism, Health, and Technoscience*. Durham, NC: Duke University Press, 2012.

Naftali, Orna. *Children, Rights, and Modernity in China: Raising Self-Governing Citizens*. New York: Palgrave Macmillan, 2014.

Nakano, Lynne. "Happiness and Unconventional Life Choices." In *Happiness and the Good Life in Japan*, ed. Wolfram Manzenreiter and Barbara Holthus, 53–66. New York: Routledge, 2017.

——. "Single Women and the Transition to Marriage in Hong Kong, Shanghai and Tokyo." *Asian Journal of Social Science* 44, no. 3 (2016): 371–72.

National People's Congress Standing Committee (NPCSC). "Law on Protection of Minors" (未成年人保护法), ed. NPCSC (全国人民代表大会常务委员会). Beijing: Zhong guo fa zhi chu ban she (中国法制出版社), 2007.

Naughton, Barry. *The Chinese Economy: Adaptation and Growth*, 2nd ed. Cambridge: MIT Press, 2018.

Nautz, Jürgen, Paul Ginsborg, and Ton Nijhuis, eds. *The Golden Chain: Family, Civil Society, and the State.* New York: Berghahn, 2013.

Oakley, Ann. *The Captured Womb: A History of the Medical Care of Pregnant Women.* Oxford: Basil Blackwell, 1986.

——. *Women Confined: Towards a Sociology of Childbirth.* Oxford: Martin Robertson, 1980.

OReilly, Michael. "Internet Addiction: A New Disorder Enters the Medical Lexicon." *Canadian Medical Association Journal* 154, no. 12 (1996): 1882–83.

Osburg, John. *Anxious Wealth: Money and Morality Among China's New Rich.* Stanford, CA: Stanford University Press, 2013.

O'Shaughnessy, Sara, and Emily Huddart Kennedy. "Relational Activism: Reimagining Women's Environmental Work as Cultural Change." *Canadian Journal of Sociology* 35, no. 4 (2010): 551–72.

Owen, Lara, and Aidila Razak. "Why Chinese Mothers Turned Away from C-Sections." *BBC World Service*, March 2, 2019. https://www.bbc.com/news/world-asia-china-46265808.

Oxfeld, Ellen. "Life-Cycle Rituals in Rural and Urban China: Birth, Marriage and Death." In *Handbook on Religion in China*, ed. Stephan Feuchtwang, 110–31. Cheltenham, UK: Edward Elgar, 2020.

Pan, Xiaoyu. *Quan Huli: Hao Yun an Chan Bai Ke* (Complete nursing: good pregnancy and safe birth). Beijing: Beijing Llianhe Chubanshe, 2017.

Phillips, Rachel, Cecilia Benoit, Helga Hallgrimsdottir, and Kate Vallance. "Courtesy Stigma: A Hidden Health Concern Among Front-Line Service Providers to Sex Workers." *Sociology of Health & Illness* 34, no. 5 (2012): 681–96.

Piketty, Thomas, Li Yang, and Gabriel Zucman. "Capital Accumulation, Private Property, and Rising Inequality in China, 1978–2015." *American Economic Review* 109, no. 7 (2019): 2469–96.

Polanyi, Karl. *The Livelihood of Man.* London: Academic, 1977.

Poo, Mu-Chou. "Ideas Concerning Death and Burial in Pre-Han and Han China." *Asia Major* 3, no. 2 (1990): 25–62.

Pritzker, Sonya E. "New Age with Chinese Characteristics?: Translating Inner Child Emotion Pedagogies in Contemporary China." *Ethos* 44, no. 2 (2017): 150–70.

Pritzker, Sonya E., and Whitney L. Duncan, "Technologies of the Social: Family Constellation Therapy and the Remodeling of Relational

Selfhood in China and Mexico." *Culture, Medicine, and Psychiatry* 43, no. 3 (2019): 468–95.

Pugh, Allison. *Longing and Belonging: Parents, Children, and Consumer Culture*. Berkeley: University of California Press, 2009.

Ran, Tao, Xiuqin Huang, Jinan Wang, Huimin Zhang, Ying Zhang, and Mengchen Li. "Proposed Diagnostic Criteria for Internet Addiction." *Addiction* 105, no. 3 (2010): 556–64.

Rao, Yichen. "E-sports vs. Exams: Competition Ideologies Among Student Gamers in Neo-Socialist China." *Social Analysis* 66, no. 4 (2022): 69–90.

——. "From Confucianism to Psychology: Rebooting Internet Addicts in China." *History of Psychology* 22, no. 4 (2019): 328–50.

Rawls, Ann, and Waverly Duck. *Tacit Racism.* Chicago: University of Chicago Press, 2020.

Roberts, Tom. "The Rise of the Catholic Right." *Sojourners*, March 2019. https://sojo.net/magazine/march-2019/rise-catholic-right.

Rose, Nikolas. *The Politics of Life Itself.* Princeton, NJ: Princeton University Press, 2006.

Rothman, Barbara K. *A Bun in the Oven: How the Food and Birth Movements Resist Industrialization.* New York: NYU Press, 2016.

——. *In Labor: Women and Power in the Birthplace.* New York: Norton, 1982.

Rozelle, Scott, Yiran Xia, Dimitris Friesen, Bronson Vanderjack, and Nourya Cohen. "Moving Beyond Lewis: Employment and Wage Trends in China's High- and Low-Skilled Industries and the Emergence of an Era of Polarization." *Comparative Economic Studies* 62 (2020): 555–89.

Sahlins, Marshall. *Stone Age Economics.* Chicago: Aldine-Atherton, 1972.

Sangren, Steven P. "The Chinese Family as Instituted Fantasy: Or, Rescuing Kinship Imaginaries from the 'Symbolic'." *Journal of the Royal Anthropological Institute* 19, no. 2 (2013): 279–99.

Santos, Gonçalo. "Birthing Stories and Techno-Moral Change Across Generations. Coping with Hospital Births and High-Tech Medicalization in Rural South China, 1960s–2010s." *Technology and Culture* 61, no. 2 (2020): 581–616.

——. *Chinese Village Life Today: Building Families in an Age of Transition.* Seattle: University of Washington Press, 2021.

——. "Love, Family, and Gender in 21st Century China." In *Socialism with Neoliberal Characteristics*, ed. K. W. Endres and C. Hann, 31–35. New York: Max Planck Institute for Social Anthropology, 2017.

——. "Multiple Mothering and Labor Migration in Rural South China." In *Transforming Patriarchy: Chinese Families in the Twenty-First Century*, ed. Gonçalo Santos and Stevan Harrell, 31–65. Seattle: University of Washington Press, 2017.

——. "On Intimate Choices and Troubles in Rural South China." *Modern Asian Studies* 50, no. 4 (2016): 1298–1326.

Santos, Gonçalo D., and Suzanne Z. Gottschang. "Rethinking Reproductive Technologies and Modernities in Time and Space." *Technology and Culture* 61, no. 2 (2020): 549–58.

Santos, Gonçalo, and Stevan Harrell, eds. *Transforming Patriarchy: Chinese Families in the Twenty-First Century*. Seattle: University of Washington Press, 2017.

Santos, Gonçalo D., Yichen Rao, Jack L. Xing, and Jun Zhang. "Capitalism, Overwork, and Polanyi's Dialectics of Freedom. Emerging Visions of Work-Life Balance in Contemporary Urban China." In *Work, Ethics and Freedom: Chimeras of Freedom in the Neoliberal Era*, ed. Chris Hann, 132–57. Oxford: Berghahn, 2021.

Santos, Gonçalo D., and Jun Zhang. "Who Is Requesting Cesarean Delivery? The Political Economy of Childbirth Medicalization in Late Reform China." Manuscript

Scarry, Elaine. *The Body in Pain: The Making and Unmaking of the World*. New York: Oxford University Press, 1987.

Shanghai Statistics Bureau. *2015 nian shanghaishi 1 percent renkou chouyang diaocha ziliao* (2015 Shanghai 1 percent population sample survey). Beijing: China Statistics Press, 2015.

Sharma, Devika, and Frederik Tygstrup, eds. Introduction to *Structures of Feeling: Affectivity and the Study of Culture*, 1–19. Berlin: Walter De Gruyter, 2015.

Shi, Lihong. "Losing an Only Child: Parental Grief Among China's *Shidu* Parents." In *Chinese Families Upside Down: Intergenerational Dynamics and Neo-Familism in the Early 21st Century*, ed. Yunxiang Yan, 176–93. Amsterdam: Brill, 2021.

Shirai, Chiaki. "Historical Dynamism of Childbirth in Japan: Medicalization and Its Normative Politics, 1868–2017." *Technology and Culture* 61, no. 2 (2020): 559–80.

——. *Umisodateto josan'no rekisi* 産み育てと助産の歴史 (History of childbirth: childrearing and midwifery in Japan). Tokyo: Igakushoin, 2016.

Simmel, Georg. "Fashion." *American Journal of Sociology* 62, no. 6 (1904): 541–58.

Spires, Anthony J. "Regulation as Political Control: China's First Charity Law and Its Implications for Civil Society." *Nonprofit and Voluntary Sector Quarterly* 49, no. 3 (2020): 571–88.

Stafford, Charles, ed. *Ordinary Ethics in China.* London: Routledge, 2013.

Strathern, Marilyn. *The Gender of the Gift: Problems with Women and Problems with Society in Melanesia.* Berkeley: University of California Press, 1988.

——. *Reproducing the Future: Anthropology, Kinship and the New Reproductive Technologies.* Manchester, UK: Manchester University Press, 1990.

Sun, Longji. "The Deep Structure of Chinese Culture." In *Seeds of Fire: Chinese Voices of Conscience,* trans. Geremie Barme and John Minford, 30–35. New York: Farrar, Straus, and Giroux, 1988.

Sun, Lynn Lin. "The Happiness Impasse: Exploring Middle-Class Women's Pursuits of Marital Happiness in Urban China and Japan." PhD diss., Chinese University of Hong Kong, 2021.

Sun, Peidong. *Shei lai qü wo de nüer?: shanghai xiangqinjiao yü "baifa xiangqin"* (Who's going to marry my daughter?: Shanghai matchmaking corner and "gray-hair matchmaking"). Beijing: China Social Sciences Press, 2012.

Survey and Research Center for China Household Finance. *Guomin xinfu baogao 2014* (Chinese People's Happiness Report 2014). February 13, 2015.

Swidler, Ann. "Culture in Action: Symbols and Strategies." *American Sociological Review* 51, no. 2 (1986): 273–86.

——. *Talk of Love: How Culture Matters.* Chicago: University of Chicago Press, 2003. First published in 2001.

Throop, Jason C. "Ambivalent Happiness and Virtuous Suffering." *HAU: Journal of Ethnographic Theory* 5, no. 3 (2015): 45–68.

Torres, Jennifer M., and Raymond G. De Vries. "Birthing Ethics: What Mothers, Families, Childbirth Educators, Nurses, and Physicians Should Know About the Ethics of Childbirth." *Journal of Perinatal Education* 18, no. 1 (2009): 12–24.

Tu, Fangjing. "WeChat and Civil Society in China." *Communication and the Public* 1, no. 3 (2016): 343–50.

Vallor, Shannon. *Technology and the Virtues: A Philosophical Guide to a Future Worth Wanting.* Oxford: Oxford University Press, 2016.

Vance, J. D. *Hillbilly Elegy: A Memoir of a Family and Culture in Crisis.* New York: Harper Collins, 2016.

Van Hollen, Cecilia. *Birth on the Threshold: Childbirth and Modernity in South India.* Berkeley: University of California Press, 2003.

Verbeek, Peter-Paul. "Materializing Morality: Design Ethics and Technological Mediation." *Science, Technology and Human Values* 31, no. 3 (2006): 361–80.

Wajcman, Judy. *Feminism Confronts Technology.* Cambridge: Polity, 1991.

Wang, Eileen. "Requests for Cesarean Deliveries: The Politics of Labor Pain and Pain Relief in Shanghai, China." *Social Science & Medicine* 173, suppl. C (2017): 1–8.

Wang, Qi. *Huaiyun, Anchan, Yuezi: Yi Ji Shen* (Pregnancy, safe birth, postnatal confinement: do's and don'ts). Beijing: Zhongguo Renkou Chubanshe, 2011.

Wang, Xie Xiangnan. *Iron Moon: An Anthology of Chinese Worker Poetry,* trans. Eleanor Goodman and ed. Qin Xiaoyu. Buffalo, NY: White Pine, 2017.

Watson, Rubie. "Remembering the Dead: Graves and Politics in Southeastern China." In *Death Ritual in Late Imperial and Modern China,* ed. James Watson and Evelyn Rawski, 203–27. Berkeley: University of California Press, 1988.

Weber, Max. "Religious Rejections of the World and Their Directions." In *From Max Weber: Essays in Sociology,* trans. and ed. Hans H. Gerth and C. Wright Mills, 323–59. New York: Oxford University Press, 1949.

——. "Science as a Vocation." In *From Max Weber: Essays in Sociology,* trans. and ed. Hans H. Gerth and C. Wright Mills, 129–56. New York: Oxford University Press, 1949.

Wei, Wei, and Yunxiang Yan. "Rainbow Parents and the Familial Model of *Tongzhi* (LGBT) Activism in Contemporary China." *Chinese Sociological Review* 54, no. 5 (2021): 451–72.

Weinstein, Deborah. *The Pathological Family: Postwar America and the Rise of Family Therapy.* Ithaca, NY: Cornell University Press, 2013.

Whyte, Martin King. "Continuity and Change in Urban Chinese Family Life." *China Journal,* no. 53 (2005): 9–33.

——. *Myth of the Social Volcano: Perceptions of Inequality and Social Injustice in Contemporary China.* Stanford, CA: Stanford University Press, 2010.

———. *Small Groups and Political Rituals in China*. Berkeley: University of California Press, 1974.

Williams, Raymond. *Marxism and Literature*. Oxford: Oxford University Press, 1978.

Wolf, Jacqueline. *Cesarean Section: An American History of Risk, Technology, and Consequence*. Baltimore, MD: John Hopkins University Press, 2018.

Wu, David Y. H. "Parental Control: Psychocultural Interpretations of Chinese Patterns of Socialization." In *Growing Up the Chinese Way*, ed. Sing Lau, 1–26. Hong Kong: Chinese University Press, 1996.

Wu, Fei. "Suicide, a Modern Problem in China." In *Deep China: The Moral Life of the Person, What Anthropology and Psychiatry Tell Us About China Today*, ed. Arthur Kleinman, Yunxiang Yan, Jing Jun, Sing Lee, and Everett Zhang, 213–36. Berkeley: University of California Press, 2011.

Xiangnan, Xie. *Iron Moon: An Anthology of Chinese Worker Poetry*, trans. Eleanor Goodman and ed. Qin Xiaoyu. Buffalo, NY: White Pine, 2017.

Xiaotong, Fei. *From the Soil: The Foundations of Chinese Society*, trans. Gary G. Hamilton and Wang Zheng. Berkeley: University of California Press, 1992. First published in 1947.

———. *Xiangtu Zhongguo* (Shanghai, 1948). Translation from "Chinese Social Structure and Its Values." In *Changing China: Readings in the History of China from the Opium War to the Present*, ed. J. Mason Gentzler, 211–13. New York: Praeger, 1977.

Xie, Kailing. *Embodying Middle Class Gender Aspirations: Perspective from China's Privileged Young Women*. Singapore: Palgrave Macmillan, 2021.

Xie, Yu. "Understanding Inequality in China." *Chinese Journal of Sociology* 2, no. 3 (2016): 327–47.

Xu, Bin. *Culture of Democracy*. Cambridge: Polity, 2022.

———. "Grandpa Wen: Scene and Political Performance." *Sociological Theory* 30, no. 2 (2012): 114–29.

———. *The Politics of Compassion: The Sichuan Earthquake and Civic Engagement in China*. Stanford, CA: Stanford University Press, 2017.

Xu, Jing. *The Good Child: Moral Development in a Chinese Preschool*. Stanford, CA: Stanford University Press, 2017.

Xu, Jingjing. "The Self-Cultivation of a Psychological Counselor" (*Xinli zixunshi de ziwo xiuyang*). *Sanlian shenghuo zhoukan* 18, no. 46 (November 2019): 50–54.

Xu, Qiong, and Wei-Jun Jean Yeung. "Hoping for a Phoenix: Shanghai Fathers and Their Daughters." *Journal of Family Issues* 34, no. 2 (2013): 184–209.

Yan, Yunxiang. "The Changing Moral Landscape." In *Deep China: The Moral Life of the Person*, ed. Arthur Kleinman, Yunxiang Yan, Jing Jun, Sing Lee, and Everett Zhang, 36–77. Berkeley: University of California Press, 2011.

——. "The Chinese Path to Individualization." *British Journal of Sociology* 61, no. 3 (2010): 489–512.

——. "Dislocation, Reposition and Restratification: Structural Changes in Chinese Society." *China Review* 15 (1994): 1–24.

——. "Doing Personhood in Chinese Culture: The Desiring Individual, Moralist Self, and Relational Person." *Cambridge Anthropology* 35, no. 2 (2017): 1–17.

——. *The Individualization of Chinese Society*. New York: Berg, 2009.

——. "Intergenerational Intimacy and Descending Familism in Rural North China." *American Anthropologist* 118, no. 2 (2016): 244–57.

——. "Introduction: The Inverted Family, Post-Patriarchal Intergenerationality and Neo-Familism." In *Chinese Families Upside Down: Intergenerational Dynamics and Neo-Familism in the Early 21st Century*, ed. Yunxiang Yan, 1–30. Leiden: Brill, 2021.

——. "Introduction: The Rise of the Chinese Individual." In *The Individualization of Chinese Society*, ed. Yunxiang Yan, xv–xl. New York: Berg, 2009.

——. "Neo-Familism and the State in Contemporary China." *Urban Anthropology and Studies of Cultural Systems and World Economic Development* 47, no. 3 (2018): 181–224.

——. "Of Hamburger and Social Space: Consuming McDonald's in Beijing." In *The Consumer Revolution in Urban China*, ed. Deborah Davis, 201–25. Berkeley: University of California Press, 2000.

——. "Parents-Driven Divorce and Individualization Among Urban Chinese Youth." *International Social Science Journal*, no. 213–214 (2015): 317–30.

——. *Private Life Under Socialism: Love, Intimacy, and Family Change in a Chinese Village 1949–1999*. Stanford, CA: Stanford University Press, 2003.

——. "Three Discourses on Neo-Familism." In *Chinese Families Upside Down: Intergenerational Dynamics and Neo-Familism in the Early 21st Century*, ed. Yunxiang Yan, 253–74. Amsterdam: Brill, 2021.

Yang, Jie. "'Happy Housewives': Gender, Class, and Psychological Self-Help in China." In *Chinese Discourses on Happiness*, ed. Gerda Wielander and Derek Hird, 129–49. Hong Kong: Hong Kong University Press, 2018.

——. *Unknotting the Heart: Unemployment and Therapeutic Governance in China*. Ithaca, NY: Cornell University Press, 2015.

Yang, Mayfair. *Re-enchanting Modernity: Ritual Economy and Society in Wenzhou, China*. Durham, NC: Duke University Press, 2020.

Yiwu, Liao. "The Leper." In *The Corpse Walker: Real Life Stories, China from the Bottom Up*, 49. New York: Anchor, 2009.

Young, Kimberley. *Caught in the Net*. New York: Wiley, 1998.

Zelizer, Viviana A. *The Purchase of Intimacy*. Princeton, NJ: Princeton University Press, 2007.

Zhang, Bichun, and Baojun Xu. "失独父母的非制度化政治参与及其分类治理" (The noninstitutional political participation of *shidu* parents and the differentiated governance). *Jianghan Forum*, no. 8 (2015): 132–37.

Zhang, Everett. "China's Sexual Revolution." In *Deep China: The Moral Life of the Person*, ed. Arthur Kleinman, Yunxiang Yan, Jing Jun, Sing Lee, Everett Zhang, Pan Tianshu, Wu Fei, and Guo Jinhua, 106–51. Berkeley: University of California Press, 2011.

——. "Grieving at Chongqing's Red Guard Graveyard: In the Name of Life Itself." *China Journal* 70 (2013): 24–47.

Zhang, Jing. "公共性与家庭主义: 社会建设的基础性辨析" (The public and familism: An analysis of basic principles in the construction of public society). 北京工业大学学报-社会科学版 (Journal of Beijing University of Technology: Social Science Edition) 11, no. 3 (2011): 1–4, 10.

Zhang, Jun. "(Extended) Family Car, Filial Consumer-Citizens: Becoming Properly Middle Class in Post-Socialist South China." *Modern China* 43, no. 1 (2017): 36–65.

Zhang, Li. *Anxious China: Inner Revolution and Politics of Psychotherapy*. Berkeley: University of California Press, 2020.

——. "Bentuhua: Culturing Psychotherapy in Postsocialist China." *Culture, Medicine and Psychiatry* 38 (2014): 283–305.

——. "Cultivating Happiness: Psychotherapy, Spirituality, and Well-Being in a Transforming Urban China." In *Handbook of Religion and the Asian City: Aspiration and Urbanization in the Twenty-First Century*, ed. Peter van der Veer, 315–32. Berkeley: University of California Press, 2015.

——. "Cultivating the Therapeutic Self in China." *Medical Anthropology* 37, no. 1 (2018): 45–58.

——. *In Search of Paradise: Middle-Class Living in a Chinese Metropolis.* Ithaca, NY: Cornell University Press, 2010.

——. "Private Homes, Distinct Lifestyles: Performing a New Middle Class." In *Privatizing China: Socialism from Afar*, ed. Li Zhang and Aihwa Ong, 23–40. Ithaca, NY: Cornell University Press, 2008.

Zhang, Weiguo. "Is Death Taboo for Older Chinese Immigrants?" *OMEGA–Journal of Death and Dying* 84, no. 4 (2022): 1061–80.

Zhao, Xudong 赵旭东. "The Sino-German Comparison on the Views of Therapeutic Relationship in Systemic Family Therapy" (系统家庭治疗中有关治疗关系的观点—— 附中德比较). *Foreign Medicine: Psychiatry* (国外医学: 精神病学分册) 22, no. 2 (1995): 65–70.

Zheng, Yuqiao. *Zheng Yuqiao Yu'er Baihuo* (Zheng Yuqiao's encyclopedia of childcare). Beijing: Huaxue Gongye Chubanshe, 2015.

Zhu, Jinghui, and Zhu Qiaoyan. "温和的理性： 当代浙江农村家庭代际关系研究" (Mild rationality: A study of intergenerational relationships among rural families in Zhejiang province). 《浙江社会科学》 (*Zhejiang Social Sciences*), no. 10 (2013): 99–105, 129, 158.

Zigon, Jarrett. "How Is It Between Us? Relational Ethics and Transcendence." *Journal of the Royal Anthropological Institute* 27, no. 2 (2021): 384–401.

CONTRIBUTORS

Becky Yang Hsu is an associate professor of sociology at Georgetown University, where she is also affiliated with the Asian Studies Program. She is interested in the relationship between social practices and the social relationships that are taken for granted as natural and ordinary. Her current work is on grave sweeping in China. She is the author of *Borrowing Together: Microfinance and Cultivating Social Ties* (2017) and coeditor of *The Chinese Pursuit of Happiness: Anxieties, Hopes, and Moral Tensions in Everyday Life* (2019). She is a senior fellow at the Berkley Center for Religion, Peace, and World Affairs. She convenes the Research Group on Culture and Society for the Initiative for U.S.-China Dialogue in the Office of Global Engagement at Georgetown University.

Teresa Kuan is an associate professor of anthropology at the Chinese University of Hong Kong. She is interested in the social life of psychological ideas and practices, and she has conducted research projects on popular parenting advice as well as the development of family therapy in mainland China. Her work contributes to the development of an anthropological approach to the study of ethics in everyday life, focusing on "moral luck" and distributions of responsibility in particular. She is the author of *Love's Uncertainty: The Politics and Ethics of Child Rearing in Contemporary*

China (2015), and coeditor of the special issue "Moral (and Other) Laboratories," published in the journal *Culture, Medicine, and Psychiatry* (2017). She is a co-convener of the Research Group on Culture and Society for the Initiative for U.S.-China Dialogue in the Office of Global Engagement at Georgetown University.

Richard Madsen sociology emeritus, distinguished research professor and director of the U.C.-Fudan Center for Contemporary Chinese Studies at the University of California, San Diego. He is a coauthor (with Robert Bellah et al.) of *The Good Society* (1991) and *Habits of the Heart* (1985), which received the Los Angeles Times Book Award and was jury nominated for the Pulitzer Prize. His other books include *Morality and Power in a Chinese Village* (1984), *China and the American Dream* (1995), *China's Catholics: Tragedy and Hope in an Emerging Civil Society* (1998), and *Democracy's Dharma: Religious Renaissance and Political Development in Taiwan* (2007). He is a participant in the Initiative for U.S.-China Dialogue on Global Issues Research Group on Culture and Society.

Yichen Rao is an assistant professor of anthropology at Utrecht University. He examines China's digital economy in its sociocultural context and unravels how digital capitalism interacts with human affect and subjectivity. His dissertation fieldwork and book project on China's financial technologies have both been funded by the Wenner-Gren Foundation for Anthropological Research. His articles on China's digital finance and internet addiction have been published in *Economy and Society*, *Economic Anthropology*, *History of Psychology*, and *Social Analysis*.

Gonçalo Santos teaches social-cultural anthropology in the Department of Life Sciences at the University of Coimbra in Portugal. He is also a researcher at the Research Centre for Anthropology and Health, University of Coimbra, where he coordinates the Research Cluster "Technoscience, Society, and the Environment." He held previous positions at the London School of Economics, the Max Planck Institute for Social Anthropology, and the University of Hong Kong. He is the author or editor of four books, including *Chinese Village Life Today* (2021) and *Transforming Patriarchy* (2017, coedited with Stevan Harrell). He is the director of the Sci-Tech Asia International Research Network and is a participant in the Initiative for U.S.-China Dialogue on Global Issues Research Group on Culture and Society.

Lynn Lin Sun is an anthropologist and lecturer at the Centre for China Studies at the Chinese University of Hong Kong. Her research interests lie in ordinary ethics and moral experience embedded in intimate lives, focusing particularly on the affective dimension. Her comparative fieldwork on how "marital happiness"—a set of dominant warm and fuzzy logics—is constructed, experienced, and negotiated by married people in contemporary urban China and Japan has been supported by the Japanese Association of University Women and the Chinese University of Hong Kong. She is a research fellow in the Initiative for U.S.-China Dialogue on Global Issues Research Group on Culture and Society.

Yunxiang Yan is a professor of anthropology at the University of California, Los Angeles, and adjunct professor at Renmin University, China. Unpacking and understanding the moral experiences of ordinary people in our rapidly changing world has been the abiding theme of his anthropological career for more than twenty years. His research interests include family and kinship, economic anthropology, social change and development, cultural globalization, and the individual-society relationship. He is the author of *The Flow of Gifts: Reciprocity and Social Networks in a Chinese Village* (1996), *Private Life Under Socialism: Love, Intimacy, and Family Change in a Chinese Village, 1949–1999* (2003), and *The Individualization of Chinese Society* (2009). He was awarded a Guggenheim fellowship in 2010. He is a participant in the Initiative for U.S.-China Dialogue on Global Issues Research Group on Culture and Society.

INDEX

AA. *See* Alcoholics Anonymous
"About the Demands and
    Application for Compensation
    from Parents Who Have Lost
    Their Only Child," 39–40
action, 3
activism, 57; for common good, 23,
    26; of *shidu* parents, 29. *See also*
    advocacy
activist parents, 13–14; dignity of, 30;
    NHFPC relation to, 39–40
activists: government relation to,
    19n10; public/private dichotomy
    relation to, 24
addict identity, 165
addiction, 164–65, 168. *See also*
    internet addiction
advocacy, 28; civil society relation to,
    56; moral authority relation to,
    55; neo-familism relation to, 48,
    49, 52, 53–54; of rainbow parents,
    29–30, 31–32, 35–36; of *shidu*
    parents, 26, 38–39, 55
affect amplifier, 179–80, 212

"affective intervention," 184
affectivity, 214n6
aging, 270–71
agrarian communities, 71, 88
Ahmed, Sara, 178, 211
Ah Qiang, 29
Al-Anon, 168
Alcoholics Anonymous (AA),
    164–65, 168
alienation, 105n19
alternative imaginaries, of
    happiness, 203–4
alternative lifestyles, 207, 208–9
Alzheimer's disease, 58n5
ambiguity, in mainstream
    media, 81
amoral familism, 23–24
Anna Karenina (Tolstoy), 186
anxiety, 283; C-section and, 224;
    depression and, 147; marriage
    and, 182, 187; of parents, 11–12;
    success, 153
apathy, 23–24, 41
arbitrariness, 202

pain, 250n9; C-section relation to, 231, 238; isolation and, 139n38; of vaginal birth, 244, 250n9
parental authority, 8, 158
parental pressure, 181, 183
parent-child bonding, 54; neo-familism and, 48
parent-child bonds, 22–23; *shidu* parents and, 33–34; in *tongzhi* community, 32
parent-child communication, 169–70
parenting styles: IA relation to, 145, 157; inner psyche and, 156–57
parents, 10, 25, 112; activist, 13–14, 30, 39–40; anxiety of, 11–12; of autistic children, 37; children relation to, 159, 166; civic engagement of, 26; communicator role of, 163–64; IA relation to, 155–56; identity shift of, 160; instant gratification relation to, 161–63; moral authority of, 55; one-child policy relation to, 9; personal growth of, 35–36; preparation for funeral, 267; residential treatment and, 167–69. *See also* rainbow parents; shidu parents
Parents and Friends of Lesbians and Gays (PFLAG), 25, 29–30, 37; hotline service of, 31–32, 35; training programs of, 36
particularistic exclusion, 95
party-state, 100; Cao Xi relation to, 140n55; common good

relation to, 103. *See also* Chinese Communist Party
pathology, of IA, 143
patriarchal family, 153, 238–39
patriarchy, 10
patrilineal structure, 53, 240
patriotism, 48
peasant society, familism in, 42
Perel, Esther, 187
perfectionist ideology, 102, 103
personal growth: counseling certification program for, 112–13; of parents, 35–36
personal guanxi, 68
personality cult, 98–99
personalization, of political conflict, 98
personal liberty, 247; moral responsibility and, 246; mother-in-law relation to, 248
personal networks, 10, 13
PFLAG. *See* Parents and Friends of Lesbians and Gays
"phoenixes," 211, 220n61
pluralism, 68, 81
polarization, 72, 102–3; in U.S., 90
political community, 83–84, 85
political conflict, personalization of, 98
political economy, 91
political submission, 7
politics, 74; communication in, 85; economy relation to, 96–97
Pontifical Academy of Social Sciences, 110
popular culture, children relation to, 171

GPSR Authorized Representative: Easy Access System Europe, Mustamäe tee 50, 10621 Tallinn, Estonia, gpsr.requests@easproject.com